D1274950

INTELLECTUAL ORIGINS OF
AMERICAN NATIONAL THOUGHT

INTELLECTUAL ORIGINS OF AMERICAN NATIONAL THOUGHT

Pages from the Books Our Founding Fathers Read

EDITED, WITH COMMENTARY, BY

WILSON OBER CLOUGH

Second Revised Edition

The American Experience Series

CONSULTING EDITOR: HENRY BAMFORD PARKES

CORINTH BOOKS
NEW YORK

WILSON OBER CLOUGH was born in New Brunswick, New Jersey, received his A.B. at Union University in 1917, and his A.M. at the University of Colorado. He has been Professor of English at the University of Wyoming since 1938, and William Robertson Coe Professor of American Studies at the University of Wyoming since 1956. He received his Litt. D. at Union University in 1957 and his LL.D. at the University of Wyoming in 1961. His published books include *History of the University of Wyoming, 1887-1937*, and *Grammar of English Communication*.

Library of Congress Catalog Card No.: 61-14984

INTELLECTUAL ORIGINS OF AMERICAN NATIONAL THOUGHT
is a revised second edition of *Our Long Heritage* originally published by the University of Minnesota Press for the William Robertson Coe American Studies Program of the University of Wyoming.

NOTE ON COVER ILLUSTRATION

The illustration on the cover is a detail from John Trumbull's *The Declaration of Independence, July 4, 1776* and is reproduced with the kind permission of the Yale University Art Gallery.

THE AMERICAN EXPERIENCE SERIES
Published by Corinth Books, Inc.
32 West Eighth Street, New York 11, New York
Distributed by The Citadel Press
222 Park Avenue South, New York 3, New York

Manufactured in the United States of America

"*Let us look to our schools, not to purge them of ideas, but to purge them of trivialities. Let us make sure that the history of our country, from the remotest origins to the present, is studied with the amplitude it deserves.*" THOMAS JEFFERSON.

"*That nations should be informed of their Rights is of the most absolute necessity: because the happiness or infelicity of any People entirely depends upon the enjoyment or deprivation of liberty.*" ALGERNON SIDNEY, Preface, *Discourses Concerning Government.*

"*Rara temporum felicitas, ubi sentire quae velis et quae sentias dicere licet.*" (*Rare good fortune of the times, when you may think what you wish and may say what you think.*) MOTTO, *Philadelphia Chronicle,* 1767. FROM TACITUS.

PREFACE

AMERICAN colleges and universities have recently witnessed a marked growth in courses variously labelled American Studies, American Civilization, or The American Heritage. Similarly, the general public, in the form of adult education groups, great books courses, or library borrowings, has shown a heartening revival of interest in our national history. This is all to the good, and meets in some measure Walter Lippman's complaint that our education has progressively removed from the curriculum the very Western heritage which gave us our democratic state. Yet a difficulty arises. We must avoid a narrow chauvinism; nevertheless, we must concentrate on the somewhat specialised heritage available to our founding fathers in the eighteenth century. It is the thesis of this book that it is precisely that heritage which links us with the larger Western world, and which gave strength and sinew to the political philosophy of our political ancestors. This heritage was embodied in the books in their libraries; books, however, not always easily available to the modern reader outside of the great library centers.

Hence this text, which aims first of all to furnish the general reader with some characteristic passages from eighteenth century libraries, together with a minimum of notes intended to suggest the pertinence of the given selection. The result is admittedly selective, as their reading was selective for a purpose and a need. History records, it is true, no final victories, only a perpetual readjustment among forces. Yet it is the American heritage to have spoken for the "party of hope" and the reasonableness of the effort to preserve those larger liberties toward which mankind gropes.

Our founding fathers made no pretense of having invented their political wisdom *de novo*, but admitted freely that they had drawn from the lessons of history and the past. To this common inheritance they added the judgment of their own practical experience, common sense and reason. Hence, such questions as the following soon arise: What did the founding fathers read, and to what degree did such reading contribute to their conclusions? What was their political education, their knowledge of history and political thought? From what sources did they imbibe those determinations which were to make such a stir in history? Had their ideas a past, or were they solely a product of the New World, by a kind of mutation without precedent?

It does not take long to discover that those colonists who played the major roles in our history between roughly 1740 and 1790 were very considerable readers; and that from such reading and deliberation, whether done in solitude or in committees, emerged a body of political ideas that became common property and that reached expression in certain simple but hitherto startling words, "We the people."

Such a transformation did not come about all at once. Indeed, it was part of a long and often discouraging story, with roots far back in history. For that reason, we must scan, as they did, the ancient records of tyranny and wrong, as well as the persistent efforts of men to define the good society. We cannot neglect the struggle that tore England apart in the seventeenth century, nor the Renaissance stream on the continent, nor the emergent liberalism of eighteenth century Europe and America. Such are the major divisions of our reading.

In the preparation of this book I have made almost no use of certain excellent collections of the documents of political history, many of which range over a longer period or cover a more diverse heritage. For this reason it may appear that our colonial readers oversimplified the picture or limited their interest to what met a special need. This is quite possible. Revolutionary thought was not merely an amiable blending of any and every point of view. It was eclectic; but that is not the same as irresolute. The purpose of the founding fathers was not academic. Rather, it was first and foremost a practical one of devising some form of government that would preserve their gains and discourage arbitrary incursions upon their freedoms. History to them was utilitarian; they read it for purposive selection, and to conclusions which still merit our attention.

PREFACE

This book traces our heritage to about 1790 only. What follows after that date is better known and better documented. The evidence as to what books were most often read and referred to during the earlier period was gathered primarily from diaries, letters, journals, papers, political documents, library lists, and similar sources, supplemented by recourse to such works as the Evans *American Bibliography, 1639–1820* (Chicago, 1903–1959), now happily reinforced by the *Early American Imprints, 1639–1800*, in the form of microprints. Some studies of colonial reading are also mentioned in the Appendices.

Like any anthology worth the effort, this one should lead the reader to the authors represented for a more exhaustive knowledge. The intent is less to offer a conclusive philosophy of colonial culture than to supply some documentation from which readers may proceed to the larger discussion. Coming to this study from English and American literature rather than from specialization in political philosophy, history, or law, I have aimed more at the general student than at the specialized scholar; and I have been rewarded by the enthusiasm with which many have responded to the discovery that the heritage of ideas is indeed long. That this should be a discovery implies a need. To assist such students, the Index treats the major terms of the text in some detail so that those who use the book as a text may, if they wish, assign exercises in tracing, at least in skeleton form, the historical stages of such concepts.

The issues within these pages are still pertinent. If we cannot today draw so glibly upon the long metaphysical tradition of "nature's laws" and "certain inalienable rights," there still remain with us certain very real and empirical difficulties if human society is to survive. How shall we arrive at some unanimity on what man may reasonably expect of society; how shall we impose some limits on the irresponsibility of men and nations? The American political theorists asserted often that they spoke in the name of a common humanity. They prefaced their documents with sturdy affirmations of the grand principles that were assumed to bind all men and nations alike. They waited for no authoritative permissions; but asserted more frankly than ever a nation had done before in history the necessity of freedom to assemble and to exercise judgment on their own affairs. These are still the basic freedoms.

It is a pleasant task to acknowledge here the aid and encouragement given me by others: my wife for her patience; students in my classes;

the late Willani Robertson Coe and the Coe Foundation of New York City for a generous interest in the American Studies program at the University of Wyoming; President G. D. Humphrey of this same University. I am indebted to many scholars by indirection; and to a few for generous suggestions by correspondence, though the latter, since they did not read my manuscript, can in no way be held responsible for its limitations. I should like to thank, among others, Harry Hayden Clark, David Potter, Clinton Rossiter, and Daniel Boorstin for kindly letters. To the books of the last two I should have been more deeply indebted had I encountered them before my first draft was completed.

I must also pay especial tribute to the unfailing courtesy and helpfulness of the library staffs of the University of Wyoming, the University of Colorado, and the Bibliographical Center of Denver; and again to the great libraries of Harvard and Yale Universities (the Widener and the Houghton libraries of Harvard, where I uncovered many of these early works, and the Yale University Library), also the Newberry Library of Chicago, for free access to the riches on their shelves. The staff of the University of Minnesota Press was most helpful and considerate in editorial direction and suggestion on my first edition. Bibliographical notes in the Appendices and footnotes must suffice to suggest certain useful works, though I have concentrated by preference upon the older works which were the inspiration for this study. Errors in transcription or judgment must be throughout my own responsibility.

In this second printing, through the courtesy of Mr. Elias S. Wilentz of Corinth Books, I have been able to correct a few errors, and append certain revisions or additional matter in the Appendix B and C; but I have in no way altered my original thesis. Indeed, as I review the original plan and as I have profited by subsequent class discussions, I have more confidence than ever in this approach as at least *one* valid means among many of reminding Americans that our national history is linked with the aspirations of human beings over the centuries, and has still its meaning and import for humanity at large. If I have in any measure contributed to that understanding, I shall not regret my labors.

WILSON O. CLOUGH

Laramie, Wyoming
February 1955
Revised, (April) 1961.

TABLE OF CONTENTS

Part II. The English Tradition to 1700, page 93

TABLE OF CONTENTS

INTELLECTUAL ORIGINS

TABLE OF CONTENTS

Conclusion, page 257

GENERAL INTRODUCTION

"Let us study the law of nature; search into the spirit of the British constitution; read the histories of the ancient sages; contemplate the great examples of Greece and Rome; set before us the conduct of our own British ancestors, who have defended for us the inherent rights of mankind against foreign and domestic tyrants and usurpers." John Adams, *Dissertation on the Canon and the Feudal Law*, 1765

"Having been initiated, in youth, in the doctrines of civil liberty, as they were taught by such men as Plato, Demosthenes, Cicero and other renowned persons among the ancients, and such as Sidney and Milton, Locke and Hoadley among the moderns, I liked them; they seemed rational." Jonathan Mayhew, "The Snare Broken," sermon, 1766

"I give to my son, when he shall arrive to the age of fifteen years, Algernon Sydney's works, John Locke's works, Lord Bacon's works, Gordon's Tacitus, and Cato's Letters. May the spirit of liberty rest upon him." Josiah Quincy, Jr., will, dated 1774

"If you will follow my advice, there still may be hopes of your reformation. Apply yourself, without delay, to the study of the law of nature. I would recommend to your perusal, Grotius, Pufendorf, Locke, Montesquieu and Burlamaqui. I might mention other excellent writers on the subject; but if you will attend diligently to these, you will not require any others." Alexander Hamilton to Samuel Seabury, "The Farmer Refuted," 1774

". . . not to find out new principles, or new arguments, never before thought of, not merely to say things which had never been said before; but to place before mankind the common sense of the subject, in terms so plain and firm as to command their assent. . . Neither aiming at originality of principles or sentiment, nor yet copied from any particular and previous writing, it was intended to be an expression of the American mind. . . All its authority rests then on the harmonizing sentiments of the day, whether expressed in conversation, in letters, printed essays, or the elementary books of public right, as Aristotle, Cicero, Locke, Sidney, etc." Thomas Jefferson, to Henry Lee, on the Declaration of Independence, May 8, 1825

GENERAL INTRODUCTION

Much has been made in American history of the impact of the frontier upon the transplanted Europeans who became Americans with a new way of life and a new philosophy of government. The origin of American institutions has been traced to this feature of American experience, sometimes to a degree that would lead the young student, especially as one goes westward from the Atlantic seaboard, to believe that everything American is wholly indigenous.

There is no need to minimize the contribution of the frontier to American life. Indeed, in the end, such a study as this one might even serve to reinforce the conviction that something new in history did take place. Nevertheless, there has been a corresponding danger that Americans might deny or largely forget their common heritage with the past. It is the purpose of this book of selected readings, taken from the shelves of our colonial ancestors, to remind us once again that we are indubitably a part of the great inheritance of western Europe, and to furnish the evidence that some of our most cherished traditions of liberty have behind them a long history to link us with a past far beyond Jamestown and Plymouth.

Take, for example, the great body of words and phrases used over and over in the heat of revolutionary oratory and pamphleteering: natural law, the law of nature, natural rights, man in the state of nature, the law of nations, reason and nature, Nature's God, self-evident (i.e., natural) truths, the rights of man, the right of resistance, the will of the people, the authority of the people, a government of laws not men, public office as a trust, the consent of the governed, covenant and compact and contract theories of government, constitutional rights, no taxation without representation, no taxation without consent, the election of representatives of the people, magistrates as servants of the people, the liberties of the people, freedom of the press, objections to standing armies, and, in sum, the end and aim of government as the preservation of these rights. Not a single one of these terms is American in origin. Not a single phrase is without its long history, often running back far into the life of ancient Greece and Rome.

How, then, did these and other concepts get into the American stream of history? The answer is to be found, directly or indirectly, in books, the inheritance of colonial Englishmen of the great books and ideas of their own past. That answer may be summarized in two sentences:

1. American political wisdom was the fruit of a long inheritance, stretching back to classical times, re-emergent in the Renaissance, blended opportunely with a sturdy British tradition of common law, reinforced by the studies of continental scholars, and crossing as a whole to America as a common heritage.

2. American leaders were fortunate in this heritage, wise in selection from it, fortunate again in the climate of eighteenth-century liberalism and in the freedoms of a new world; and were thus able to forge from their opportunity a whole new, revolutionary and dynamic synthesis of their own.

Hence, though popular opinion often appears to favor some sort of political revelation for a time of need, the true answer is at once less mystical and more profoundly moving. Madison stated the American contribution in a sentence (Federalist Paper No. 14): "Is it not the glory of the people of America that, while they have paid a decent regard to the opinions of former times and other nations, they have not suffered a blind veneration for antiquity, for custom or for names, to overrule the suggestions of their good sense and knowledge of their own situations, and the lessons of their own experience?"

Adams recognized the power of "opinions of former times" when he asserted that American rights were founded on "the principles of Aristotle and Plato, of Livy and Cicero, and Sidney, Harrington and Locke; the principles of nature and eternal reason."[1] The first half of his assertion acknowledges the classical and British inheritance; the second appeals to an eighteenth-century confidence in observation, experience, and common sense, a confidence no less rooted in a long tradition.

GENERAL INTRODUCTION

Did Americans Draw on Their Heritage?

Directly or indirectly, Americans drew heavily on the heritage of the past, especially as it was embedded in the British tradition, for the language and the argument of their cause. In a sense, American political history was but an extension of the European past, though an American might supplement that statement by a reminder that (1) it was from the liberal tradition that the American more specifically drew, and (2) adaptations and remodelings did result in new features.

At the risk of a dangerous oversimplification, let us put the argument thus: The ancient Greek world produced a body of political and philosophical literature which became the property of the Roman world at the time of the late republic and the earlier empire, and which, under the needs of an imperial expansion over the known Mediterranean world (Europe, Asia, Africa), took the form of a philosophy of a universal law common to all mankind, a law of nature, of man, and of nations. Elements of this philosophy could be assimilated by Christianity under the term "law of God," as might be shown by Augustine and Thomas Aquinas, to reappear later in some form in such diverse figures, for example, as John Calvin, Grotius, or Richard Hooker. But it was destined to reappear more dynamically in Renaissance thinking and Renaissance humanism, where it leaned more directly on the great new texts of the ancient classics, and where, under the impact of the new science and mathematics, it could take once again a new secular form as natural law, and reason and nature.

In the meantime, in England a long struggle between a medieval logic of authoritarian royal power and a sturdy native tradition of common law emerged to violence in the seventeenth century, and ended in a new concept of government. Seventeenth-century man, caught in an economic revolution, in part fostered by New World concerns, and dragging with him still the shreds of old rationalizations and abstractions, nevertheless worked his way to a new synthesis. In the process and in the search for a modern platform, the native religious and political strains blended with the classical argument for the law of nature, and produced a typical British compromise in government and church. This philosophy found expression religiously in Hooker and Milton and in more secular terms in Harrington, Sidney, and especially Locke.

This British resolution the Americans inherited as their own right, a right intensified, if anything, by their own history of religious independency and social cosmopolitanism, and by the frontier opportunity for political autonomy. As the original settlement motivation and theocratic drive yielded to a rising practicality and self-confidence, the Americans, seeking but failing to find relief in the old British tradition, turned once more to the ancient language of the law of nature and of nations, that is, the classical and Renaissance heritage. This new surge of an old tradition, perhaps its last forceful revival in history, was immensely aided by two important factors: the eighteenth-century climate of liberalism, rationalism, and empiricism, which made possible an American eclecticism that ignored much of the medieval inheritance; and the freedom to experiment without too much traditional restraint. Up to and through the American revolutionary era, then, the stream of a long heritage flows vigorously in a New World setting.

There is a certain duality, therefore, in the American story: on the one hand, the hard lessons of self-reliance which fostered independence and the empirical spirit; on the other, the growing culture which turned to the long heritage for its language and its argument. It is the dichotomy of East and West which has often been pointed out in our history. As we turn, then, to the records of the past, we do not forget that the temper of the time was empirical and eclectic. Yet it is equally important to recall how thoroughly British was the cultural climate of the American eighteenth century.

We must begin, then, with the reminder that American colonials were British from the outset. Whatever the motivations for settlement, they brought with them the traditions of the motherland. Printing, as we know, was slow to start, and was limited to sermons and civil statutes. The Puritan press printed little else from its beginning in 1639 up to at least 1715. Yet the General Laws of the Massachusetts Colony, the Fundamental Orders of Connecticut (see text, p. 113), the Plantation Agreement at Providence, Bacon's rebellion in Virginia, the proposed New England confederation, or the Frame of Government of the Province of Pennsylvania, all of them seventeenth century, prove how English were these colonists.

Their language, that is, is in the British civil tradition. However rigorous the laws of Massachusetts in the name of their faith, they also strongly affirm the traditional liberties—"free fruition of such Liberties, Immunities, Privileges, as Humanity, Civility and Christianity call for, as due to every man in his place and proportion, without impeachment and infringement"; and they order that "no man's life shall be taken away, no man's honor or good name shall be stained, no man's person shall be arrested, restrained, banished, dismembered, nor any ways punished, no man shall be deprived of his wife or children, no man's goods or estate shall be taken away from him, nor any ways indamaged, under color of law or countenance of authority, unless it be by virtue of equity of some express law of the country, warranting the same established by a general court." [2]

In like wise, the Connecticut orders of 1638 reaffirm the ancient British rights; the Plantation Agreement at Providence of 1640 stipulates liberty of conscience and government by arbitration; and the Pennsylvania charter of 1701 asserts that "liberty of conscience shall be kept and remain, without any alteration, inviolable forever." Thus the traditions of civil law and civil liberties forge the links with the past of British history.

But it is with American libraries, at first largely dependent on importations, that we are most concerned. *Literary Culture in Early New England, 1620–1730,* by T. G. Wright (New Haven, Conn.: Yale University Press, 1920), records numerous titles of books imported to Harvard and to private libraries before 1730. Harvard had early the works of Bacon and Erasmus, North's Plutarch, Epictetus, Aquinas, and Cicero's *De Officiis.* Brewster in Plymouth owned Bacon and Cicero, Seneca and Machiavelli, and Raleigh's histories. Cicero is also in the libraries of Sewell and Cotton Mather, and the latter has also More's *Utopia,* Plutarch, and Richard Hooker. Samuel Lee's library, sold in 1693, included 124 works in physics, 83 in philosophy, 112 of history in Latin and 45 in English, and so on, including the works of Plato, Aristotle, Xenophon, Seneca, Sophocles, Tacitus, Plutarch, and Bacon.

Southern planters, too, took pride in their libraries and could point in the seventeenth century to Montaigne, Erasmus, Bacon, Hobbes, Locke, Descartes, Grotius, and Machiavelli. The Robert Beverly estate in Virginia in 1734 showed classical and British works, including Bacon, Milton, Locke, Pope and Shaftesbury; and William Byrd's library is said to have possessed 394 volumes of ancient classics alone.

The Eighteenth-Century Climate of America

There was, as we have noted, little printing in America before 1735, though the appearance in 1717 of John Wise's *Vindication* (see page

7

226), or the difficulties experienced by the Franklins around 1720, or the printing in 1721 of Henry Care's *English Liberties*, a documentation of the political heritage (see below, p. 106), would indicate that the American press was already aware of issues to come.

In Philadelphia, the new atmosphere of religious liberalism found early expression in Andrew Bradford's publication in 1728 of *A Few Words in Favor of Free Thinking* and Samuel Keimer's *A Looking Glass for the Modern Deists*; and in Boston, James Franklin offered *Faults on All Sides: The Case of Religion Considered*. Evidently, the rising Whig and deistic temper of the mother country was already abroad.

In 1735 appeared the first bit of American translation from the Latin, James Logan's *Moral Distichs* of Cato. In the same year, the *Narrative of Peter Zenger's Case and Trial in New York* began the issue of the freedom of the press in the new world. Zenger was defended by the aging Andrew Hamilton of Philadelphia, who reverted to the ancient British right to remonstrate against "arbitrary attempts of men in power," and cited the infamous Star Chamber of the past. He defended, he said, the cause of "every freeman that lives under British government on the main of America." Gouverneur Morris called this case "the morning star of liberty which subsequently revolutionized America." As in the expostulation against Governor Andros in 1689, British "natural rights" were invoked.

We should note, too, the rise of American newspapers and magazines: the *New England Courant* (1721) of the Franklins, already quoting Trenchard on freedom of speech (see *Cato's Letters*, page 222); the *Pennsylvania Journal* (1741), vigorous spokesman of English liberties; the Maryland and Virginia gazettes, dating from 1727 and 1736. Peter Zenger we have mentioned. The first magazines, appearing in Philadelphia in 1741, Andrew Bradford's *American Magazine* and Franklin's *General Magazine*, show a lively awareness of political issues. Franklin's publication ran commentaries on European affairs and on colonial complaints; and Bradford's three issues were rich in references to free inquiry, liberty, religious freedom, and the "religion of Nature." A review of legislative proceedings in Maryland provoked a summary of government from Athens and Sparta down to the English revolution, with Locke, Harrington, and Cicero as authorities. It was a theme destined to become familiar to Americans, the subject, indeed, of many a revolutionary document, as of the *Federalist Papers*, numbers 18–20.

The tide of importation swelled in the eighteenth century, and every ship to England carried its order for books. Yale by 1714 had the complete works of Boyle, Locke, Newton and Milton, Spenser and Bacon. Grotius appeared everywhere after 1700. By 1750 Franklin was proposing that the youth of Pennsylvania be taught the classics through translations, as well as the English Locke, Milton, Pope, Addison, Swift, Sidney, and Tillotson. By 1755 the newer colleges of Philadelphia and King's (Columbia) openly argued for a broadly humanitarian education; and within the decade religious tests for entrance were removed by King's and Rhode Island (Brown). The tide of pamphlets, sermons, Acts of Parliament, and small magazines grew at home; and by 1755 some twenty-four presses were busy in the colonies, publishing twelve hundred titles in that one year. They dealt with practical problems like western lands and Indians, freedom of the press, relations with the mother country, trade and British restrictions, eighteenth-century science, local government, Whitefield and the Great Awakening, liberalism and deism. They also included reprints of European writings. For example, Addison's *Cato* (see page 219) was printed in Boston in 1750, a symbol of the popularity of the Stoic conception of republican virtue.

Thus we must assume that Americans of the century were readers, though we may deduct a portion of Franklin's claim that in America farmers were as well read as gentlemen elsewhere; or of Joel Barlow's "There are not five men in Europe who understand the nature of liberty and theory of government as well as they are understood by five hundred men in America." Yet these gentlemen may not have been wholly wrong. Noah Webster and Timothy Dwight, traveling at a later date about New England and New York, commented on the wide distribution of books and newspapers. The new country, they concluded, was a remarkably literate one.

But it is from 1750 on that American readers begin to consult their heritage; and it is from the same date that library lists become impressive. Politics, population, economic activities, new immigration, and a concern for ideas rose simultaneously. Franklin's proposal of 1754 for colonial federation recognized the rising power of the New World. Though the plan failed of execution because the time was not ripe either in the colonies or in the home government, it gave sufficient warning that Americans were no political illiterates. The French and Indian Wars had convinced the colonists of their mutual interests and their growing importance; and the literature of liberty flourished from that date.[3]

The colonial case was at first prosecuted in British terms and in the language of the "late revolution." John Dickinson's draft of the Pennsylvania Assembly Action on the Stamp Act of 1765, for example, opens with the "Resolved, first, That the Constitution of Government in this Province is founded on the Rights of Mankind, and the noble Principles of English Liberty, and is therefore perfectly true." Back of this emphasis was the fact that American law was British law, in the tradition of Coke, British secular law, and the parliamentarian habit. Only as events convinced the Americans that their claims to the full status of British citizens were being denied did they turn to the broader metaphysical heritage, that of Cicero and Locke, Grotius and Montesquieu, the law of nature and of nations.*

By the time of the Revolution, then, we may assume a considerable awareness on the part of American patriots of the general heritage. Let us glance, for example, at the fifty-six signers of the Declaration of Independence. Over one half were college graduates, a high showing for the time. They represented Harvard, Yale, Princeton, William and Mary, and Philadelphia, as well as Cambridge, Edinburgh, and the Temple Court of London. Carroll of Maryland, the one Roman Catholic of the group, was well educated in Belgium, France, and England. A few had medical training; more were lawyers, often prepared by reading with older men. Some of those without formal schooling, such as Franklin, Hopkins, Francis Lee, Walton, and Gwinnett, were reputed to be "prodigious" readers. Nearly half of them were by religious affiliation not members of the Anglican Church, despite its official status; and of those who were members, no doubt many shared the "latitudinarian" and deistic spirit of the day. Such men were no isolated rustics. Without this literate and liberal complexion, the story might have been quite different.

And what of the clergy of the day? The prevailing temper of the colonies was dissidence. Encouraged by a liberal British mercantile policy designed to get the colonies settled, dissidents flocked from Europe

* See, for example, Adams' testimony below (p. 259) on the Congressional debates of 1774.

GENERAL INTRODUCTION

to America, Pilgrim and Puritan, Presbyterian and Congregationalist, Baptist, Quaker, Dutch Calvinist and French Huguenot, German Lutheran and German Pietist, and English Catholic—none of them anxious to support the established church of England. One thing they had in common, an opposition to an English episcopate. Add to this a habit of appeal to a law higher than state, and a resolution to endure each in his own persuasion, and one can readily understand that conformity was not the watchword.[4]

Largest of these groups around 1775 were the Congregationalists and Presbyterians, followed by Baptists and Anglicans (the latter about one sixth of the whole), the Quakers, the foreign groups (German and Dutch), then a lesser number of Methodists, Roman Catholics, and scattered smaller bodies, such as Moravian, Dunker, Huguenot, and Jewish. No one single group was dominant over all the colonies. In this lack of religious uniformity lay the true source of religious freedoms— in this and in the rising current of liberalism.

Yet the Revolution could not have been accomplished without clerical support. Even Anglican clergy at times participated. But most militant were the descendants of the Puritans, and the Baptists, Methodists, and frontier Scotch-Irish. Even the inner light of Quakers and Pietists encouraged self-reliance and simplicity over authoritarianism, and foreign groups must have appreciated the general tolerance. Thus the authoritarian voices of Jonathan Boucher or Samuel Seabury were in the minority.

Boucher of Virginia and Governor Hutchinson of Massachusetts alike laid the blame for American sedition at the door of the Puritan clergy. "Election sermons" were usually printed, and there is in them abundant evidence of familiarity with Sidney, Harrington, Milton, and Locke, as with the classics. John Wise's *Vindication* of 1717 won a reprinting in 1772. By 1748, Jonathan Mayhew was claiming the right to religious freedom as "absolutely unalienable in nature"; and in 1750 he presented his *Discourse Concerning Unlimited Submission*. Whitefield, quite apart from politics, was nevertheless preaching in the 1740s the right of disobedience to those who break the laws of God. Definition of such "higher law" might and did vary considerably from speaker to speaker, but the general tone was not one of a passive acquiescence.

We are not surprised, then, to find that libraries flourished and that they included the literature of the European past. Some, as we have said, are impressive collections. Jefferson lost one library by fire and began another. In 1769 he ordered a varied list of books, including Locke, Montesquieu, and Burlamaqui. His well-known list for Robert Skipworth runs to 140 items in the fields of fine arts, politics, religion, history, and law, with the familiar names and titles of Milton, Addison, Pope, Locke, Sidney, Bolingbroke, Hume, Blackstone, Montesquieu, Mrs. Carter's Epictetus, L'Estrange's Seneca, Guthrie's Cicero, Gordon's Tacitus, Langhorne's Plutarch, and many another.

Noah Webster lists his reading: Plato, Tacitus, Cicero, Montesquieu, Rousseau, and others; and James Sullivan, jurist and one-time governor of Massachusetts, and author of *Observations* on our government (1791), is said to have been well grounded long before this date in Grotius, Pufendorf, Vattel, Burlamaqui, Hume, and Price. John Dickinson and James Wilson were sound students of history and law, and admirers of the classics and of Burlamaqui. These are but samplings.

Perhaps the libraries of Samuel and John Adams are the most impressive. Samuel, who for his graduation thesis at Harvard had studied as early as 1743 the doctrine of resistance, had more than superficial acquaintance with Plato, Cicero, Locke, Harrington, Coke, Grotius, Pufendorf, Montesquieu, and Blackstone. But the library of John Adams, as later catalogued for presentation to the town of Quincy in 1822, outdoes all others. Here are the complete works in their original languages of Cicero, Livy, Tacitus, Plato, Demosthenes, Aristotle, and Plutarch, the Greek often in parallel columns with the Latin, as was the Renaissance custom. Here, too, are the translations into English of Plato, Aristotle's *Politics* (the Ellis translation), Cicero, Thucydides, Mrs. Carter's Epictetus, Homer, Horace, Creech's Lucretius, Spens' Plato, Gordon's Sallust and Tacitus, and Murphy's Tacitus. Here are French authors in French and English: Bodin, Montesquieu, Nugent's Burlamaqui, Diderot, Grotius, Montaigne, Mably, Condillac, Raynal, Voltaire, Rousseau, Pufendorf in Latin and English, Farnesworth's Machiavelli, and Justinian's *Institutes*. And here are English works: the *Anglo-Saxon Chronicle* in Latin and English, Coke's *Commentaries*, Newton, the complete Milton, Hobbes, Locke, Harrington's *Oceana*, Gibbon, Hume, Tillotson, Bolingbroke, Burke, Blackstone, and Priestley. Adams read omnivorously and marked his margins generously.[5]

GENERAL INTRODUCTION
Eighteenth-Century Empiricism

The temper of the century was indubitably empirical. The roots of that empiricism lay both in the hard, practical facts of a frontier and in the mind and logic of the European Age of Enlightenment. Again, the threads cannot be easily disentangled. On the one hand were the lessons of self-reliance: the translation of peasant, indentured servant, and serf to free landholder, artisan, and merchant; the freedom from court, military, legal, and ecclesiastical controls; the very air and room of a vast continent. On the other was the whole body of eighteenth-century literature, science, and philosophy.

"Study governments as you do astronomy by facts, observations and experiments," wrote John Adams. Such was the expression of the new thesis. A Newtonian mathematics and a successful science had predicated an orderly universe, discoverable by reason and experience. Why, then, should not man and his political and social institutions be submitted to the same stimulating examination? On all sides, the rationalists taught that governments were but human phenomena, to be regulated by men for their own security and improvement. They were but agents of man, designed to preserve the rights of man in an orderly society, and their authority was delegated by those who instituted them. Human rights were not gifts of king or government, but inalienable, as a long tradition had argued. History was the record, to be examined by reason and common sense for its lessons and its warnings; and the present was the laboratory of experiment. To these theories America gave a new vitality.

Adams and Jefferson alike repudiated mystical and supernatural explanations for the American result. The common sense of the matter, said Jefferson, was a first concern. "The United States of America," wrote Adams in his Preface to his *Defense of the Constitutions of the United States of America* (1787–1788), "have exhibited, perhaps, the first example of governments erected on the simple principles of nature. . . . It will never be pretended that any persons employed in that service had interviews with the gods, or were in any degree under the inspiration of Heaven, more than those that work upon ships and houses, or laboring in merchandise and agriculture; it will forever be acknowledged that these governments were contrived merely by the use of reason and the senses. . . . Thirteen governments thus founded on the natural authority of the people alone, without a pretence of miracle or mystery, and which are destined to spread over the northern part of that whole quarter of the globe, are a great point gained in favor of the rights of mankind. The experiment is made, and has completely succeeded." Franklin, shrewd and politically observant, could but marvel in his turn how commonplace men, freed from the traditional threats of authority and given time and information, could arrive at sound conclusions by a pooling of their native good sense and experience. Perhaps in this literal confidence in the empirical synthesis of the century lay a part of the difference between Europe and America.

No doubt it is permissible today to smile at that confidence of another century in the fictions of "reason and nature." Carl Becker, in his *Heavenly City of the Eighteenth Century Philosophers*, treats them with a certain amused condescension. Yet J. R. Randall, in his *Making of the Modern Mind*, says, "The scientific culture of the eighteenth century marks the closest approach in modern times to the universal and cosmopolitan spirit that marked the Roman Empire and, in a different way, the Middle Ages." [6] John Adams, never without a residue of Puritan suspicion of human nature, nevertheless wrote to Jefferson in 1815 that the eighteenth century, "notwithstanding all its errors and vices, has been of all that are past the most honorable to human nature." As the older scholastic habit of footnoting faded from American documents, the experience of a new day replaced it with the new authority. Now Europe might quote America as the object lesson of practical government, founded on consent. As Madison wrote in the *National Gazette* (January 19, 1792): "In Europe charters of liberty have been granted by power. America has set the example . . . of charters of power granted by liberty."

The Lockean emphasis on property has often been treated as if it were crass materialism or some sort of ethical scandal. Yet consider for a moment the significance of property as a symbol of a new day. The word *freeman* had a special meaning to the New World settler, precisely because it represented a status difficult to acquire and precariously held in the Old World. Had not court, nobility, and cleric combined for centuries to seize time and again the humble man's property, and without recourse, making confiscation a major form of punishment for crimes political and ecclesiastical? Property, in the Lockean sense, included the rights to one's own person. To envision a society in which one's person and the fruits of one's labor were inviolable was no mean achievement. Must "rights" be forever limited to the privileged? Yet the founding fathers, in their optimism, took property for granted as a "right," and extended the horizon to the more inclusive, if more abstract, goal of "happiness."

The Plan Followed Below

We need not pretend at this point that the American founding fathers gave their days and nights to historical research, nor that they evolved a tight philosophical system, in the formal sense. If, in the heat of debate, orators and pamphleteers leaned on references to the Grecian states, Roman republican virtues, the ancient rights of Englishmen, the learning of Locke or Montesquieu, these do not necessarily prove scholarly depth. Perry Miller has wisely remarked of the Puritans that they not so much founded their society on the Scriptures as searched the Scriptures for corroboration of the society they had founded. So it might be said of the colonists that they not so much built on classical, Renaissance, and British learning as selected therefrom whatever might encourage them in the turn of events.

It is not always possible, therefore, to assert with literal confidence that a given American idea stems directly from a given author or book. The aim in this study is rather to make available a body of readings from the shelves of American libraries of around 1750 to 1780, from which selections we may savor the spirit and temper of that period, as well as its reference to its heritage.

On what basis, then, were the authors and excerpts below chosen? Primarily, on the evidence, admittedly sometimes inferential, as to the favored reading of the American eighteenth century: the evidence of libraries, papers, journals, diaries, letters, autobiographies, and political pamphlets. Graduate students aided not a little in such researches. Where reference is found to occur with some frequency and forcefulness to a Cicero, a Sidney, or a Burlamaqui, for example, the assumption is valid of acquaintance with that author, especially when his works are known to have been reasonably accessible. Some of the American documents incorporated into Part IV or the Appendix will illustrate such links. Though it might be difficult to produce statistical arguments for the relative influence of this or that author, I believe that further research would not greatly dispute the right of those found here to their representation, nor their relevancy to the issues which occupied the minds of thoughtful Americans in the period.[7]

Excerpts from such authors were suggested first by actual or near quotation: for example, John Wise's almost verbatim use of Pufendorf in his *Vindication* of 1717; Stephen Hopkins' or John Adams' quotations from Thucydides; the similarity of the opening words of the Declaration of Rights of 1688 and of the American Declaration of 1774; or the condensations of the language of "natural rights" (e.g., in the American "Rights of the Colonists" of 1772); and a dozen other such echoes of the past. There is admittedly a subjective element here, as actual quotation is not the rule and footnote substantiation not the general practice. Hence, a part of the intention is to immerse ourselves for a time in the library habits of the eighteenth century in America.

A word may be said of the recurrent term "natural law." There is a vast and complex literature on the subject of "natural law" and the "law of nature," which it is not the purpose of this book to debate. Colonial Americans were not scholastic in temper, nor were they given to subtleties and distinctions between Platonic, Aristotelian, or Aquinian connotations. The modern concern for some unassailable "system" of thought was less their goal than that of a practicable and workable political pattern. "A law of nature was acknowledged on all sides," wrote Basil Kennet of England early in the century; and its validity was as little questioned as are many of our own nationalistic assumptions. The applications of such a "law," it is true, might be far from consistent; and the opposition might be summarily labeled (as in the Declaration of 1772) "utterly irreconcilable to these principles." Such polemic thunderings are the not infrequent weakness of any large generalization labeled Truth. We must not be surprised, then, if to some, reason and nature meant a Newtonian universe of mathematical order; to others, inalienable rights and freedoms; and to still others, perhaps a majority, a heavy artillery piece, loaded with utility in the political arena.

Notwithstanding the ambiguities of "natural law," therefore, or of the "laws of nature and of nature's God" of the Declaration of Independence, few can ignore the weight of this concept in the eighteenth century. Excerpts had to be given, therefore, to show its very ancient roots and its persistence.

The division followed below seems a practicable one: first, the clas-

sical inheritance; second, the British seventeenth-century body of political writings; third, the continental stream; and finally, eighteenth-
century contributions, including some British colonial or American
documentation. A few American papers are added for convenience in
the Appendix. Prefatory comments throughout are intended to give
a minimum of setting or link with the over-all story.

The classical stream was a part of the traditional colonial education,
itself inherited from Cambridge and Oxford, and was augmented in the
seventeenth and eighteenth centuries by translations, often of considerable merit.

The British inheritance is of prime importance. The revolutionary
era began with an insistence on British rights; and up to the point of
open rebellion Americans seemed aggrieved and surprised that their
claim was not immediately recognized. They were, if anything, more
aware of the "late revolution" than the British themselves. Colonial life
was British, and in nothing so much as in the practice of civil government. To ask the origin of American political ideas is to ask a review
of British political history before 1775.

Continental works were by no means negligible in the growing libraries of the colonies; and names like Grotius, Pufendorf, Vattel,
Montesquieu, and Burlamaqui appear too frequently to be ignored. Nor
were the later French *philosophes* entirely without representation.

Finally, eighteenth-century British and American documents blend
and bring the argument up to the point of separation. The old documents had served a solid purpose. For a time the new country rode the
tide of a fine balance between authority and a frontier individualism,
between a static conservatism and a reckless romanticism. Distrustful
still of "democracy," yet encouraged by a new vision of the potential-
ities of the common man, happy in its distance from Old World re-
straints, aroused by endless vistas of opportunity, yet checked by the
balanced temper of the Age of Reason, a new world worked out its
own answers. How fortunate the little colonies were in their time, situation, and leadership.

It is unfortunate that space would not permit some further glimpse
of the literary and cultural currents of the day. Americans read also
some Shakespeare, Milton's poetry, or Greek drama, and more of Pope,
Swift, Goldsmith or Watts, and the British latitudinarian religious writers than I have been able to suggest. But these streams contributed less

directly to the political and pragmatic interests of the day, and so have
been necessarily minimized here.*

Obviously the story could not end with 1789, and the best minds
were quick to see that they had but inaugurated a new chapter in history. The larger volume they contemplated with confidence, because
they believed that the start had been wise and sound. Such a study as
this one, therefore, should be but the launching of a more comprehensive effort. The pages that follow, as has been said, are more particularly concerned with the intellectual stimulus that Americans found in
the books on their shelves: the classical inheritance, more alive to them
than to us, the Renaissance humanistic impulse, as filtered through the
history and intellect of England down to the day of the American testing. If certain key words appear repetitious, that but proves our major
point—the living persistence of the long heritage. Perhaps such a reading as this might serve, too, in some small degree to illuminate the
subsequent development of the American political, social, and cultural
patterns into the nineteenth and even the twentieth century.

* See further comment on colonial reading, Appendix C.

PART I · THE CLASSICAL HERITAGE

"This it is which is particularly salutary and profitable in the study of history, that you behold instances of every variety of conduct displayed on a conspicuous monument; that from thence you may select for yourself and for your country that which you may imitate; thence note what is shameful in the undertaking, and shameful in the result, which you may avoid." Livy, Preface to *History of Rome* (*c.* 25. B.C.)

"By reading of these Greek and Latin authors, men from their childhood have gotten a habit (under a false show of liberty) of favoring tumults, and of licentious controlling the actions of their sovereigns." Thomas Hobbes, *Leviathan*, II, 21 (1651)

"Two republican powers, Athens and Rome, have done more honor to our species than all the rest of it." John Adams, 1782

"To read the Latin and Greek authors in their original is a sublime luxury." Thomas Jefferson, letter to Joseph Priestley, January 27, 1800

"This is true liberty, when free-born men,
Having to advise the public, may speak free,
Which he who can, and will, deserves high praise;
Who neither can nor will, may hold his peace;
What can be juster in a State than this?"
Euripides, *The Suppliants* (5th century B.C.)

"Europe shall mourn her ancient fame declined
And Philadelphia be the Athens of mankind."
Titan's *Almanac*, 1730.

THE CLASSICAL HER[

THAT Americans read, and read seriously, the classic authors is beyond dispute. Their writings and debates are full of analogies drawn from the literature of the ancients, both for suggestion and warning. Demosthenes, Tiberius Gracchus, Brutus, Cato the Younger, and Cicero were symbols of excellence, and the tyrants of Greece, Caesar, and the decadent Emperors of Rome their abhorrence. Thucydides, Livy, and Tacitus they read for precept and example, and Plutarch supplied many an illustration of resistance to tyranny. Cicero and Seneca gave expression to the Stoic ideal of virtue in public office, and even the sententious morality of the eighteenth century echoed the old philosophers.

Cicero's oft quoted definition of law as the highest reason implanted in nature, which orders that which should be done and prohibits the contrary, could be used to justify rebellion against palpable injustice. Such a "law," labeled variously Nature's law, the law of nature, natural law, or the law of reason, had classical authority and contemporary usefulness. When it was called also God's law, it could be made palatable to those who possessed in their faiths a concept of a law above man. Thus we find John Dickinson quoting Sophocles:

> I could never think
> A mortal's law of power or strength sufficient
> To abrogate the unwritten law divine,
> Immutable, eternal, not like these
> Of yesterday, but made e'er time began.[1]

American acquaintance with the classics, like American education and much of American thinking, it can never be too strongly empha-

...irect inheritance from the Renaissance, fostered by the ...s, and given vitality by an obvious appropriateness to the ...t event.[2]

To say that the Renaissance was a rebirth of the ancient literature and the beginning of the modern world is a historical cliché, but none the less true. It was truly as if an ancient relative, forgotten and somewhat tarnished, had suddenly been found to have left an immense inheritance for his descendants, capable of reviving ambitions and financing exploits. Without that inheritance one can hardly imagine the modern world of science and political freedom. This, I think, is a point that one must unhesitatingly accept in any consideration of the American heritage.

The advent and growth of printing coincided most fittingly with the rise of the Renaissance spirit, and also with the Protestant Reformation, a fact not without its significance for the settlement of America. Humanism is a Renaissance word, and referred first to the new studies in the "humanities," or the ancient non-Christian writers who dealt with a man as man, primarily in terms of his needs and his welfare here on this earth, his social, intellectual, and moral living here and now. And if both Reformation and Counter Reformation had the unfortunate effect of dimming somewhat the first illuminations of the great Humanists, and of attaching censorship and disapproval to their eclecticism and philosophic tolerance, the Renaissance impact upon education lingered long both in Europe and America, and entered into universities everywhere.[3] It accounts for the tremendous importance given to the study of Greek and Latin, and eventually to secular subjects of all kinds. It is well to recall the great Humanists like the Catholic Erasmus and Sir Thomas More, or the Puritan Milton, for to such the later centuries owed not a little of their admiration for the past and their tolerance toward new ideas.

It is probably difficult for a mid-twentieth-century young generation to appreciate the extent and the impact of a classical education upon our ancestors. Hebrew and New Testament Greek were studied at Cambridge and Harvard for their religious associations, but Latin and Greek otherwise signified the great masculine, pagan contributions to the civilization of Western Europe. References to Greece and Rome abound in early American political papers and pamphlets, and they must indicate some general knowledge. Jefferson accounted his ability to read Greek a supreme luxury; Madison, John Dickinson, and Monroe carefully examined the political history of the ancients; and John Adams perused the old authors for relaxation and instruction. Even Patrick Henry, who was no scholar, claimed to have reread his Livy each year.

One gazes with respect on the great quartos and folios in Greek and Latin from the early days of printing, set by hand and pressed out by manual labor. Here, as elsewhere, America was the fortunate heir of the past. Collections of ancient literature had begun before the advent of printing, it is true; nevertheless, printing was the great stimulus to the editing and publishing of the ancients. The pioneer presses of Italy, Germany, Switzerland, France, Belgium, Holland, and finally England made available one ancient author after another. Only later did modern languages enter into the story. The rise of printing in England, already a center of Greek at Oxford, coincided with the era of important translations.[4] North's Plutarch and Florio's Montaigne, for example, were Shakespeare's companions; and the King James Bible threw its influence over all subsequent English literature.

A word should be said of the translations below. The aim was to make available the pages read by eighteenth-century Americans; hence, though modern translations might be both more accurate and more readable, the excerpts below come mostly from texts that circulated in the eighteenth century. For the translations of the period manage to sound often like the eighteenth century; and for that reason, despite some qualms, I have risked using in this book the more crabbed old texts, some of them not easily come by. Except for minor liberties with spelling and punctuation, taken in the interests of clarity, I have followed carefully the older texts. It is suggested that readers occasionally compare some more modern rendering of these classic authors, or read any larger quantities of classic authors in modern translations.

Thucydides

471?–400? B.C.

&§ Few ancient historians held so high a place as Thucydides. Facts were his concern; he drew no trite moral, and he had no recourse to supernaturalism. In him one might view the beginnings of democracy in manageable form—that is, the Greek city-state, with its shifts from king to freedom and again to tyranny. Athenian treatment of colonies was also a subject of interest to Americans (see Stephen Hopkins, page 242). The modernity of Thucydides is still pointed out, as are the resemblances between the speech of Pericles and that of Lincoln at Gettysburg. His history covered the years 431–404 B.C.

For Pericles, as reported by Thucydides, Athenian democracy meant government for all, equity of laws, selection of magistrates on merit, free private speech, freedom of circulation in the city—even for strangers—a vigorous native spirit, and a general participation in citizenship.

The passages below will illustrate (1) Thucydides' aim as historian; (2) the funeral oration of Pericles; and (3) the melancholy collapse of Athenian power, and of all Greece, into the horrors of anarchy, tyranny, and cruelty.

Herodotus the traveler, Thucydides the objective recorder, Xenophon the soldier, these men inaugurated in the fifth century B.C. the manner of modern history. Thucydides has gone through many editions since the Venetian one in Greek of 1502. Thomas Hobbes put him into English in 1634. Excerpts below are from the translation of William Smith, second edition, London, 1781. This translation first appeared in 1753, and was published in Philadelphia in 1818.[5] 〰

Thucydides as Historian

[Bk. I]. Thucydides an Athenian hath compiled the history of the war between the Peloponnesians and the Athenians, as managed by the contending parties. He began to write upon its first breaking out, from an expectation that it would prove important, and the most deserving regard of any that ever happened. He grounded his conjecture on the earnestness of both the flourishing parties to make all necessary preparations for it; and he saw that all the rest of Greece was engaged on one side or the other, some joining immediately, and others intending soon to do it; for this was the greatest commotion that ever happened amongst the Grecians, since in it some Barbarians, and it may be said the greatest part of mankind were concerned. . . .

From the testimonies alleged in support of what I have hitherto advanced, any one may depend on my account of things, without danger of false opinions. Let him withhold his credit from the songs of poets, whose profession it is to give all possible enlargements to their subjects. Let him do so farther by the writers of prose who study more that artful composition which captivateth the ear than the plain and simple recital of truth, where proper attestations are never found, and many things through length of time have incredibly sallied out into mere fable; and then he will be convinced upon the plainest proofs that the state of ancient Greece was very nearly the same as I have described it. And this present war, when considered in all its operations, notwithstanding the propensity of mankind to imagine that war in which they are personally engaged to be the greatest that ever happened, and so soon as it is over to replace their admiration upon others more ancient, will easily be owned to have been the most important of all.

As to the *speeches* of particular persons either at the commencement or in the prosecution of the war, whether such as I heard myself or such as were repeated to me by others, I will not pretend to recite them in all their exactness. It hath been my method to consider principally what might be pertinently said upon every occasion to the points in debate, and to keep as near as possible to what would pass for genuine by universal consent. And as for the *actions* performed in the course of this war, I have not presumed to describe them from casual narratives or my own conjectures, but either from certainty, where I myself was a spectator, or from the most exact informations I have been able to collect from others. This indeed was a work of no little difficulty, because even such as were present at those actions disagreed in their accounts about them, according as affection to either side or memory prevailed.

My relation, because quite clear of *fable*, may prove less delightful to the ears. But it will afford sufficient scope to those who love a sincere account of past transactions, of such as in the ordinary vicissitudes of human affairs may fully occur, at least be resembled again. I give it to the public as an *everlasting possession*, and not as a contentious instrument of temporary applause.

Pericles' Funeral Oration

[Bk. II, Ch. 6. 431 B.C.]. But the same winter, the Athenians, in conformity to the established custom of their country, solemnized a public funeral for those who had been first killed in this war, in the manner as follows:

The bones of the slain are brought to a tabernacle * erected for the

* Crawley has "tent." See *Complete Writings of Thucydides*, Crawley translation, in the Modern Library edition (New York: Random House, 1934), p. 102.

purpose three days before, and all are at liberty to deck out the remains of their friends at their own discretion. But when the grand procession is made, the cypress coffins are drawn on carriages, one for every tribe, in each of which are separately contained the bones of all who belonged to that tribe. One sumptuous bier is carried along empty for those that are lost, whose bodies could not be found among the slain. All who are willing, both citizens and strangers, attend the solemnity. . . .

As soon as they are interred, some one selected for the office by the public voice, and ever a person in great esteem for his understanding and of high dignity amongst them, pronounces over them the decent panegyric—and this done, they depart . . . Over these, the first victims of it, Pericles son of Xantippus was appointed to speak. So, when the proper time was come, walking from the sepulchre and mounting a lofty pulpit erected for the purpose, from whence he might be heard more distinctly by the company, he thus began:

Many of those who have spoken before me on these occasions have commended the author of that law which we are now obeying, for having instituted an oration to the honor of those who sacrifice their lives in fighting for their country. For my part, I think it sufficient for men who have approved their virtue in action, by action to be honored for it. . . . It is my duty to obey the law and to endeavor to procure, as far as I am able, the good-will and approbation of all my audience.

I shall therefore begin first with our forefathers, since both justice and decency require we should on this occasion bestow on them an honorable remembrance. In this our country they kept themselves always firmly settled, and through their valor handed it down free to every since succeeding generation. Worthy indeed of praise are they, and yet more worthy are our immediate fathers; since enlarging their own inheritance into the extensive *empire* which we now possess, they bequeathed that, their work of toil, to us their sons. . . . I mean not here to recite those martial exploits by which these ends were accomplished, or the resolute defences we ourselves and our fathers have made against the formidable invasions of Barbarians and Greeks—your own knowledge of these will excuse the long detail. But by what methods we have risen to this height of glory and power; by what polity and by what conduct we are thus aggrandized, I shall first endeavor to show; and then proceed to the praise of the deceased. These, in my opinion, can be no impertinent topics on this occasion; the discussion of them must be beneficial to this numerous company of Athenians and strangers.

We are happy in a form of government which cannot envy the laws of our neighbors; for it hath served as a model to others, but is original at Athens. And this our form, as committed not to the *few*, but to the whole body of the people, is called a *democracy*. How different soever in a private capacity, we all enjoy the same general equality our laws are fitted to preserve, and superior honors just as we excel. The public administration is not confined to a particular family, but is attainable only by merit. Poverty is not a hindrance, since whoever is able to serve his country meets with no obstacle to preferment from his first obscurity. The offices of the *state* we go through without obstructions from one another; and live together in the mutual endearments of private life without suspicions; not angry with a neighbor for following the bent of his own humor, nor putting on that countenance of discontent which pains though it cannot punish—so that in private life we converse without diffidence or damage, whilst we dare not on any account offend against the public, through the reverence we bear to the magistrates and the laws, chiefly to those *enacted* for redress of the injured, and to those *unwritten*, a breach of which is allowed a disgrace. Our laws have further provided for the mind most frequent intermissions of care by the appointment of public recreations and sacrifices throughout the year, elegantly performed with a peculiar pomp, the daily delight of which is a charm that puts melancholy to flight. The grandeur of this our Athens causeth the produce of the whole earth to be imported here, by which we reap a familiar enjoyment not more of the delicacies of our own growth than those of other nations.

In the affairs of war we excel those of our enemies, who adhere to methods opposite to our own. For we lay open Athens to general resort, nor ever drive any stranger from us whom either improvement or curiosity hath brought amongst us, lest any enemy should hurt us by seeing what is never concealed. We place not so great a confidence in the preparatives and artifices of war as in the native warmth of our souls impelling us to action. In point of education, the youth of some people are inured by a course of laborious exercise to support toil and exercise like men; but we, notwithstanding our easy and elegant way of life, face all the dangers of war as intrepidly as they. . . .

In our manner of living we show an elegance tempered with frugality, and we cultivate philosophy without enervating the mind. We display our wealth in the season of beneficence, and not in the vanity of discourse. A confession of poverty is disgrace to no man; no effort to avoid it is disgrace indeed. There is visibly in the same persons an attention to their own private concerns and those of the public; and in others engaged in the labors of life, there is a competent skill in the affairs of government. For we are the only people who think him that does not meddle in state affairs, not indolent, but good for nothing. And yet we pass the soundest judgments, and are quick at catching the right apprehensions of things, not thinking that words are prejudicial to actions, but rather the not being duly prepared by previous debate, before we are obliged to proceed to execution. Herein consists our distinguishing excellence, that in the hour of action we show the greatest courage, and yet debate beforehand the expediency of our measures. The courage of others is the result of ignorance; deliberation makes them cowards. . . .

I shall sum up what yet remains by only adding—that our Athens in general is the school of Greece; and that every single Athenian amongst us is excellently formed by his personal qualifications for all the various scenes of active life, acting with a most graceful demeanor and a most ready habit of dispatch. . . .

In the just defence of such a State these victims of their own valor, scorning the ruin threatened to it, have valiantly fought and bravely died. And every one of those who survive is ready, I am persuaded, to sacrifice life in such a cause. And for this reason have I enlarged so much on national points, to give the clearest proof that in the present war we have more at stake than men whose public advantages are not so valuable, and to illustrate by actual evidence how great a commendation is due to them who are now my subject. . . .

As for you who now survive them, it is your business to pray for a better fate, but to think it your duty also to preserve the same spirit and warmth of courage against your enemies . . . making the daily-increasing grandeur of this community the object of your thoughts and growing quite enamoured of it. And when it really appears great to your apprehensions, think again that this grandeur was acquired by brave and valiant men. . . . Now let every one respectively indulge the decent grief for his departed friends, and then retire.

THE CLASSICAL HERITAGE

The Nature of Corruption

[Bk. III, Ch. 10. 427 B.C. It would be pleasant to record that the outcome of a war begun so confidently was a happy one. Instead, Thucydides recounts a melancholy story of a long-drawn-out struggle, the disastrous Athenian expedition to Sicily, and the final victory of Sparta. Book VI is the account of an early naval expedition. Here, in Book III, we have a first-hand observation of the nature of war's progress and corruption. From this passage John Adams quoted in his *Defense of the Constitutions of the United States* (1787–1788), remarking of it that "It is impossible to read in Thucydides his account of the factions and confusions . . . without horror."]

When the Corcyreans had discovered the approach of the Athenian reinforcement, and the departure of the enemy, they received the Messenians within their walls who till now had lodged without; and having ordered the ships which they had manned to come about into the Hyllaic harbor, while they were going about in pursuance of this order, they put all the adverse faction whom they found to the sword. Those further who had been taken in on the ships at their persuasion, they threw into the sea and then retired. They afterwards went to Juno's temple and persuaded a party of suppliants there, to the amount of fifty, to undergo a judicial trial, in which they were all condemned to die. The majority of suppliants, who refused to hear such persuasion, no sooner saw the fate of their brethren than they either slew one another in the temple, or hung themselves upon the trees within its verge; each finding some expedient for his own dispatch. During those seven days that Eurymedon with his reinforcement continued at Corcyra, the people of that city extended the massacre to all whom they judged their enemies. The crime on which they justified their proceedings was *their* attempt to overturn the democracy.

Some perished merely through private enmity; some for the sums they had lent, by the hands of the borrowers. Every kind of death was here exhibited. Every dreadful act usual in a sedition, and more than usual, was perpetrated now. For fathers slew their children; some were dragged from altars; and some were butchered at them. And a number of persons immured in the temple of Bacchus were starved to death. So cruel was the progress of this sedition, and so excessively cruel did it appear, because the first of so black a nature that ever happened. But afterwards the contagion spread, one may say, through the whole ex-

tent of Greece, when factions raged in every city, the *popular* demagogues contending for the Athenians, the aspiring *few* for the Lacedaemonians. In peace, it is true, they were void of all pretext, of all
opportunity to invite these rivals. But now, amidst declared hostilities,
and the quest of alliance to afflict their enemies and add an increase of
strength to themselves, opportunities were easily found by such as were
fond of innovations to introduce the side they favored. The consequence of this was sedition in cities, with all its numerous and tragical
incidents. Such were now, and such things ever will be, so long as
human nature continues the same. . . . War, which snatcheth from
them their daily subsistence, is the teacher of violence, and assimilates
the passions of men to their present condition.

By these means were cities harassed with seditions. And those to
whose fate the later commotions fell, through enquiry what had happened in such instances before, grew enormously ambitious to suppress
the machinations of others, both in policy of attempts and extravagance
of revenge. Even words lost now their former significance, since to
palliate actions they were quite distorted. For truly, what before was
a brutal courage began to be esteemed that fortitude which becomes
a human and sociable creature; prudent consideration, to be specious
cowardice; modesty, the disguise of effeminancy; and being wise in
every thing, to be good for nothing. The hot fiery temper was ad-
judged the exertion of true manly vigor; cautious and calm deliberation, to be a plausible pretext for intended knavery. He who boiled
with indignation was undoubtedly trusty; who presumed to contradict,
was ever suspected. He who succeeded in a roguish scheme was wise;
and he who suspected such practices in others, was a still more able
genius. But was he provident enough so as never to be in need of such
base expedients, he was one that would not stand to his engagements
and most shamefully awed by his foes. In short, he who could prevent
[i.e., get ahead of] another in executing villainy, or could persuade a
well-designing person to it, was sure to be applauded.

Men now who were allied in blood were less valued or caressed than
such as were connected by voluntary combination; since the latter,
unscrupulous and uninquisitive, were more ready to embark in any
scheme whatever. For now associations were not formed for such
mutual advantage as is consistent with, but for the execution of such

rapines as are contrary to, human laws. In mutual trust they persisted, not out of any regard to religious obligations, but from the bond of communicated guilt. To the fair and honest proposals of adversaries they hearkened indeed, when such by active strength could control them, but never through candid ingenuity.* Revenge upon another was a more valued possession than never to have suffered injury. Oaths, if ever made for present reconciliation, had a temporary force, so long as neither knew how to break them; but never when either party had power to abet their violation. He who at inviting opportunity durst incur the perjury, if the adversary was off his guard, executed his rancor with higher spirit than from enmity open and avowed. Such a step was thought most secure; and, because he had thus surpassed in guile, it was certainly extolled as a masterpiece of cunning. Large is the number of villains, and such obtain more easily the reputation of dexterity than their dupes can of goodness. The latter are apt to blush; the former most impudently triumph.

The source of all these evils is a thirst for power, in consequence either of rapacious or ambitious passions. . . . Seditions in this manner introduced every species of outrageous wickedness into the Grecian manners. Sincerity, which is most frequently to be found in generous tempers, was laughed out of countenance and forever vanished. It was become the universal practice to keep up a constant enmity of intention against one another, and never to believe. No promise was strong enough, no oath sufficiently solemn, to banish such mutual diffidence. Those who excelled in shrewd consideration resigned all hope of any lasting security, and stood ever on their guard against whom it was impossible for them to trust. But persons of meaner understandings took more effectual means for their preservation. Living in constant apprehensions, from their own inferiority and the craft of their opponents, lest by words they should be overreached, or that such subtle heads might execute their treacheries upon them unawares, they boldly seized the present moment, and at once dispatched the men they dreaded; who, presuming too much on their own penetration, and that it was superfluous to aim a blow at those whom they could at any time supplant by cunning, despised them so far as to neglect a proper guard, and so contributed to their own destruction.

* Crawley has "generous confidence."

Demosthenes

384?–322 B.C.

◄§ The defeat of the Persians in 490 and 480 B.C. had made of Athens a free and powerful city, the head of the league with the Grecian cities of Asia Minor and the Agean. It was the great century, the age of art and drama, architecture and sculpture, science and oratory—Athens, the teacher of the ancient world. But rivalry with Sparta, as we have seen, ended in disaster before 400 B.C., and by mid-century, Philip of Macedon threatened all Greece. It was this threat that called forth the orator Demosthenes. The first Philippic was a call to arms, the second a warning of the designs of the northern barbarian. For a time Athens responded, but the march of Philip and his son Alexander was not to be halted.

The orations of Demosthenes have long been models of patriotism aroused, and Patrick Henry was flattered to be compared with the Greek. Demosthenes was edited in Greek as early as 1504 in Venice, and put into Latin by 1550. His orations appeared frequently, and two translations into English appeared in the eighteenth century in London: that of the Reverend Mr. Francis in 1757–1758, and that of T. Leland in 1770 in three volumes. The latter went through several editions into the nineteenth century. The excerpt below is from the third edition, London, 1777. §►

The Fourth Philippic

First, then, Athenians! be firmly convinced of these truths: that Philip does commit hostilities against us, and has violated the peace; (and let us no longer accuse each other of his crimes); that he is the implacable enemy of the whole city, of the ground on which this city stands, of every inhabitant within these walls, even of those who imagine themselves highest in his favor. . . . But it is against our constitution that his arms are principally directed; nor, in all his schemes, in all his actions, hath he anything so immediately in view as to subvert it. And there is in some sort a necessity in this. He knows full well that his conquests, however great and extensive, can never be secure while you continue free; but that if once he meets with any accident (and every man is subject to many), all those whom he hath forced into his service will instantly revolt, and fly to you for protection. For you are not naturally disposed to grasp at empire yourselves, but to frustrate the ambitious attempts of others; to be ever ready to oppose usurpation and assert the liberty of mankind; this is your peculiar char-

acter. And therefore it is not without regret that he sees in your freedom a spy upon the incidents of his fortune. Nor is this his reasoning
weak or trivial.

In the first place, therefore, we are to consider him as the enemy of
our state, the implacable enemy of our free constitution. Nothing but
the deepest sense of this can give you a true, vigorous and active spirit.
In the next place, be assured that every thing he is now laboring, every
thing he is concerting, he is concerting against our city; and that, wherever any man opposes him, he opposes an attempt against these walls.
For none of you can be weak enough to imagine that Philip's desires
are centered in those paltry villages of Thrace . . . that he endures
the severity of toils and seasons and braves the utmost dangers for these,
and has no designs upon the ports, and the arsenals, and the navies, and
the silver-mines, and all the other revenues of Athens; but that he will
leave them for you to enjoy, while, for some wretched hoards of grain
in the cells of Thrace, he takes up his winter quarters in the horrors
of a dungeon? Impossible! No; these and all his expeditions are really
intended to facilitate the conquest of Athens. . . .

Let us then approve ourselves men of wisdom; and fully persuaded
of these truths, let us shake off our extravagant and dangerous supine-
ness. Let us supply the necessary expenses; let us call upon our allies;
let us take all possible measures by keeping up a regular army; so that,
as he hath his force constantly prepared to injure and enslave the
Greeks, yours too may be ever ready to protect and assist them. . . .

If any man think that the measures I propose will require great expense and be attended with much toil and trouble, he thinks justly. Yet
let him consider what consequences must attend the state, if these measures be neglected; and it will appear that we shall really be gainers by
engaging heartily in this cause. Suppose some god should be our surety
(for no mortal ought to be relied on in an affair of such moment) that,
if we continue quiet and give up all our interests, he will not at last turn
his arms against us. It would yet be shameful, it would (I call all the
powers of heaven to witness!) be unworthy of you, unworthy the
dignity of your country and the glory of your ancestors, to abandon
the rest of Greece to slavery, for the sake of private ease. I, for my
part, would rather die than propose so mean a conduct! However, if
there be any other person who will recommend it, be it so; neglect
your defense; give up your interests! But if there be no such counsellor,

if, on the contrary, we all foresee that the farther this man is suffered to extend his conquests, the more formidable and powerful enemy we must find in him, why this reluctance? Or when, my countrymen, will we perform our duty? Must some necessity compel us? What one may call the necessity of freemen not only presses us now, but hath long since been felt: that of slaves, it is to be wished, may never approach us. And how do these differ? To a freeman, the disgrace of past misconduct is the most urgent necessity; to a slave, stripes and bodily pains. Far be this from us! It ought not to be mentioned! ...

I would gladly lay before you the whole conduct of certain politicians; but I spare them. One thing only I shall observe: the moment that Philip is mentioned, there is still one ready to start up and cry, "What a happiness to live in peace! How grievous the maintenance of a great army! Certain persons have designs upon our treasury!" Thus they delay your resolutions and give him full liberty to act as he pleases: hence you gain ease and indulgence for the present (which I fear may at some time prove too dear a purchase); and these men recommend themselves to your favor and are well paid for their service. But in my opinion there is no need to persuade you to peace, who sit down already thoroughly persuaded. Let it be recommended to him who is committing hostilities; if he can be prevailed on, you are ready to concur. Nor should we think those expenses grievous which our security requires; but the consequences which must arise if such expenses be denied. Then as to plundering our treasury, this must be prevented by entrusting it to proper guardians, not by neglecting our affairs. For my own part, Athenians, I am filled with indignation when I find some persons expressing their impatience, as if our treasures were exposed to plunderers, and yet utterly unaffected at the progress of Philip, who is successively plundering every state of Greece; and this that he may at last fall with all his fury upon you. . . .

But suppose he marches directly against us, what shall we say in that case? He will still assure that he is not at war: such were his professions to the people of Oreum when his forces were in the heart of their country; and to those of Pherae until the moment that he attacked their walls; and thus he amused the Olynthians until he marched his army into their territory. And will you still insist, even in such a case, that they who call upon us to defend our country are embroiling us in a war? Then slavery is inevitable. There is no other medium between an obstinate refusal to take arms, on your part, and a determined resolution to attack us, on the part of the enemy.

Nor is the danger which threatens us the same with that of other people. It is not the conquest of Athens which Philip aims at; no, it is our utter extirpation. He knows full well that slavery is a state you would not, or, if you were inclined, you could not submit to; for sovereignty is become habitual to you. Nor is he ignorant that at any unfavorable juncture, you have more power to obstruct his enterprises than the whole world besides.

Let us then be assured that we are contending for the very being of our state; let this inspire us with abhorrence of those who have sold themselves to this man; and let them feel the severity of public justice. For it is not, it is not possible to conquer our foreign enemy until we have punished those traitors who are serving him, within our walls. Else, while we strike on these, as so many obstacles, our enemies must necessarily prove superior to us.

Plato

427–347? B.C.

⥲ Plato and Aristotle—these names loom high in the ancient and medieval worlds, and into the modern. Wherever men have laid the city perfect in the future, Plato's *Republic* has made itself felt, whether it be Augustine's *City of God*, More's *Utopia*, or Campanella's *City of the Sun*; and Aristotle's mantle has fallen on all who have attempted to define the state as a natural human phenomenon, whether it be Harrington's *Oceana*, Montesquieu, or the American debates. As the historians recorded the Greek city-state in its actuality, so Plato and Aristotle gave the first important political philosophies in history.

Plato might with justice have been omitted from these readings, since he seems not to have exerted much positive influence on American political thought. Though his *Republic* was surely well known, the somewhat contemptuous dismissal of his writings by Adams and Jefferson indicates the empirical temper of the day; and, indeed, Plato's idealism lent itself more strictly to conservative uses, and had long been associated with a scholastic philosophy. His *Republic* was not truly a republic; and his philosopher-kings could be more easily transmuted into "divine rights" of kings than into "consent of the governed." Yet Franklin's admiration for the Socratic method is well known; and the passage below has its own special interest because of its theme of the rise of a human society from natural wants, a thesis easily demonstrated on the American frontier, and consistent with Aristotle's empiric view of man as by nature a political animal. Plato was not wholly without empirical hints; nor Aristotle without idealism, since his city-state, too, ends in virtue.

Plato was first printed in Greek in Venice in 1513, following upon earlier editions in Latin. Fragments of his work were, of course, known from ancient times. Translations into modern languages were not numerous, and the first real appearance in English seems to be that of H. Spens of Glasgow, in 1763. This is the translation followed below, excerpted, in fact, from Jefferson's own copy, now in the Library of Congress. Paragraphing has been modernized, and an occasional awkward passage annotated by reference to Jowett's translation, which may be found in the Modern Library edition of Plato's *The Republic*.

Socrates died in 399 B.C., and Plato, his pupil, lived into the sadder days of the decay of the Athenian state, expressing in his *Republic* his distrust of the popular will and his ideal society. The book begins with a casual discussion of the Golden Age and justice, until Thrasymachus interrupts to denounce Socrates as a quibbler, and to assert that justice is whatever the stronger make it, and that the unjust always seize power and property without scruple. "For such as revile wickedness [i.e., injustice] revile it not because they are afraid of doing, but because they are afraid of suffering, unjust things," says he. Socrates, in rebuttal, assumes that "every government, in as far as it is government, considers what is best for nothing else but the governed." This is a theme with a long history, involving Aristotle, Cicero, Thomas Aquinas, Hooker, and many who follow them.

The argument continues into Book II, in which Glauco considers the naturalistic explanation of justice as follows: after men had experienced injustice, both toward themselves and in themselves toward others, it seemed desirable "to agree among themselves neither to do injustice nor to be injured, and that hence laws begun [*sic*] to be established, and their compacts" (Spens). Socrates then suggests that the disputants start all over by examining the gradual formation of a city-state. This is the famous passage below, from Book II. In its translation Spens uses "city" where Jowett has "state."[6] ✌

The Republic

[Bk. II: Origin of the City]. A city, then, said I, as I imagine, takes its rise from this, that none of us happens to be self-sufficient, but is indigent [i.e., in need of] of many things; or do you imagine there is any other origin of building a city?

None other, said he.

Thus then, one taking in one person for one indigence, and another for another, as they stand in need of many things, they assemble into one habitation many companions and assistants; and to this joint-habitation we give the name city, do not we?

Certainly.

And they mutually exchange with one another; each judging that if he either gives or takes in exchange, it will be for his advantage.

Certainly.

Come then, said I, let us, in our discourse, make a city from the beginning. And, it seems, our indigence hath made it.*

Why not?

But the first and the greatest of wants is the preparation of food, in order to subsist and live.

By all means.

The second is of lodging. The third, of clothing, and such like.

It is so.

But come, said I, how shall the city be able to make so great a provision? Shall not one be a husbandman, another a mason, some other a weaver; or shall we add to them a shoemaker, or some other of those who minister to the necessaries of the body?

Certainly.

So that the most indigent city † might consist of four or five men?

It seems so.

But what now? must each of these do his work for them all in common: As the husbandman, being one, shall he prepare food for four, and consume quadruple time and labor in preparing food, and sharing it with others; or, neglecting them, shall he for himself alone make the fourth part of this food, in the fourth part of the time; and, of the other three parts of time, shall he employ one in the preparation of a house, the other in that of clothing, the other of shoes, and not give himself trouble in sharing with others, but do his own affairs by himself?

Adimantus said: And probably, Socrates, this way is more easy than the other. . . .

And hence it appears that more will be done, and better, and with

* Jowett is much better here: "yet the true creator is necessity." Another translation, that of Davies and Vaughan, 1852, rendered it "our natural wants."
† Jowett: "the barest notion of a State."

greater ease, when every one does but one thing, according to their genius, and in proper season, and freed from other things.

Most certainly, said he.

But we need certainly, Adimantus, more citizens than four for those provisions we mentioned. For the husbandman, it would seem, will not make a plough for himself, if it is to be handsome; nor yet a spade, nor other instruments of agriculture; as little will the mason, for he likewise needs many things; and in the same way the weaver and the shoemaker likewise. Is it not so?

True.

Joiners, then, and smiths, and other such workmen being admitted into our little city, make it strong.

Certainly.

But it would be no very great matter neither, if we did not give them neatherds likewise, and shepherds, and those other herdsmen, in order that both the husbandmen may have oxen for ploughing, and that the masons, with the help of the husbandmen, may use the cattle for their carriages, and that the weavers, likewise, and the shoemakers may have hides and wool.

Nor yet, said he, would it be a very small city, having all these.

But, said I, it is almost impossible to set down such a city in any such place as that it shall need no importations.

It is impossible.

It shall then certainly want others still who may import from another state what it needs.

It shall want them.

And surely this service would be empty if it carry out nothing which these want from whom they import what they need themselves. It goes out empty in such a case, does it not?

To me it seems so.

But the city ought not only to make what is sufficient for itself, but such things, and so much also, as may answer for those things they need.

It ought.

Our city, then, certainly wants a great many more husbandmen and other workmen?

A great many more.

And other servants besides, to import and export the several things: and these are merchants, are they not?

Yes.

We shall then want merchants likewise?

Yes, indeed.

And if the merchandise is by sea, it will want many others, such as are skillful in sea affairs.

Many others, truly.

But what as to the city within itself? How will they exchange with one another the things which they have each of them worked; and for the same of which, making a community, they have built a city?

It is plain, said he, in selling and buying.

Hence we must have a mercat-place [i.e., market-place], and money, as a symbol, for the sake of exchange.

Certainly.

If now the husbandman, or any other workman, bring any of his work to the mercat [i.e., market], but come not at the same time with those who want to make exchange with him, must he not be set idle from his work, sitting in the mercat?

By no means, said he. But there are some who, observing this, set themselves to this service; and in well-regulated cities they are mostly such as are weakest in their body, and unfit to do any other work. There they are to attend about the mercat, to give money in exchange for such things as any may want to sell, and things in exchange for money to such as want to buy.

This indigence, said I, procures our city a race of shopkeepers. [Hirelings, laborers, are also added.] . . .

Hath our city now, Adimantus, already so increased upon us as to be complete?

Perhaps.

Where, now, at all, should justice and injustice be in it; and in which of the things that we have considered does it appear to exist?

I do not know, said he, Socrates, if it be not in a certain use, somehow, of these things with one another.*

Perhaps, said I, you say right. But we must consider it, and not weary.

[Here follows a description of daily living, labor, social gatherings, food and feasting, and the introduction of the luxuries demanded by civilization, so that, according to Socrates, it is no longer a "healthy" city, but demands "beds and tables, seasonings, ointments, and perfumes, mistresses, and confections." Socrates continues:]

* Jowett: "in the dealings of these citizens with one another."

39

Must not the city, then, be larger? For that healthy one is no longer sufficient, but is already full of luxury, and of a crowd of such as are no way necessary to cities; such as all kind of sportsmen, and the imitative artists, many of them imitating in figures, and color; and others in music; poets, too, and their ministers, rhapsodists, actors, dancers, undertakers, workmen of all sorts of instruments; and what hath reference to female ornaments, as well as other things. We shall need likewise many more servants. Do you not think they will need pedagogues, and nurses, and tutors, hair-dressers, barbers, victuallers too, and cooks? And further still, we shall want swineherds likewise; of these there were none in the other city (for there needed not), but in this we shall want these, and many other sorts of herds likewise; if any eats the several animals, shall we not?

Why not?

Shall we not, then, in this manner of life be much more in need of physicians than formerly?

Much more.

And the country, which was then sufficient to support the inhabitants, will instead of being sufficient, become too little; or how shall we say?

In this way, said he.

Must we not then encroach upon the neighboring country, if we want to have sufficient for plough and pasture, and they in like manner on us, if they likewise suffer themselves to accumulate wealth to infinity, going beyond the boundary of necessaries?

There is great necessity for it, Socrates.

Shall we afterwards fight, Glauco, or how shall we do?

We shall certainly, said he.

But we say nothing, said I, whether war does any evil or any good; but this much only, that we have found the origin of war, from whence most especially arise the greatest mischiefs to states, both private and public.

Yes, indeed.

We shall need, then, friend, still a larger city, not for a small, but for a large army, who in going out may fight with those who assault them for their whole substance, and every thing we have now mentioned.

What, said he, are not these sufficient to fight?

No; if you, at least, said I, and all of us, have rightly agreed when we formed our city; and we agreed, if you remember, that it was impossible for one to perform many arts handsomely.

You say true, said he.

What then, said I, as to that contest of war; does it not appear to require art?

Very much, said he.

[There follows a discussion of the qualities needed by the guardians of the state, bravery, spirit, gentleness toward friends, philosophic disposition, and education, avoiding false fables and teaching the nature of the good and the true. Book VIII, after a caustic description of the ways of tyrants, attacks Democracy (i.e., mob rule) as the root of despotism and tyranny. The ideal is found, then, in the kingly rule, by the philosopher-king. For this ideal Plato is willing to sacrifice something of the "rights of men."]

Aristotle

384–322 B.C.

◦§ Aristotle, pupil of Plato, rose with Alexander the Great, and ranged the world of his time for his encyclopedic knowledge. Well known in Europe before the Latin and Greek editions of the late fifteenth century, he had come back into the European stream by way of the Spanish-Arabian scholar Averrois, who is said to have made Thomas Aquinas necessary. Certainly, though politics is not a major part of Aquinas' great work, what he has to say about the subject owes much to Aristotle and Cicero, perhaps particularly his distinction between natural law and divine law, on the first of which his thought in no small measure follows the Greek, and admits once more into the European stream the ancient concept of "natural law," with consequences reflected in Hooker, and so, indirectly, in Locke. Nevertheless, as is well recognized, the eighteenth-century adaptation of "natural law" was in part a deliberate attempt to rescue this classical concept from its theological overtones. Thus a duality which had long kept political theory linked with ecclesiastical complications could not be resolved until the American frank secularization of politics and separation of state and church.

Aristotle's *Opera Omnia* were edited by Erasmus in 1531. The *Ethics*, which preceded the *Politics*, appeared in English in 1547. The *Politics* was translated in 1598 from the French of Louis le Roy (Regius) of 1586. Two eighteenth-century translations were those of Ellis and Gillies. William Ellis published his in 1776, Gillies his in 1798. Excerpts below are from the Ellis translation, second edition, of 1778, which was used in the Everyman's Library in 1912.[7]

This essay on Politics recorded all the known forms of states, their evolution, their strength and weakness, in a way hitherto unequalled in the Western world. It is thus seminal for all subsequent studies of government; and Aristotle's major divisions became the conventional ones for centuries to follow, even in American political literature. References of a general sort to Aristotle are frequent, and nothing better shows the central position of this essay than the differences in interpretation. What Ellis translates as "democracy," Jowett calls "republic." Where Jowett has "community," Ellis has "political society," and Gillies "commonwealth." In Ellis, this society aims first at "good"; in Gillies, at "utility." Gillies, following the French Revolution, filled his Introductions with Tory remarks aimed at Locke's theory as "admirably fitted for producing revolutions and seditions."

Yet all perceived that Aristotle's genius lay in his concept of government as natural to man, or, as Gillies put it, "as congenial to the nature of man as it is natural for a plant to fix its roots in the earth" (introduction, II,1). Aristotle, that is, inaugurated the discussion of governments on the level of man's activities, derived from man's needs and his experience in the common enterprise of society.

Aristotle, though referred to oftener in American political writings than Plato (Franklin mentioned the *Politics* as early as 1721), is likewise a kind of secondary source of reference. Yet that may be because reference to, and acceptance of, his political divisions were almost universal, and called for no peculiar emphasis. ❧

Definitions

[I, 1]. As we see that every city is a society, and every society is established for some good purpose (for an apparent good is the spring of all human actions), it is evident that this is the principle upon which they are everyone founded, and this is more especially true of that which has for its object the best possible, and is itself the most excellent, and comprehends all the rest. Now this is called a city, and the society thereof a political society. . . . As, in an inquiry into every other subject, it is necessary to separate the different parts of which it is compounded, till we arrive at their first elements, which are the most minute parts thereof; so by the same proceeding we shall acquire a knowledge of the primary parts of a city and see wherein they differ from each other, and whether the rules of art will give us any assistance in examining into each of these things which are mentioned. . . .

[I, 2]. For what every being is in its most perfect state, that certainly is the nature of that being, whether it be a man, a horse, or a house; besides, whatsoever produces the final cause and the end which we desire must be best. Hence it is evident that a city is a natural production,* and that man is naturally a political animal, and that whatsoever is naturally and not accidentally unfit for society must be either inferior or superior to man. Thus the man in Homer who is reviled for being "without Society, without Law, without Family." Such a one must naturally be of a quarrelsome disposition, and as solitary as the birds. The gift of speech also evidently proves that man is a more social animal than the bees, or any of the herding cattle; for Nature, as we say, does nothing in vain, and man is the only animal who enjoys it. . . . He that is incapable of society, or so complete in himself as not to want it, makes no part of a city, as a beast or a god. There is then in all persons a natural impetus to associate with each other in this manner, and he who first founded civil society was the cause of the greatest good. . . .

[III, 1]. As a city is a collective body and, like other wholes, composed of many parts, it is evident that our first inquiry must be what a citizen is: for a city is a number of citizens. . . . There is nothing that more characterizes a complete citizen than having a share in the judicial and executive part of the government. . . .

[III, 6, 7]. We proceed next to consider whether one form of government only should be established, or more than one; and if more, how many, and of what sort, and what are the differences between them. The form of government is the ordering and regulating of the city, and all the offices in it, particularly those wherein the supreme power is lodged; and this power is always possessed by the administration; † but the administration itself is that particular form of government which is established in any state. Thus in a democracy the supreme power is lodged in the whole people; on the contrary, in an oligarchy it is in the hands of a few. . . .

It is evident that every form of government or administration, for the words are of the same import, must contain a supreme power over the whole state, and this supreme power must necessarily be in the hands of one person, or a few, or many; and when either of these apply

* Jowett: "a creation of nature," and "man is by nature," etc.
† Jowett says "constitution."

their power for the common good, such states are well governed; but when the interest of the one, the few, or the many who enjoy this power, is alone consulted, then ill . . . We usually call a state which is governed by one person for the common good, a Kingdom; one that is governed by more than one, but by a few only, an Aristocracy; either because the government is in the hands of the most worthy citizens, or because it is the best form for the city and for its inhabitants. When the citizens at large govern for the public good, it is called a State, which is also a common name for all other governments, and these distinctions are consonant to reason. . . . Now the corruptions attending each of these governments are these: a Kingdom may degenerate into a Tyranny, an Aristocracy into an Oligarchy, and a State into a Democracy. Now a Tyranny is a monarchy where the good of one man only is the object of government, an Oligarchy considers only the rich, and a Democracy only the poor; but neither of them have a common good in view. . . .

[III, 9]. A City is a society of people joining together with their families and their children to live agreeably for the sake of having their lives as happy and as independent as possible. . . . It is not therefore founded for the purpose of men's merely living together, but for their living as men ought. . . .

[III, 16]. He who would place the supreme power in mind would place it in God and the laws; but he who entrusts man with it, gives it to a wild beast, for such his appetites sometimes make him; for passion influences those who are in power, even the very best of men: for which reason, law is reason without desire.

Democracy

[IV, 4]. The most pure democracy is that which is so called principally from that equality which prevails in it; for this is what the law in that state directs: that the poor shall be in no greater subjection than the rich; nor that the supreme power shall be lodged with either of these, but that both shall share it. For if liberty and equality, as some persons suppose, are chiefly to be found in a democracy, it must be so by every department of government being alike open to all; but as the people are the majority, and what they vote is law, it follows that such a state must be a democracy. . . .

Where a democracy is governed by stated laws, there is no room for

them [demagogues], but men of
but where power is not vested in
for there the people rule with kingl)
body; for they are supreme, not as i.
capacity. When the people possess this
gether absolute, that they may not be un&
this is the time when flatterers are held in
government is not in the laws, then there i
ought to be supreme over all things; and p.
arise should be determined by the magistrates \

The Golden Mean

[IV, 11]. We proceed now to inquire what form of government and
what manner of life is best for communities in general, not adapting it
to that superior virtue which is above the reach of the vulgar, or that
education which every advantage of nature and fortune only can furnish, nor to those imaginary plans, which may be formed at pleasure;
but to that mode of life which the greater part of mankind can attain
to. . . . The opinions which we form upon these subjects must depend
upon one common principle: for if what I have said in my treatise on
Morals is true, a happy life must arise from an uninterrupted course of
virtue; and if virtue consists in a certain medium, the middle life must
certainly be the happiest; which medium is attainable by everyone. . . .

It is the genius of a city to be composed as much as possible of equals;
which will be most when the inhabitants are in the middle state. . . .
It is plain, then, that the most perfect political community must be
amongst those who are in the middle rank, and those states are best instituted wherein these are a larger and more respectable part, if possible, than both the other; or if that cannot be, at least than either of
them separate; so that being thrown into the balance, it may prevent
either scale from preponderating.

The Nature of Tyranny

[V, 11]. What has already been mentioned is as conducive as anything can be to preserve a tyranny; namely, to keep down those who
are of an aspiring disposition, to take off those who will not submit, to
allow no public meals, no clubs, no education, nothing at all, but to
guard against everything that gives rise to high spirits or mutual con-

e learned meetings of those who are at leisure
on with each other; and to endeavor by every pos-
keep all people strangers to each other; for knowledge
confidence; and to oblige all strangers to appear in public . . .
those who are kept like slaves seldom entertain any noble thoughts;
in short, to imitate everything which the Persians and barbarians do, for
they all contribute to support slavery; and to endeavor to know what
every one who is under power does and says, and for this purpose to
employ spies. . . . A tyrant also should endeavor to engage his subjects in a war, that they may have employment, and continually depend
upon their General. A King is preserved by his friends, but a tyrant
is of all persons the man who can place no confidence in friends, as
every one has it in his desire, and these chiefly in their power, to destroy him. . . .

Tyrants always love the worst of wretches, for they rejoice in being
flattered, which no man of a liberal spirit will submit to, for they love
the virtuous, but flatter none. Bad men too are fit for bad purposes;
"like to like," as the proverb says. A tyrant also should show no favor
to a man of worth or a freeman; for he should think that no one deserved to be thought these but himself; for he who supports his dignity
and is a friend to freedom encroaches upon the superiority and the
despotism of a tyrant. Such men, therefore, they naturally hate, as destructive to their government.

[Aristotle finds best of his four kinds of democracy, that composed
of husbandmen (farmers) holding small properties, following their own
business and not desiring another's, and not meddling in government
if left alone. Liberty he finds in governing and being governed alter-
nately, living as one likes, chosing magistrates from the people, with
appointments for short times only, except where special skills are
needed. Finally, he inquires what life is best, and ends with a definition
of virtue.]

The Good Life

[VII, 1, 2]. As what is good, relative to man, may be divided into
three sorts, what is external, what appertains to the body, and what to
the soul, it is evident that all these must conspire to make a man happy.
For no one would say that a man was happy who had no fortitude, no
temperance, no justice, no prudence, but was afraid of the flies that
flew around him; nor would abstain from the meanest theft if he was

either hungry or dry, or would murder his dearest friend for a farthing; and also was in every particular as wanting in his understanding as an infant or an idiot. These truths are so evident that all must agree to them. . . . Let us therefore be well assured that every one enjoys as much happiness as he possesses virtue and wisdom, and acts according to their dictates. . . . It is evident that government must be the best which is so established that every one therein may have it in his power to act virtuously and live happily.

Polybius
205?–123? B.C.

◄§ Polybius appears to have been the earliest admirer of Roman political institutions as seen from the outside. Though he follows closely Aristotle's classification of political forms, we cannot fail to be interested, as colonial Americans were, in his cyclic theory of governments and his belief that Rome by trial and error had discovered the answer in a mixed form of government, an equilibrium consistent with the principle of checks and balances. His discussion of the natural origin of government, and of its behavior under natural law, has a distinctly eighteenth-century flavor, especially so in Hampton's translation, first published in 1756, and again in 1764 with Book VI, from which the excerpt below is taken (fifth edition, London, 1811). The writings of Polybius early appeared in Latin, and were clearly known to Cicero and others. Polybius was first Englished by Edward Grimeston in 1633.[8] ঽ►

[Bk. VI]. There are therefore six different kinds of government: three, which are in the mouths of all men [i.e., royalty, aristocracy, and democracy], and which have now been mentioned; and three more that are allied to these by nature; monarchy, oligarchy, and the government of the multitude. Of all these, the first in order is monarchy; which is established by the bare work of nature, without any preparation or design. From monarchy arises royalty, when art has been applied to correct the vices of the former. And when royalty has degenerated into congenial evil, which is tyranny, the destruction of the latter gives birth to aristocracy. This again being changed, according to the natural order of things, into oligarchy, the subjects, roused to vengeance by oppression, resist the injustice of their governors, and establish a democracy. And, in the last place, when the people themselves become haughty and untractable, and reject all law, to democracy succeeds in the course of time the government of the multitude.

That this deduction is agreeable to truth will be clear to everyone who considers with attention the commencement and first rise, as well as the changes, which nature has appropriated to each particular kind of government. And indeed there is no other way but by observing what was the natural birth of every state to judge with certainty concerning the progress of it towards perfection, and from thence to decline and ruin; and to discern at what time, in what manner, and into what different form it will at last be changed. Above all others, the Roman government may best be illustrated by such a method of inquiry: because this state, both in its first establishment and subsequent increase, displays a close conformity with the settled laws and regular course of nature. . . .

What then are the commencements, and what the original rise, of political societies? When a deluge, a pestilential disease, a famine, or any other similar cause, has brought destruction upon the human race, as tradition assures us it has happened in former times, and as it is probable it will again hereafter happen; and when all arts and institutions are extinguished also in the same calamity, from the few that are left alive another progeny of men springs up who, being conscious of their natural weakness, and attracted like all other animals to a union with their own kind, associate themselves together in a body. At this time, therefore, it is manifest that he who is superior both in strength and courage must govern and conduct the rest. For that this is indeed the genuine work of nature is most clearly seen in the examples of the several kinds of animals, which are led by natural instinct only, unimproved by reason. . . . Such, therefore, is the original state of men, when they assemble together in a manner not unlike to that of other animals, and are led by those that are the bravest and the most powerful. And this state may properly be called a monarchy, in which the authority of those that govern is measured by their strength. But afterwards, when in these societies a common education and mutual intercourse have produced new sentiments and habits, then first commences royalty; then first arise in the human mind the notions of honorable and base, of just and unjust. . . .

[Here Polybius traces the sense of duty and justice from gratitude or ingratitude in children toward parents, or of men toward those who have saved them in danger, or of people toward the bravest to defend them in warfare; for by reason, man alone of animals cannot be indifferent to these things, since he, too, may next be exposed to danger.]

When he, therefore, who possesses the greatest power and is placed at the head of all the rest, is found always to comply with the general sentiments, in supporting fortitude and merit, and in distributing to every one impartial justice, the people, no longer dreading his superior force but paying a willing obedience to his wisdom, submit themselves to his authority, and with one consent maintain him in his government against all invaders, even to extreme old age. And thus the monarch, by insensible degrees, becomes a king, when reason takes the rule in the place of strength and violence. Such are the first perceptions among mankind of justice and injustice, of base and honorable; and such the origin and rise of genuine royalty. For the people not only confirm these leaders in the possession of the power to which they have been raised, but preserve it to their children likewise; being persuaded that those who have received their birth and education from virtuous parents cannot but resemble them in manners. And if at any time they are displeased at the conduct of these descendents, they then choose other magistrates and kings. But having been taught to discern by past experience the difference between external faculties and the endowments of the mind, they now appoint to the supreme command not those that excel in bodily strength and vigor, but those who are distinguished by their wisdom and superior reason. . . .

[Polybius next shows how descendents of kings plunge into self-gratification and admit of no contradiction, and so arouse hatred and dissolve into tyranny; and so are destroyed by a few nobility and give way to aristocracy, to whom the people are grateful. But the children of aristocracy repeat the same abuses, and fall into an oligarchy, and in turn arouse rebellion, led by some brave citizen. Not daring to try monarchy or aristocracy again, they now trust to themselves and frame a democracy. In time, this liberty and equality gives way to ambition and power, whose holders corrupt the people by gifts until all yields to violence and force and anarchy, and so again to a single leader, or monarch and arbitrary control.]

Such is the circle in which political societies are revolved, and such the natural order in which the several kinds of government are varied, till they are at last brought back to that original form from which the progress was begun. With the help of being acquainted with these principles, though it may not perhaps be easy to foretell the exact time of every alteration that may happen in a state, yet, if our sentiments are free from prejudice and passion, we shall very rarely be deceived in judging of the degree either of exaltation or decline in which it actually subsists, or in declaring the form into which it must at last be changed. With regard especially to the commonwealth of Rome, this view of things cannot fail to lead us into the knowledge both of the original constitution and the gradual progress of it towards perfection, as well as of the future revolution also that awaits it. For as this government above all others received, as we have already observed, both its first establishment and subsequent increase from the settled laws of nature, it is reasonable to believe that it will follow the same laws likewise in being changed hereafter into a contrary form. But this will be more distinctly seen in the following parts of this discourse. I shall now give a short account of the frame of government that was established by Lycurgus. Such a digression will not be foreign to my design.

This legislator, then, having considered with himself that, according to the necessary and established course of all things, the several accidents and changes that have now been mentioned were inevitable, formed this conclusion: that every simple and single kind of government was insecure, on account of its proneness to degenerate into that more vicious kind which was most nearly allied to it by nature. . . .

Lycurgus, therefore, foreseeing this necessity, instead of adopting either of the single forms of government, collected what was excellent in them all; and so joined together the principles that were peculiar to each several form, that no one of them might be extended beyond proper bounds . . . but that each separate power, being still counteracted by the rest, might be retained in due position, and the whole government be preserved in equal balance; as a vessel, when impelled to either side by the wind, is kept steady by a contrary force. Thus the dread of the people, to whom a certain share was allotted in the government, restrained the excesses and abuse of royalty. The people, on the other hand, were maintained in a due submission to the kings by their apprehension of the power of the senate. For the members of the senate, being all selected from the best among the citizens, were always ready to support the cause of justice; and, by throwing their own weight into the scale, when either side was in danger of being oppressed by the other, to give such strength to the weakest party as the constitution of the state required. By these means, the Lacedaemonians preserved their liberty entire for a much longer time than any other people. . . .

The Romans, on the other hand, though they arrived indeed at the same perfection in the constitution of their state, were not led to it by foresight or by reason. But, during the course of many contests and disorders in which they were engaged, having been careful always to adopt upon every change such improvements as the occasion itself suggested to them, they at last obtained the same end likewise as that which Lycurgus had proposed; and completed the most beautiful frame of government of all that are in our times known.

Cicero

106–43 B.C.

"As all the ages of the world have not produced a greater statesman and philosopher united than Cicero, his authority should have great weight." John Adams, *Defense of the Constitution*

⤚§ Few men have touched political expression and literary style over so long a period as Cicero. An orator of first rank, he set the standard for the Latin of succeeding generations. A lawyer, Roman consul, and Senator, he defended the Roman constitution amid the decay of the republic and the rise of dictatorships, and lost his life in that struggle. Study in Greece and a brief governorship in Asia Minor had widened his horizons, and when exile and disappointment sent him to his country villa, he turned to the writing of philosophical essays. Like his younger friend, Virgil, he felt that Rome's mission was great, to give the world the lessons of universal peace under law;[9] and in consequence his writings summarize for us the best of the ancient world. Wherever men have discussed government and political science, the influence of Cicero has been felt. American references to him were frequent.

Cicero's *De Natura Deorum* ("On the Nature of the Gods") shows him to be a lover of Plato, with a large admixture of Stoicism, with its concept of a common humanity under one universal law. His *De Legibus* ("On Laws"), composed from 52 B.C. on, uses the dialogue method to expose the highest conception of law in the ancient world. His *De Officiis* ("On Offices"), written just before his death for his son who was a student in Athens, consists of practical advice on politics and ethics, as viewed by a conservative in both fields.

Editions of Cicero have been very many, especially in Latin, both of his total works and of individual essays. His *De Officiis* was in English as early as 1534 and variously published before 1700. In 1699 it was translated by Thomas Cockman, and reached six editions by 1739. Excerpts from *De Officiis* below are from Cockman's translation (edition of New York, Harper's, 1833). Though *De Legibus* was known widely in Latin, few translations into English appeared before 1800, and excerpts below are therefore from the translation of Francis Barham of 1841, as revised by C. D. Yonge (London, 1853).[10] ❧

De Legibus ("On Laws")

[Bk. I]. The whole subject of universal law and jurisprudence must be comprehended in this discussion, in order that this which we call civil law may be confined in one small and narrow space of nature. For we shall have to explain the true nature of moral justice, which must be traced back from the nature of man. And laws will have to be considered by which all political states should be governed. And last of all, shall we have to speak of those laws and customs of nations which are framed for the use and convenience of particular countries, which are known by the title of civil laws. . . .

It is not so much the science of law that produces litigation as the ignorance of it. At present let us examine the first principles of Right.

Now many learned men have maintained that it springs from law. I hardly know if their opinion be not correct, at least according to their own definition: "for law," say they, "is the highest reason implanted in nature, which prescribes those things which ought to be done, and forbids the contrary." And when this same reason is confirmed and established in men's minds, it is then law. . . .

There exists, therefore, since nothing is better than reason, and since this is the common property of God and man, a certain aboriginal rational intercourse between divine and human natures. But where reason is common, there right reason must also be common to the same parties; and since this right reason is what we call law, God and men must be considered as associated by law. Again, there must also be a communion of right where there is a communion of law. And those who have law and right thus in common, must be considered members of the same commonwealth. . . .

There is no one thing so like or so equal to another as in every instance man is to man. And if the corruption of customs and the variation of opinions did not induce an imbecility of minds and turn them aside from the course of nature, no one would more nearly resemble himself than all men would resemble all men. Therefore, whatever definition we give of man will be applicable to the whole human race. And this is a good argument that there is no dissimilarity of kind among men; because if this were the case, one definition could not include all men.

In fact, reason, which alone gives us so many advantages over beasts, by means of which we conjecture, argue, refute, discourse, and accomplish and conclude our designs, is assuredly common to all men; for the faculty of acquiring knowledge is similar in all human minds, though the knowledge itself may be endlessly diversified. By the same senses we all perceive the same objects, and those things which move the senses at all, do move in the same way the senses of all men. And those first rude elements of intelligence which, as I have observed, are the earliest development of thought, are similarly impressed upon all men; and that faculty of speech which is the interpreter of the mind, agrees in the ideas which it conveys, though it may differ in the words by which it expresses them. And therefore there exists not a man in any nation who, if he adopts nature for his guide, may not arrive at virtue. . . .

[Men are also alike, says Cicero, in errors, fear of pain and death, superstition, and also in a regard for kindness and dislike of cruelty.]

But if, as nature prompts them to, man would with deliberate judgment, in the words of the poet, "being men, think nothing that concerns mankind indifferent to them," then would justice be cultivated equally by all. For to those to whom nature has given reason, she has also given right reason, and therefore also law, which is nothing else than right reason enjoining what is good, and forbidding what is evil. And if nature has given us law, she hath also given us right. But she has bestowed reason on all, therefore right has been bestowed on all. And therefore did Socrates deservedly execrate the man who first drew a distinction between utility and nature, for he used to complain that this error was the source of all human vices, to which this sentence of Pythagoras refers—"The things belonging to friends are common"—and that other, "Friendly equality." From whence it appears that when a wise man has displayed this benevolence which is so extensively and widely diffused towards one who is endowed with equal virtue, then that phenomenon takes place which is altogether incredible to some people, but which is a necessary consequence, that he loves himself not more dearly than he loves his friend. . . .

But there is no expiation for the crimes and impieties of men. The guilty therefore must pay the penalty and bear the punishment; not so much those punishments inflicted by the courts of justice, which were not always in being, do not exist at present in many places, and even where established are frequently biased and partial, but those of *conscience*; while the furies pursue and torment them, not with burning torches as the poets feign, but with remorse of conscience and the tortures arising from guilt.

But were it the fear of punishment and not the nature of the thing itself that ought to restrain mankind from wickedness, what, I would ask, could give villains the least uneasiness, abstracting from all fears of this kind? And yet none of them was ever so audaciously impudent but what he either denied that the action in question had been committed by him, or pretended some cause or other for his just indignation, or sought a defence of his deed in some right of nature. And if the wicked dare appeal to this principle, with what respect ought not good men to treat them?

But if either direct punishment or the fear of it be what deters men from a vicious and criminal course of life, and not the turpitude of the thing itself, then none can be guilty of injustice, and the greatest offenders ought rather to be called imprudent than wicked.

On the other hand, those among us who are determined to the practice of goodness, not by its own intrinsic excellence but for the sake of some private advantage, are cunning rather than good men. . . .

It is therefore an absurd extravagance in some philosophers to assert that all things are necessarily just which are established by the civil laws and the institutions of nations. Are then the laws of tyrants just, simply because they are laws? . . . For my own part, I do not think such laws deserve any greater estimation than that passed during our own interregnum, which ordained that the dictator should be empowered to put to death with impunity whatever citizen he pleased, without hearing them in their own defence.

For there is but one essential justice which cements society, and one law which establishes this justice. This law is right reason, which is the true rule of all commandments and prohibitions. Whoever neglects this law, whether written or unwritten, is necessarily unjust and wicked.

But if justice consists in submission to written laws and national customs, and if, as the same school affirms, everything must be measured by utility alone, he who thinks that such conduct will be advantageous to him will neglect the laws, and break them if it is in his power. And the consequence is that real justice has really no existence if it have not one by nature, and if that which is established as such on account of its utility is overturned for some other utility.

But if nature does not ratify law, then all the virtues may lose their sway. . . .

[Bk. II]. Therefore, as that Divine Mind, or reason, is the supreme law, so it exists in the mind of the sage, so far as it can be perfected in man. But with respect to civil laws, which are drawn up in various forms, and framed to meet the occasional requirements of the people, the name of law belongs to them not so much by right as by the favor of the people. For men prove by some such arguments as the following that every law which deserves the name of law ought to be morally good and laudable. It is clear, say they, that laws were originally made for the security of the people, for the preservation of states, for the peace and happiness of society; and that they who first framed enactments of that kind persuaded the people that they would write and publish such laws only as should conduce to the general morality and happiness, if they would receive and obey them. And then such regulations, being thus settled and sanctioned, they justly entitled *Laws*. From which we may reasonably conclude that those who made unjustifiable and pernicious enactments for the people acted in a manner contradictory to their own promises and professions, and established anything rather than *laws*, properly so called, since it is evident that the very signification of the word *law* comprehends the whole essence and energy of justice and equity.

De Officiis ("Concerning Offices")

STATE AS TRUSTEE

[Bk. I, 25]. Those who design to be partakers in the government should be sure to remember those two precepts of Plato; first, to make the safety and interest of their citizens the great aim and design of all their thoughts and endeavors, without ever considering their own personal advantage; and secondly, so to take care of the whole collective body of the republic as not to serve the interest of any one party, to the prejudice or neglect of all the rest. For the government of a state is much like the office of a guardian or trustee, which should always be managed for the good of the pupil, and not of the persons to whom he is intrusted; and those men who, whilst they take care of one, neglect or disregard another part of the citizens do but occasion sedition and discord, the most destructive things in the world to a state. Whence it comes to pass that while some take part with the popular faction, and others make their court to every great one, there are but few left who are concerned for the benefit and good of the whole. . . . Eager ambition and contending for honor is of all things most ruinous and destructive to a state.

CICERO'S EXCUSE FOR WRITING

[Bk. II, 1]. So long as the republic was governed by those to whose care and management she had intrusted herself, I was ever diligent, and employed all my thought for her good and preservation. But when one man [Caesar] had seized her wholly to himself, and there was no place left for my counsel or authority, and when I had lost those extraordinary persons who had been my companions in laboring for her interest, I resolved not to sink into anguish and despair, which had wholly overwhelmed me if I had not resisted them; nor to follow such pleasures or idle ways of living as were improper and unbecoming a man of learning. I could heartily wish, had it so pleased the gods, that the republic had continued in its ancient condition, and never fallen into the hands of those men who are not so much for changing as overturning everything! . . . But when the poor state, which had taken up all my care and thoughts, and for which I had labored with all my power, was utterly ruined and sunk into nothing, there was quickly no room left for such orations, either at the bar or in the senate-house; and my active mind, which had always been employed in that kind of studies, now not being able to lie wholly idle, I thought I could find no better way to get rid of those troubles which oppressed my mind than by returning again to the studies of philosophy.

ON TYRANTS

[Bk. II, 7]. As it was very well observed by Ennius, whom men fear they also hate; and whom they hate they wish out of the world. But that no force of power or greatness whatever can bear up long against a stream of public hate, if it were not sufficiently known before, was of late made appear by an instance of our own [i.e., Caesar]; and not the violent death of that tyrant only, who by force of arms oppressed the city, which now most obeys him when he is taken out of the world, but the like untimely ends of most other tyrants, who have generally been attended by the same ill fate, is a manifest token that the hatred of the people is able to ruin the most absolute authority. For obedience proceeding from fear cannot possibly be lasting; whereas that which is the effect of love will be faithful for ever. . . .

For those who are magistrates in a free city to endeavor to make themselves feared by the people is one of the maddest and most desperate attempts on the face of the earth. For though a man should by his power and greatness oppress the laws and overawe liberty by terror and threatenings, yet still they will find time to recover again; first, by the private resentment of the citizens, and afterward by their choosing in secret counsels some worthier persons to free them from the oppressor. And Liberty, after she has been chained up a while, is always more fierce, and sets her teeth in deeper than she would otherwise have done if she had never been restrained.

FOLLY OF INJURING OTHERS

[Bk. III, 5]. But to return to our general rule or measure: there is nothing on earth then so contrary to nature, neither death nor poverty nor pain, nor whatever other evil can befall a man, either in his body or fortune, as to take away any thing wrongfully from another, and to do oneself a kindness by injuring one's neighbor. . . . For though it is no more than what Nature will allow of that each man should look after himself in the first place, and furnish himself with the necessaries of life before he takes care to provide for other people, yet the same Nature will by no means permit that anyone should rise by his thrusting down another and increase his own fortune by the spoils of his neighbors. And not only Nature, that is the universal law or consent of nations, but particular laws, by which several countries and commonwealths are governed, have commanded likewise, that no one be suffered to do an injury to another for the sake of procuring an advantage to himself. For the very design and end of laws is to keep up agreement and union amongst citizens; which whoever destroys is by them punished, not with the loss of his goods alone, but with prisons, banishment, or even death itself.

[Bk. III, 6]. We should all of us therefore propose the same end, and everyone think his own interest, in particular, to be the same with that of the community in general; which, if each one endeavor to draw solely to himself, all union and agreement amongst men will be dissolved. And if Nature enjoin us that every man should desire and procure the advantage of another, whoever he be, though for no other reason than because he is a man, it necessarily follows that all men are joined by the self-same nature in one common interest; which, if it be true, then all men are subject to, and live equally under, the same law of nature. And if this be true, too, then certainly they are forbid, by that same law of nature, any ways to injure or wrong one another. But the first of these is undoubtedly certain, therefore the last must needs be so likewise. For as to what is usually said by some men, that they would not take any thing away from a father or brother for their own advantage, but that there is not the same reason for their ordinary citizens, it is foolish and absurd. For they thrust themselves out from partaking of any privileges, and from joining in common with the rest of their citizens, for the public good; an opinion that strikes at the very root and foundation of all civil societies. Others there are who are ready to confess that they ought to bear such a regard to fellow-citizens, but by no means allow of it in relation to strangers. Now these men destroy that universal society of all mankind which, if once taken away, kindness, liberality, justice and humanity must utterly perish; which excellent virtues whoever makes void is chargeable with impiety toward the immortal gods; for he breaks that society which they have established and settled amongst men.

De Republica

[Though the *De Republica* was not discovered until 1822 in the Vatican library, it was quoted fragmentarily by ancient writers, notably Lactantius and St. Augustine, from whom comes apparently the following paragraph, taken like the Laws from the 1853 edition of Barham's translation.]

DEFINITION OF TRUE LAW

[III, 2]. True law is right reason conformable to nature, universal, unchangeable, eternal, whose commands urge us to duty, and whose prohibitions restrain us from evil. Whether it enjoins or forbids, the good respect its injunctions and the wicked treat them with indifference. This law cannot be contradicted by any other law, and is not liable either to derogation or abrogation. Neither the senate nor the people can give us any dispensation for not obeying this universal law of justice. It needs no other expositor and interpreter than our own conscience. It is not one thing at Rome, and another at Athens; one thing today, and another tomorrow; but in all times and nations this universal law must for ever reign, eternal and imperishable. It is the sovereign master and emperor of all beings. God himself is its author, its promulgator, its enforcer, and he who does not obey it flies from himself, and does violence to the very nature of man.

Stoic and Epicurean

"The most esteemed sects of ancient philosophy . . . Socrates, Epicurus, Cicero, Epictetus, Seneca, Antoninus." Thomas Jefferson to Benjamin Rush

"Homo sum, nihil humani a me alienum puto." Terence

"Only the Stoics set up the doctrine of the original unity of the whole human family, and insist on being citizens of the world." E. Zeller, *Stoics, Epicureans and Skeptics*

The influence of Stoic and Epicurean upon the ancient Roman world can scarcely be given adequate treatment in this brief space, yet it must not be ignored. Greek philosophy, man's first emergence into free discussion, centered about the nature of the universe, and questions of permanence and change. Heraclitus (525?–475? B.C.) sought behind his famed *panta rei*, all things flow, some laws of permanence. Democritus (460?–370? B.C.) tried to reconcile change and permanence by postulating tiny, indestructible atoms governed by impersonal law and basic to all matter. From them came Stoic and Epicurean.

From the fourth and third centuries B.C., reaching Rome by the second century B.C., four great schools of Greek thought existed: the Academy (Plato), the Lyceum or Peripatetics (Aristotle), the Porch or Stoa (Zeno, the Stoics), and the Garden (Epicurus). Though Christianity eventually replaced them, they left their mark upon Rome at its height and even upon our world.

The Stoics advocated *apathia*, freedom from pain by self-control; the Epicureans, *ataraxia*, an untroubled serenity. Both sought how the individual man might live (and die) with self-respect and dignity, the

Stoic in an active life, the Epicurean in aloofness from the world's turmoil.

Of peculiar interest to us, however, is the Stoic emphasis upon the law of nature and the community of nations. Living in the Roman Empire, which extended over a vast area of Africa, Asia, and Europe, and themselves prominent in Roman government, the Stoics asked the question: can a governing law find a common denominator among men? Cicero said yes (see page 51), and denominated it, as did the Stoics, the *jus gentium,* the law of nations. It could also be thought of as natural law, consistent with the Stoic concept of a universal law which governed all, to be understood by reason (*logos*) without passion, and teaching conformity to necessity without complaint. For the Stoic aim was to rise above custom, prejudice, nationalism, and personal concern to a realm of universal reason. Even Greek and Latin were no longer nationalistic languages, but pervaded the known world. All men were one, they argued.

The Stoic view, not without fatalism, was vaguely pantheistic, blending God and universal mind, soul, reason, nature, law, and necessity, in a world which left individual man without freedom over events, but only over his will and self-control within events. Hence the connotation of Stoic as enduring with grim courage. In psychology, the Stoics contributed the conception of the *tabula rasa* upon which sensory data built all our knowledge, a theory later appropriated by John Locke. But above all the Stoic believed in public service from superior men, and placed action above contemplation. Hence the admiration of the eighteenth century for the figures of Cicero, Brutus, and Cato, and the frequent references in America to the virtues of the Roman republic.

Such an austere conception was understandably limited to the aristocracy of ancient Rome. Yet in its contempt for worldly goods and its resignation to a higher law, it entered even into Christianity, perhaps into Calvinism, and surely as natural law into Deism. In modified form, it appears in Cicero, Seneca, and the sad emperor, Marcus Aurelius. "I am a man," said Terence, "and I hold nothing human foreign to me." All men are brethren, taught Epictetus, and have one origin and one father. The stories of pagan gods, said the Stoics, are allegories; the gods, if they exist, said the Epicureans, dwell aloof and indifferent to man. Thus the philosophers undermined the ancient beliefs and prepared the way in the Greek and Roman worlds for a new religion. Yet they were not wholly forgotten, and many an eighteenth-century concept is traceable to these ancient speculations.[11] ß∾

Epictetus (60?–120? A.D.)

∾ß Epictetus, freed slave, contemplated suffering and the power of tyrants with a sturdy independence that at times approached eccentricity. All, said he, lies in the will, for man has no power over events. Banished from Rome with other Stoics, because of their resistance to tyrannical emperors, he never wrote, but is remembered by the *Manual* or *Enchiridion* compiled by disciples.

The *Manual* was early published in Greek and Latin, and several times put into English in the eighteenth century. Best of these translations was that of Elizabeth Carter, whose work sold 1250 copies within a short time after its publication in 1749–1750, and has been often reprinted since then. An edition in the Harvard Library bears the autograph of John Hancock. Extracts here are from the edition of 1768 (2 volumes, London). ॐ

REASON AND WILL

[Bk. I, Ch. I]. As it was fit then, this most excellent and superior faculty alone [i.e., Reason], a right use of the appearance of things, the gods have placed in our own power; but all other matters not in our power. Was it because they would not? I rather think that if they could, they had granted us these too; but they certainly could not. For, placed upon earth, and confined to such a body and to such companions, how was it possible that, in these respects, we should not be hindered by things without us?

But what says Jupiter? O Epictetus, if it were possible, I had made this little body and property of thine free, and not liable to hindrance. But now do not mistake: it is not thy own, but only a finer mixture of clay. Since, then, I could not give thee this, I have given thee a certain portion of myself; this faculty of exerting the powers of pursuit and avoidance, of desire and aversion, and, in a word, the use of the appearance of things. Taking care of this point, and making what is thy own to consist in this, thou wilt never be restrained, never be hindered; thou wilt not groan, wilt not complain, wilt not flatter anyone. . . .

What then is to be done?

To make the best of what is in our power, and take the rest as it naturally happens.

And how is that?

As it pleases God.

What, then, must *I* be the only one to lose my head?

"Why, would you have all the world, then, lose their heads for your consolation? . . .

What then should we have at hand upon such occasions? Why, what else but what is mine, and what not mine: what is permitted me, and what not. I must die: and must I die *groaning* too? Be fettered. Must it be *lamenting* too? Exiled. And what hinders me, then, but that I may go smiling, and cheerful, and serene? "Betray a secret." I will not betray it; for this is in my own power. "Then I will fetter you." What do you say, man? Fetter *me*? You will fetter my leg; not Jupiter himself can get the better of my choice [i.e., free will]. "I will throw you in prison: I will behead that paltry body of yours?" Did I ever tell you that I alone had a head not liable to be cut off? These things ought philosophers to study; these ought they daily to write; and in these to exercise themselves. . . .

[Ch. II]. To a reasonable creature, that alone is insupportable which is unreasonable; but everything reasonable may be supported. . . .

But it happens that different things are reasonable and unreasonable, as well as good and bad, advantageous and disadvantageous, to different persons. On this account, chiefly, we stand in need of a liberal education, to teach us to adapt the preconceptions of reasonable and unreasonable to particular cases, comformably to nature. . . .

[Ch. IV]. The only real thing is studying how to rid his life of lamentation and complaint, and "Alas!" and "I am undone," and misfortune and disappointment; and to learn what death, what exile, what a prison, what poison is: that he may be able to say in a prison, like Socrates, "My dear Crito; if it thus pleases the gods, thus let it be;" and not, "Wretched old man, have I kept my gray hairs for this!" . . . For what else is tragedy but the sufferings of men, struck by an admiration [i.e., wonder] of externals?

OF TYRANTS

[Ch. XIX]. When a person is possessed of some either real or imaginary superiority, unless he hath been well instructed, he will necessarily be puffed up with it. A tyrant, for instance, says, "I am supreme over all." And what can you do for me? Can you exempt my desires from disappointment? How should you? For do you never incur your own aversions? Are your own pursuits infallible? Whence should you come by that privilege? Pray, on shipboard, do you trust to yourself or to the pilot? In a chariot, to whom but to the driver? And to whom in all other arts? Just the same. In what, then, doth your power consist? "All men pay regard to me." . . .

Why, do I not pay regard to an ass? Do I not wash his feet? Do I not clean him? Do not you know that every one pays regard to himself; and to you just as he doth to an ass? For who pays regard to you as a man? Show that. Who would wish to be like *you*? Who would desire to imitate *you*, as he would Socrates? "But I can take off your head." You say right. I had forgot that one is to pay regard to you as to a fever or the cholic; and that there should be an altar erected to you, as there is to the Goddess Fever, at Rome.

[Bk. II, Ch. X]. Examine who you are. In the first place, a man: that is, one who hath nothing superior to the faculty of choice, but all things subject to this; and this itself unenslaved and unsubjected to anything. Consider then, from what you are distinguished by reason. You are distinguished from wild beasts: you are distinguished from cattle. Besides, you are a Citizen of the Universe, and a part of it: not a subservient but a principal part. You are capable of comprehending the Divine economy, and of considering the connections of things. What then doth the character of a citizen promise? To hold no private interest; to deliberate of nothing as a separate individual, but like the hand or the foot, which, if they had reason, and comprehended the constitution of nature, would never pursue or desire but with a reference to the whole.

[Bk. II, Ch. XXV]. When one of the company said to him, "Convince me that logic is necessary," Would you have me demonstrate it to you, says he? "Yes." Then I must use a demonstrative form of argument. "Granted." And how will you know, then, whether I argue sophistically? On this, the man being silent, You see, says he, that even by your own confession, logic is necessary; since without its assistance, you cannot learn so much as whether it be necessary or not.

THE ENCHIRIDION

[Sec. V]. Men are disturbed not by things, but by the principles or notions which they form concerning things.

[Sec. XLI]. It is a mark of want of genius to spend much time in things relating to the body; as to be long in our exercises, in eating, and drinking, and in the discharge of other animal functions. These should be done incidentally, and slightly; and our whole attention be engaged in the care of the understanding.

[Sec. XLVIII]. The condition and characteristic of a vulgar person is that he never expects either benefit or hurt from himself; but from externals. The condition and characteristic of a philosopher is that he expects all hurt and benefit from himself.

[Sec. CXXXI]. All things obey and are subservient to the world [i.e., to the laws of the universe]; the earth, the sea, the sun, and other stars, and the plants and animals of the earth. Our body likewise obeys it in being sick, and well, and young, and old, and passing through the other changes, whenever that decrees. It is therefore reasonable that what depends on ourselves, that is, our judgment, should not be the only rebel to it. For the World [i.e., the universe] is powerful and superior, and consults the best for us, by governing us in conjunction with the whole. Farther: opposition, besides that it is unreasonable, and produces nothing except a vain struggle, throws us likewise into pain and sorrows.

Epicurus (343–270 B.C.)

"Epicurus makes the two blessings of life to be a sound body and a quiet mind." Seneca, *Epistles*, XXI

"I too am an Epicurean. I consider the genuine (not the imputed) doctrines of Epicurus as containing everything rational in moral philosophy which Greece and Rome have left us. Epictetus indeed, has given us what was good of the stoics; all beyond, of their dogmas, being hypocrisy and grimace. Their great crime was in their calumnies of Epicurus and misrepresentation of his doctrine." Thomas Jefferson to William Short, 1819

◄§ We are led to consider Epicurus because of two items relating to Thomas Jefferson. Why did he label himself Epicurean; and did his substitution of "pursuit of happiness" for Locke's "property" in the Declaration of Independence owe anything to his Epicureanism?

The second, as we shall see, may owe something to Burlamaqui. The first is supplemented by Jefferson's own "syllabus" of Epicureanism, made around 1799. Summarized, it ran as follows:

Physical—The universe is eternal, the elements of bodies in eternal circulation.

Moral—Happiness is the aim of life. Virtue is the foundation of happiness. Utility is the test of virtue. The *summmum bonum* is to be not pained in body, nor troubled in mind. Man is a free agent. Virtue consists in Prudence, Temperance, Fortitude, Justice. To which are opposed Folly, Desire, Fear, Deceit.

This is a good summary of the ethics of Epicurus, though it omits his materialism. For Epicurus taught that all knowledge comes through the senses, and that sensory experience leads by repetition to notions, concepts, and a knowledge of causes; and that knowledge is the way of escape from fear, anxiety, and superstition. Central, too, was his theory of innumerable minute and indivisible atoms, combining and recombining to form all existence, and governed by impersonal law.

Epicureanism was a gentle philosophy, valuing friendship above all, and freedom from sensuous turmoil. Its key word, *hedone*, often translated as sensual pleasure, was in reality a quiet happiness from living in moderation, rather than the Stoic insensitivity to pain. Epicureanism was bitterly attacked by Stoics and Christians, for it taught that there was no personal immortality, that the gods, if they existed at all, were indifferent, and that the physical universe consisted of material atoms only. It was also contemptuous of the elaborate pagan rites of ancient Greece and Rome. On Lucretius, see Appendix C.

A Restoration court in England equated Epicureanism with sensuous indulgence and brought the word into disfavor. A twentieth-century atomic physics has seen in Lucretius, greatest exponent of Epicureanism, a remarkable foreshadowing of modern science.

Not much remains from Epicurus himself. The three maxims below are taken from John Digby's translation of *Epicurus' Morals*, London, 1712, a book padded with Digby's own comments. Note the utilitarian tone of the definitions. ઠ&

MAXIM XX

Common Right is nothing else than that utility which has been acknowledged by universal consent to be the cause of that justice men have observed one towards another. It is by the help thereof, that without offending others, or being offended themselves, they lived free from insult, because in all their desires they had Nature for their guide.

MAXIM XXII

Justice is nothing in itself: Mankind united in society discovered the utility and advantage of agreeing among themselves, to observe certain conditions for their living inoffensively one towards another.

MAXIM XXV

Whatever experience teaches us to be useful and beneficial in reference to the community, ought to be esteemed just, provided that it be so contrived that every one may find an advantage in it; from whence it is manifest that whoever makes a law by which no benefit accrues in the prosecution thereof, does that which is unjust in its nature.

Lucretius

96–55 B.C.

◄§ This strange and apparently solitary figure gives us in his *De Rerum Natura* ("Concerning the Nature of Things") most of what we know about Epicureanism. Combining a keen observation of nature's ways with an atomic theory of the indestructibility of matter, he argues that reason and natural law will free man from superstition and terror. *"Felix qui potuit rerum cognoscere causas"*—"Happy he who can know the causes of things"—said Virgil of him. His account of the emergence of the universe from the whirl of atoms, and the evolution of plants, animals, and primitive man is astonishingly readable and modern.

Much maligned by Christian writers of all sects, Lucretius has nevertheless survived and been frequently edited since the discovery in the fourteenth century of the manuscript of his poem.[12] His influence reappears in Hobbes, in Gassendi and Boyle and the new science, in Jefferson, and perhaps even in Locke, in the latter's effort to see political forms without recourse to supernaturalism. The American poet Philip Freneau was attracted by Lucretius, translating some of him, and adapting the opening lines of Book II.

Excerpts below are from the verse translation of Thomas Creech, first published in 1682, taken here from the London edition of 1714. Creech, who felt obliged to protest that he did not accept Lucretius' materialism, was often republished. His verse was not the smoothest nor the most literal translation, but it was the best known version of the eighteenth century. For his "seeds" or "principles," read "atoms." §►

Nature's Rule

[Bk. I]. I treat of things abstruse, the Deity,

The vast and steady motions of the sky;

The rise of things; how curious Nature joins

The various Seeds, and in one mass combines

The jarring Principles: what new supplies

Bring nourishment and strength: how she unties

The Gordian knot, and the poor compound dies:

Of Seeds or Principles (for either name

We use promiscuously; the thing's the same)

Of which she makes, to which she breaks the Frame.

For whatsoe'er's divine must live in peace,

In undisturbed and everlasting ease:

Not care for us; from fears and dangers free,

Sufficient to Its own felicity:
Nought here below, nought in our power It needs:
Ne'er smiles at good, ne'er frowns at wicked deeds.

Long time men lay oppressed with slavish fear;
Religion's tyranny did domineer,
And being placed in Heaven looked proudly down,
And frighted abject spirits with her frown.
At length a mighty Man of Greece began [i.e., Epicurus]
T' assert the natural Liberty of Man,
By senseless terrors and vain fancies led
To slavery: straight the conquered phantom fled!
Not the famed stories of the Deity,
Not all the thunder of the threatening sky,
Could stop his rising soul; through all he passed,
The strongest bounds that powerful Nature cast:
His vigorous and active Mind was hurled
Beyond the flaming limits of this World
Into the Mighty Space, and there did see
How things begin, what can, what can not be . . .

[Here Lucretius tells the story of the sacrifice of Iphigenia, her own father assisting in the sacred "murder," as proof of the cruelty of religions—"Such devilish acts Religion could persuade!"]

These fears, that darkness, which o'erspreads our souls,
Day can't disperse; but those eternal Rules,
Which from firm premises true Reason draws,
And a deep insight into Nature's laws.
And now let this as the first Rule be laid:
Nothing was by the Gods of Nothing made.
From hence proceeds all our distrust and fear;
That many things in heaven and earth appear,
Whose causes far remote and hidden lie,
Beyond the ken of vulgar Reason's eye;
And therefore men ascribe them to the Deity.
But this once proved, it gives an open way
To Nature's secrets, and we walk in day. . . .

Besides, as Nothing Nature's power creates,
So death dissolves, but not annihilates.

For could the Substances of Bodies die,
They presently would vanish from our eye;
And, without Force dissolving, perish all,
And silently into their Nothing fall.
But now since things from Seeds eternal rise,
Their parts well joined and fitted, Nothing dies,
Unless some force break off the natural ties. . . .

  [Bk. V]. Even strongest towns and rocks, all feel the rage
Of powerful Time; even temples waste by age;
Nor can the gods themselves prolong their date,
Change Nature's laws, or get reprieve from Fate.
Even tombs grow old and waste, by years o'erthrown;
Men's graves before, but now become their own;
How oft the hardest rock dissolves, nor bears
The strength but of a few, though powerful years! . . .

The Evolution of Man and Society

[Bk. V]. Like beasts they lay in every wood and cave,
Gathering the easy food that Nature gave . . .
Contented they with the poor easy store
That sun and earth bestowed, they wished no more;
Soft acorns were their first and chiefest food,
And those red apples that adorn the wood. . . .

  But when they built their huts, when fire began,
And skins of murdered beasts gave clothes to man;
When one to one confined, in chaste embrace,
Enjoyed sweet love, and saw a numerous race;
Then Man grew soft, the temper of his mind
Was changed from rough to mild, from fierce to kind;
For used to fire, his limbs refused to bear
The piercing sharpness of the open air;
And lust enfeebled him; besides, the child,
Softened by parents' love, grew tame and mild.

  Then Neighbors, by degrees familiar grown,
Made Leagues, and bonds, and each secured his own;
And then by signs and broken words agreed
That they would keep, preserve, defend and feed
Defenseless infants, and the women too

As natural pity prompted them to do.
　　Though this fixed not an Universal Peace,
Yet many kept their faith, and lived at ease;
Or else, almost as soon as it began,
The race had fallen, this age ne'er seen a man.
　　Kind Nature power of framing sounds affords
To man, and then convenience taught us words;
As infants now, for want of words, devise
Expressive signs; they speak with hands and eyes;
Their speaking hand the want of words supplies.
All know their powers; they are by Nature shown. . . .

[In time, says Lucretius, came fire from lightning or the rubbing together of trees; in time came towns, kings, property. Kings were overthrown, and the confusion led to wars and finally laws.]

　　Those former Kings now murdered, they o'erthrown,
The glory of the sceptre and the crown
Decreased; the diadem, that sign of state,
Now wept in drops of blood the wearer's fate;
Spurned by the common feet, who feared no more;
'Tis sweet to spurn the things we feared before.
Thus Monarchy was lost.—
　　That sun once set, a thousand little stars
Gave a dim light to jealousies and wars;
While each among the many sought the throne,
And thought no head like his deserved the crown.
This made them seek for Laws, this led their choice
To Rulers; Power was given by public voice;
For men, worn out and tired by constant strife,
At last began to wish an easy life;
And so submitted of their own accord
To rigid Laws and their Elected Lord.[13]

Seneca

4 B.C.?–65 A.D.

◄§ Seneca and Marcus Aurelius are frequently mentioned in colonial reading, especially Roger L'Estrange's *Seneca's Morals*, first published in 1678. It was a translation of Seneca's often sententious moralizing, and is said to have been a favorite with George Washington. Seneca, nominally a Stoic, borrowed also from Epicureanism and Platonism, and wrote of Benefits, of the Happy Life, of Anger, etc. The passage below illustrates the Stoic emphasis on self-control and on the common humanity of all mankind. It is from the ninth edition of L'Estrange's book, London, 1705.[14]

Epistle XVII: *The Original of all Men is the Same*

It is not well done, to be still murmuring against Nature and Fortune; as if it were their unkindness that makes you inconsiderable, when it is only your own weakness, that you make your self so: For it is Virtue, not Pedigree that renders a man either valuable or happy. Philosophy does not either reject or choose a man for his quality [i.e., rank?]. Socrates was no patrician; Cleanthes, but an under-gardner; neither did Plato dignify philosophy by his birth, but by his goodness. All these worthy men are our progenitors; if we will but do our selves the honor to become their disciples. The original of all mankind was the same; and it is only a clear conscience that makes a man noble: for that derives even from Heaven it self. It is the saying of a great man that if we could trace our descents, we should find all slaves to come from princes, and all princes from slaves. But Fortune has turned all things topsy-turvy, in a long story of revolutions. It is most certain that our beginning had nothing before it; and our ancestors were some of them splendid, others sordid, as it happened. We have lost the memorials of our extraction, and in truth, it matters not whence we came but whither we go. Nor is it any more to our honor, the glory of our predecessors, than it is to their shame, the wickedness of their posterity. We are all composed of the same elements; why should we then value our selves upon our nobility of blood, as if we were not all of us equal, if we could but recover our evidence?

Tacitus

55?–120? A.D.

"Whoever wants information of the spirit, cruelty and rapine of soldiers quartered in populous cities, let them peruse the first book of the elegant and instructive history written by the masterly hand of Tacitus." Josiah Quincy, "Boston Port Bill," 1774

"Tacitus I consider as the first writer of the world without a single exception. His book is a compound of history and morality of which we have no other example." Thomas Jefferson, to Anne C. Bankhead, December 8, 1808

"But to live without having a Cicero and a Tacitus at hand seems to me as if it was a privation of one of my limbs." John Quincy Adams, *Diary*, 1819

◄§ Not a great deal is known of Cornelius Tacitus, lawyer, orator, and historian, one-time consul to Aquitania, and son-in-law of Agricola, governor of the Isle of Britain in the first century A.D. Yet his works survive by virtue of their compact style and their indignation against the usurpers of the old Roman Republic, and the emperors from Augustus through Nero (i.e., from 14 to 68, A.D.). From Tiberius through Nero, emperors deified upon death after an Oriental fashion perhaps borrowed through Alexander the Great, the Roman Senate was progressively ignored. Under Nerva and Trajan, whom Tacitus knew, the Senate regained some of its power. Tacitus was thus a late voice in favor of the old republican virtues, yet he resigned himself to the hope of benevolent monarchs.

Of great interest is his account of ancient Germany and Britain, the latter governed by Agricola until Domitian's jealousy brought about his death in 93 A.D. From these documents Montesquieu, Jefferson, and others developed their idea that the Anglo-Saxon heritage of liberty was traceable to the ancient German forests.

Editions of Tacitus were available from the Renaissance onward. The *Annals* and the *Germania* and *Agricola* appeared in English first in 1598. T. Gordon's *Works of Tacitus* (London, 1728–1731) was a favored translation, and excerpts from the *Annals* below are from the 1737 second edition of Gordon. Another translation, though later, was Arthur Murphy's (Dublin, 1794), which saw a Philadelphia edition in 1822. Murphy's is sufficiently superior to Gordon's to warrant taking the excerpts below for the *Germania* and *Agricola* from him (the London, 1807, edition).

Gordon set the tone of prefacing Tacitus with "lessons" on the uses and abuses of government; and Murphy, dedicating his work to Edmund Burke, used Tacitus to rebuke the French Revolution. Yet of the *Agricola*, Murphy wrote, "We see that holy flame of liberty, which has been for ages the glory of Englishmen, and the wonder of foreign nations"; and of the *Germania*, "We shall view the waters at their fountainhead, dark, foul and muddy; but by following them downward, we shall see them working themselves clear, and purified at length to a clear and limpid current. We shall gain a knowledge of the origin of laws." ᵹ►

The *Annals*

END OF THE REPUBLIC

[Bk. I]. Kings were the original magistrates of Rome. Lucius Brutus founded liberty and the consulship. Dictators were chosen only in pressing exigencies. . . . The authority of Pompey and Crassus was quickly swallowed up in Caesar, that of Lepidus and Antony in Augustus. The commonwealth, then long distressed and exhausted by civil dissensions, fell easily into his hands, and over her he assumed sovereign dominion, softened with the popular title of Prince of the Senate. But the several revolutions in the ancient free state of Rome, and all her happy or disastrous events, are already recorded by writers of signal renown. Nor, even in the reign of Augustus were there wanting authors of distinction and genius to have composed his story, till by the prevailing spirit of flattery and abasement they were checked. As to the succeeding princes, Tiberius, Caligula, Claudius and Nero, the dread of their tyranny whilst they yet reigned, falsified their history; and after their fall, the fresh detestation of their cruelties inflamed their historians. Hence my own design of recounting briefly certain incidents in the reign of Augustus, chiefly towards his latter end, and of entering afterwards more fully into that of Tiberius and the other three, unbiased by any resentment or any affection, the influence of such personal passions being far from me. . . .

When once he [Octavius] had secured the soldiery by liberality and donations, gained the people by store of provisions, and charmed all by the blessing and sweetness of public peace, he began by politic gradations to exalt himself, and with his own power to consolidate the authority of the Senate, jurisdiction of the magistrate, and weight and force of laws; usurpations in which he was thwarted by no man. All the most determined republicans had fallen in battle, or by the late sanguinary proscriptions; and for the surviving nobility they were covered with wealth and distinguished with public honors, according to the measure of their debasement and promptness to bondage. Add that all who in the loss of public freedom had gained private fortunes preferred a servile condition, safe and possessed, to the revival of ancient liberty with personal peril. . . . How few were then living who had seen the ancient free state!

The frame and economy of Rome being thus totally overturned, amongst the Romans were no longer found any traces of their primitive spirit or attachment to the virtuous institutions of antiquity. But as the equality of the whole was extinguished by the sovereignty of one, all men regarded the orders of the Prince as the only rule of conduct and obedience.

[Tacitus recounts how Tiberius on the death of Augustus seized power, had Agrippa murdered, and assumed the behavior of majesty. Thus begins his melancholy story of intrigue, tyranny, civil war, confusion, and the loss of liberties—a story often repeated in history.]

THE HISTORIAN'S TASK

[Bk. IV]. To me remains a straightened task and void of glory, steady peace, or short intervals of war, the proceedings at Rome sad and tragical, and a Prince careless of extending the empire. Not yet will it be without its profit to look mutely into such transactions as, however small at first view, give often rise and motion to great events.

For all nations and cities are governed either by the populace, by the nobility, or by single rulers. The frame of state chosen and compacted out of all these three is easier applauded than accomplished, or if accomplished, cannot be of long duration. So that, as during the Republic, either when the power of the people prevailed or when the Senate bore the chief sway, it was necessary to know the genius of the commonalty, and by what measures they were humored and restrained; and such too who were thoroughly acquainted with the spirit of the Senate and leading men came to be esteemed skilful in the times, and men of prowess; so now, when that establishment is changed and the present situation such that one rules all, it is of advantage to collect and record these later incidents, as matters of public example and instruction. . . .

I can only give a sad display of cruel orders, incessant accusations, faithless friendships, the destruction of innocents, and endless trials, all attended with the same issue, death and condemnation; an obvious round of repetition and satiety! Besides that, the old historians are rarely censured; nor is any man now concerned whether they chiefly magnify the Roman or the Carthaginian armies. But of many who under Tiberius suffered punishment or were marked with infamy, the posterity are still subsisting; or if the families themselves are extinct, there are others found who, from a similitude of manners, think that in reciting the evil doings of others they themselves are charged; nay, even virtue and a glorious name create foes, as they expose in a light too obvious the opposite characters.

[Bk. IV]. While Cornelius Cossus and Asinius Agrippa were consuls, Cremetius Cordus was arraigned for that "having published Annals, and in them praised Brutus, he had styled Cassius the last of the Romans;" a new crime, then first created . . . Tiberius received his defence with an implacable countenance. He began it on this wise, casting away all hopes of his life:

"As to facts, I am so guiltless, Conscript Fathers, that my words only are accused; but neither are any words of mine pointed against the Emperor or his mother, the only persons comprehended in the law concerning violated Majesty. It is alleged that I have praised Brutus and Cassius, men whose lives and actions have been compiled by a cloud of writers, and their memory treated by none but with honor. Titus Livius, an historian eminently famous for eloquence and veracity, celebrated Pompey with such abundant encomiums that he was thence by Augustus named Pompeianus; nor did this prejudice their common friendship. Neither Scipio nor Africanus, nor even this same Cassius, nor this same Brutus are anywhere mentioned by him as *traitors* and *parricides*, the common nicknames bestowed on them, but often as great and memorable men . . . That book of Cicero's . . . in which he exalted Cato to the skies, what other animadversion did it draw from Caesar the Dictator than a written reply, in the same style and equality as if before his Judges he had made it? The letters of Marc Antony and speeches of Brutus are full of reproaches and recriminations against Augustus, false in truth, but urged with signal asperity. The poems of Bibaculus and those of Catullus, stuffed with virulent satires against the Caesars, are still read. But even the deified Julius, even the deified Augustus, bore all these invectives and left them unsuppressed, whether with greater moderation or wisdom I cannot easily say. For, if they are despised, they fade away; if you wax wroth, you seem to avow them for true.

"Instances from the Greeks I bring none. With them not the freedom only but even licentiousness of speeches is unpunished; if any correction be returned, it is only by revenging words with words. It has been ever allowed, without restriction or rebuke, to pass our judgment upon those whom death has withdrawn from the influence of affection and hate. Are Cassius and Brutus now in arms? Do they at present fill with troops the fields of Phillippi? Or do I fire the Roman people by inflammatory harangues, with the spirit of civil rage? Brutus and Cassius, now above seventy years slain, are still known in the statues which even the conqueror did not abolish; and what do the historians but preserve their characters? Impartial posterity to every man repays his proper praise; nor will there be wanting such as, if my death is determined, will not only revive the story of Cassius and Brutus, but even my story."

Having thus said he withdrew from the Senate, and ended his life by abstinence. The Fathers condemned the books to be burned by the Aediles; but they still continued to be secretly dispersed. Hence we may justly mock the stupidity of those who imagine that they can, by present power, extinguish the lights and memory of succeeding time; for quite otherwise, the punishments of writers exalts the credit of the writings; nor did ever foreign Kings, or any else, who exercised the like cruelty reap other fruit from it than infamy to themselves, and glory to the sufferers.

Agricola
TYRANNY OVER BOOKS

[Written about 97 A.D.]. We have it upon record that . . . excellent authors fell a sacrifice to the tyrant's power. Persecution raged against their books, and by an order to the triumvirs, in the forum and in the place of popular convention the monuments of genius perished in the flames. The policy of the times, no doubt, intended that in the same fire the voice of the Roman people should be stifled, the freedom of the senate destroyed, and the sentiments of the human heart suppressed forever. To complete the work, all sound philosophy was proscribed, every liberal art was driven into banishment, and nothing fair and honorable was suffered to remain. Of our passive temper we gave ample proof; and as former times had tasted of liberty even to a degree of licentiousness, so we exhausted the bitter cup of slavery to the very dregs. Restrained by the terrors of a merciless inquisition from the commerce of hearing and speaking, and by consequence deprived of all exchange of sentiment, we should have resigned our memory with our other faculties if to forget had been as easy as to submit in silence.

At length, indeed, we begin to revive from our lethargy; but we revive by slow degrees, though the emperor Nerva, in the beginning of this glorious era, found means to reconcile two things till then deemed incompatible; namely, civil liberty and the prerogative of the prince. . . . And yet, such is the infirmity of the human mind that, even in this juncture, the remedy operates more slowly than the disease. . . .

Need I mention that in the course of fifteen years (a large portion of human life!) many fell by unavoidable accidents and the most illustrious men in Rome were cut off by the insatiate cruelty of a prince [i.e., Domitian]? A few of us, it is true, have survived the slaughter of our fellow citizens. I had almost said, we have survived ourselves, for in that chasm which slavery made in our existence, we cannot be said to have lived, but rather to have crawled in silence, the young towards the decrepitude of age, and the old to dishonorable graves.

DESCRIPTION OF BRITAIN

[Britain was then inhabited by Celts, not the later Germanic Anglo-Saxon invaders.]

Whether the first inhabitants of Britain were natives of the island or adventitious settlers is a question lost in the mists of antiquity. The Britons, like other barbarous nations, have no monuments of their history. They differ in the make and habit of their bodies, and hence various inferences concerning their origin. The ruddy hair and lusty limbs of the Caledonians indicate a Germanic extraction. That the Silures were at first a colony of Iberians is concluded, not without probability, from the olive tincture of the skin, the natural curl of the hair, and the situation of the country, so convenient to the coast of Spain. On the side opposite to Gaul the inhabitants resemble their neighbors on the continent; but whether that resemblance is the effect of one common origin, or of the climate in contiguous nations operating on the make and temperament of the human body, is a point not easy to be decided. All circumstances considered, it is rather probable that a colony from Gaul took possession of a country so inviting by its proximity. You will find in both nations the same religious rites and the same superstitions. The two languages differ but little. In provoking danger, they discover the same ferocity, and in the encounter, the same timidity. The Britons, however, not yet enfeebled by a long peace, are possessed of a superior courage.

THE CLASSICAL HERITAGE

THE SPEECH OF CALGACUS

[The invading Romans were finally victorious over the Britons. Of interest is the supposed speech of Calgacus, which may be compared with speeches popular among American schoolboys in our early history.]

Among the chieftains the most renowned was Calgacus. The multitude gathered round him, eager for action and burning with uncommon ardor. He harangued them to the following effect:

"When I consider the motives that have aroused us to this war, when I reflect on the necessity that now demands our firmest vigor, I expect everything great and noble from that union of sentiment that pervades us all. From this day I date the freedom of Britain. We are the men who never crouched in bondage. Beyond this spot there is no land where liberty can find a refuge. Even the sea is shut against us, while the Roman fleet is hovering on the coast. To draw the sword in the cause of freedom is the true glory of the brave, and in our condition, cowardice itself would throw away the scabbard. In the battles which have been hitherto fought with alternate vicissitudes of fortune, our countrymen might well repose some hopes in us; they might consider us as their last resource; they knew us to be the noblest sons of Britain, placed in the last recesses of the land, in the very sanctuary of liberty. We have not so much as seen the melancholy regions where slavery has debased mankind. We have lived in freedom, and our eyes have been unpolluted by the sight of ignoble bondage.

"The extremity of the earth is ours. Defended by our situation, we have to this day preserved our honor and the rights of men. But we are no longer safe in our obscurity. Our retreat is laid open; the enemy rushes on, and, as things unknown are ever magnified, he thinks a mighty conquest lies before him. But this is the end of the habitable world, and rocks and brawling waves fill all the space behind. The Romans are in the heart of the country; no submission can satisfy their pride, no concessions can appease their fury. While the land has anything left, it is the theatre of war; when it can yield no more, they explore the seas for hidden treasure. Are the nations rich? Roman avarice is their enemy. Are they poor? Roman ambition lords it over them. The east and the west have been rifled, and the spoiler is still insatiate. The Romans, by a strange singularity of nature, are the only people who invade with equal ardor the wealth and the poverty of nations. To rob, to ravage, and to murder, in their imposing language, are the arts of civil policy. When they have made the world a solitude, they call it peace. . . .

"In me behold your general; behold an army of freeborn men. Your enemy is before you, and in his train heavy tributes, drudgery in the mines, and all the horrors of slavery. Are those calamities to be entailed upon us? Or shall this day relieve us by a brave revenge? There is the field of battle, and let that determine. Let us seek the enemy, and as we rush upon him, remember the glory delivered down to us by our ancestors, and let each man think that upon his sword depends the fate of all posterity."

This speech was received, according to the custom of the barbarians, with war songs, with savage howlings, and a wild uproar of military applause.

The *Germania*
NATURE OF THE GERMANS

[Written about 98 A.D.] The Germans abound with rude strains of verse, the reciters of which, in the language of the country, are called *Bards*. With this barbarous poetry they inflame their minds with ardor in the day of action, and prognosticate the event from the impression which it happens to make on the minds of the soldiers, who grow terrible to the enemy, or despair of success, as the war-song produces an animated or feeble sound. Nor can their manner of chanting this savage prelude be called the tone of the human organs; it is rather a furious uproar, a wild chorus of military virtue. The vociferation used upon these occasions is uncouth and harsh, at intervals interrupted by the application of their bucklers to their mouths, and by the repercussions bursting out with redoubled force. . . .

I have acceded to the opinion of those who think that the Germans have hitherto subsisted without intermarrying with other nations, a pure, unmixed and independent race, unlike any other people, all bearing the marks of a distinct national character. Hence, what is very remarkable in such prodigious numbers, a family likeness throughout the nation; the same form and feature, stern blue eyes, ruddy hair, their bodies large and robust, but powerful only in sudden efforts. They are impatient of toil and labor; thirst and heat overcome them; but from the nature of their soil and climate, they are proof against cold and hunger.

THE POLITICAL INSTITUTIONS OF THE GERMANS

In matters of inferior moment the chiefs decide; important questions are reserved for the whole community. Yet even in those cases, where all have a voice, the business is discussed and prepared by the chiefs. The general assembly, if no sudden alarm calls the people together, has its fixed and stated periods, either at the new or the full moon. This is thought the season most propitious to public affairs. Their account of time differs from that of the Romans: instead of days, they reckon the number of nights; and their proclamations run in the same style. The night, according to them, leads the day.

Their passion for liberty is attended with this ill consequence: when a public meeting is announced, they never assemble at the stated time Regularity would look like obedience; to mark their independent spirit they do not convene at once, but two or three days are lost in delay. When they think themselves sufficiently numerous, the business begins. Each man takes his seat, completely armed. Silence is proclaimed by the priests, who still retain their coercive authority. The king or chief of the community opens the debate; the rest are heard in their turn, according to age, nobility of descent, renown in war or fame for eloquence. No man dictates to the assembly; he may persuade but cannot command. When anything is advanced not agreeable to the people, they reject it with a general murmur. If the proposition pleases, they brandish their javelins. This is their highest and most honorable mark of applause; they assent in a military manner, and praise by the sound of their arms.

In this council of the state accusations are exhibited and capital offenses prosecuted. Pains and penalties are proportioned to the nature of the crime. For treason and desertion the sentence is to be hanged on a tree. The coward and such as are guilty of unnatural practices are plunged under a hurdle into bogs and fens. In these different punishments the point and spirit of the law is that crimes which affect the state may be exposed to public notoriety; infamous vice cannot be too soon buried in oblivion. He who is convicted of transgressions of an inferior nature pays a mulct of horses or of cattle. Part of this fine goes to the King, or the community, and part to the person injured or his

family. It is in these assemblies that princes are chosen and chiefs elected
to act as magistrates in the several cantons of the state. To each of these
judicial officers assistants are appointed from the body of the people,
to the number of a hundred, who attend to give their advice and
strengthen the hands of justice.

Plutarch

46?–120? A.D.

&§ With Plutarch these selections from the ancient classical world
conclude, though quotations might also have been found from Livy,
the poets, or the later historians. But it was from records of Roman
republican virtues that Americans drew most willingly; and it was
Plutarch who furnished the most popular source of anecdote, biogra-
phy, narrative, and moral reflection. Everyone read him, in North's or
in the so-called Dryden translation, or in the original.

Plutarch, like Tacitus, was a product of the first and second centuries. But he was a Greek, though he had traveled in Egypt and Italy,
and he wrote in Greek, the language of philosophy and literature. His
interest was character and moral philosophy rather than politics; his
philosophy was the contemporary compound of Aristotle, Plato, and
the Stoics. His plan was to pair a Greek with a Roman for each of his
biographical sketches.

The problem here is one of selection. American interest was slanted
toward the law-givers and lovers of liberty. Hence, those most often
mentioned from Plutarch were those below: Lycurgus, Marcus Cato,
Cato the Younger (the subject of Addison's *Cato*), Tiberius Gracchus,
and Marcus Brutus.

North's *Plutarch*, from the French version of Amyot, appeared in
1575 and thereafter, with new additions. It is still readable. The so-
called Dryden translation, the work of several hands, with an introduction by Dryden, appeared in 1683–1686, and was widely read in the
eighteenth century. It was reworked by A. H. Clough in the nineteenth
century, the translation now most often used. The Langhorne translation of 1770 has also been often reprinted. Present excerpts are from the
fifth London edition of 1716 of the so-called Dryden text, admittedly
uneven, but nearest to the period we are studying. §&

Lycurgus (9th century B.C.)
AN EARLY SENATE

He [Lycurgus] was dearly missed at Lacedaemon [Sparta], and a
great many embassies were sent to pray his return. For Kings indeed

we have (said they) who wear the marks and assume the titles of royalty, but as for the inward qualities of their minds, they have nothing by which they are to be distinguished from their subjects. . . . Yet were not the kings themselves averse from his return, for they looked upon his presence as a bulwark for them against the growing insolencies of the people.

Things being in this posture at his return, he applied himself, without loss of time, to a thorough reformation, and resolved to change the whole face of the commonwealth. . . .

Amongst the many changes and alterations which Lycurgus made, the first and of greatest importance was the establishment of the Senate, which having a power equal to the king's in matters of great consequence, did (as Plato expresses it) with its phlegm allay and qualify the hot complexion of a monarchy, served as a rampart against the insolence of the people, and always kept the commonwealth in good temper. For the state which before had no firm basis to stand upon, but leaned one while toward an absolute monarchy (when the kings had the upper hand) and another while towards a pure democracy (when the people had the better of it) found in this establishment of the Senate a counterpoise, which always kept things in a just equilibrium. For the twenty-eight always adhered to the weaker side, and put themselves like a weight into the lighter scale, until they had reduced the other to a balance. . . .

For indeed the prerogative being thus kept within some reasonable bounds, at once he [the king] freed himself from the envy and secured himself from the danger to which an unlimited jurisdiction lies exposed. So that the Spartan kings fared much better after it than their neighbors at Messene and Argos; who by screwing their prerogative too high, cracked it, and for want of yielding a little to the populacy, lost all.

Indeed, whosoever shall take a prospect of the seditions and civil wars which befell these bordering nations (to whom they were as near related in blood as situation) will find good reason to admire the profound wisdom and providence of Lycurgus; for these three states in their first rise were equal, or, if there were any odds, they lay on the side of the Messenians and Argives, who in the division of their country were more fortunate than the Spartans: yet was their flourish but of small continuance, soon falling into confusion, partly by the tyrannical disposition of their kings, and partly by the ungovernableness of the people, so that now their servile and disgraceful condition makes it appear to the whole world that it is one of the greatest blessings which heaven can send down upon any nation, to give them so wise a law-giver who could set bounds to those two interfering powers, and of such jarring elements frame an orderly commonwealth. . . .

Lycurgus would never reduce his laws into writing; nay, it is expressly forbid in the Rhetra: * For he thought that the most material points, and such as most directly tended to the public welfare, being imprinted on the hearts of their youth by a good education, and by a constant and habitual observance of them, becoming a second nature, would supply the place of a law and law-giver in them all the rest of their lives; and as for things of lesser importance, as pecuniary contracts, and such like, the forms of which ought to be changed as occasion requires, and in trust of time become insufficient for the ends they were intended for, he thought it the best way to leave them to every man's discretion, and to prescribe no certain form at all. He left therefore no inviolable custom in such cases, willing that the manner and form of bargaining should be altered according to the circumstances of time, and determination of men of the soundest judgment. For he was persuaded that without good education the best laws in the world signified nothing, and where that was they were in a manner superfluous. . . .

It was not the design of Lycurgus that his city should govern a great many others; he thought rather that the happiness of a kingdom, as of a private man, consisted chiefly in the exercise of virtue, and mutual love of the inhabitants; his principal aim was to make them nobly minded, content with their own, not apt to follow vain hopes, but moderate in all their enterprises; and by consequence able to maintain themselves and continue long in safety. And therefore all those who have written well of politics, as Plato, Diogenes, Zeno, and several others, have taken Lycurgus for their model, as appears by their writings: but these great men left only projects and words behind them; whereas Lycurgus, without writing anything, left a flourishing government, which as it was never thought of before him, so can it scarcely be imitated in following ages; so that he stands for an undeniable proof that a *perfect* wise man was not so mere a notion and chimera as some thought. He hath obliged the world not with one single man, but with a whole na-

---

* *Rhetra* is translated elsewhere in the same sketch as "grand covenant."

tion of philosophers, and therefore deserves preference before all other statists, because he put that in practice of which they only had the idea.

Marcus Cato (234–149 B.C.)

A ROMAN STOIC, OLD STYLE

Now Cato grew more and more powerful by his eloquence, so that most called him the Roman Demosthenes, but his manner of life was yet more famous and talked of; for eloquence was an exercise commonly studied and affected by all the youth, but he was very rare who would endure bodily labor, a light supper, and a dinner which never saw the fire; or be in love with a poor thin garment, and a homely lodging; nay, and did more esteem a mind that wanted not great things than the real possession of them: for now the state (unable to keep its purity, by reason of its greatness, and having so many places and people from all parts under its government) was fain to receive many mixed customs, and new fashions of living. With reason therefore did everybody admire Cato, when they saw others sink under labors, and grow quite effeminate by pleasures; and yet beheld him unconquered by either, and that not only when he was young and desirous of honor, but also when old and bald, after his consulship and triumphs. As a true victor too in wrestling, he would persevere and carry on that exercise to his very last. . . .

When he entered upon the government of Sardinia, though his predecessors there used to require tents, bedding and clothes upon the public account, and to charge them heavily by furnishing provisions and entertainments for a great train of servants and friends; he, on the contrary, by his frugality showed an incredible difference, for in nothing wanted he the contribution of the public, nay, he would walk without a coach to visit the cities . . . yet though he seemed thus easy and sparing to all who were under his power, he, on the other hand, showed great severity and strictness, being always inflexible, in what related to public justice, and most upright and severe in what concerned the ordinances of the commonwealth; so that the Roman government where he was, never seemed more terrible, and yet more mild. Nay, his very manner of speaking seemed to have such a kind of idea with it; for it was courteous, and yet grave; pleasant and piercing; facetious and austere; sententious, and yet pithy. And (as Plato says) he was like Socrates, who seemed outwardly to those about him to be but a simple, blunt and sullen fellow; whilst at the bottom he was full of such gravity and matter as would even move tears, and touch the very hearts of his auditors.

Cato the Younger (95–46 B.C.)

[This Cato, equally Stoic, was the great-grandson of Marcus Cato.]

'Tis said of Cato that he did, even from his infancy, in his speech, his countenance, and all his childish pastimes, discover an inflexible temper, unmoved by any passion, and firm in every thing.

He would force himself, much beyond the strength of his age, to go through with whatever he undertook. He was rough and ungentle toward them that flattered him; but yet more stubborn and untractable to those who threatened him. He was very difficultly moved to laugh; and was rarely seen to smile. Not quickly or easily provoked to anger; but if once incensed, he was no less difficultly pacified.

When he began to learn, he proved dull and slow to apprehend; but what he once received, he very faithfully retained. . . .

Having gained an intimate acquaintance with Antipater, the Stoic philosopher, he bent himself chiefly to the study of moral philosophy and politics.

He was carried, as it were, by a kind of inspiration, to embrace every virtue; but most inclined to delight in a sort of steady justice, that was not to be wrought upon by favor or compassion. He learned also the art of speaking in public; which he looked upon as a thing no less requisite for governing than the art of war for defending a city. . . .

He accustomed his body to labor and violent exercise; would use himself to go bareheaded both in hot and cold weather. When he went abroad with any of his friends, though they were on horse-back, and he on foot, yet he would often join now one, then another, and discourse with them on the way. . . .

Cato esteemed the customs and manners of men at that time so corrupt, and a reformation in them so necessary, that he thought it requisite, in many things, to go contrary to the ordinary way of the world. Wherefore seeing the lightest and gayest colors were most in fashion, he would always wear black; and he would often go out of doors, without either shoes or coat; not that he sought vain-glory from such novelties, but he would accustom himself to be ashamed only of what deserves shame, and to despise all other sorts of disgrace.

Cato the Senator

He was always first at the senate, and went out last. Oftentimes, while others walked about there idly, he would sit and read by himself, holding his gown before his book, and was never out of town when the senate was to meet.

Pompey and his party, finding that Cato could never be either persuaded or compelled to favor their unjust designs, they contrived to keep him from so much frequenting the senate by engaging him in business for his friends, either to plead their causes, or arbitrate their differences. But he quickly discovering their contrivance, to encounter it, fairly told all his acquaintances that he would never meddle in any private business when the senate was assembled; since it was not for honor or riches, nor rashly or by chance that he engaged himself in the affairs of state, but he undertook the service of the public as the proper business of an honest man.

[Cato conducted himself as a Stoic, rebuking gaiety and refusing to cooperate with the corrupt Pompey and Caesar. His conduct led to his imprisonment, but public opinion forced his release and his appointment to command in Cyprus, to get him out of Rome. The story is told at length of Cato's gradual alignment with the party of Brutus and his resistance to Pompey and Caesar, and finally his suicide rather than to surrender to Caesar. Two excerpts must suffice.]

Cato's Incorruptibility[15]

After this, Scipio, Hypsaeus and Milo stood to be consuls, and that not only with the usual and common disorders of bribery and corruption, but with arms and slaughter were running desperately into a civil war. Whereupon it was proposed that Pompey might be empowered to preside over that election. This Cato at first opposed, saying that the laws ought not to seek protection from Pompey, but Pompey from the laws. Yet this confusion lasting a long time, the forum continually, as it were, besieged with three armies, and no possibility of putting a stop to these disorders, Cato at length agreed that rather than fall into the last extremity, the senate should freely confer all on Pompey; since 'twas necessary to make use of a lesser evil to prevent a greater. . . . Pompey, being hereupon declared consul, invited Cato to his house in the suburbs. When he came, he saluted and embraced him very kindly, acknowledged the favor he had done him, and desired his counsel and assistance, in the management of this office. Cato made answer that what he had spoken heretofore was not out of hate to Pompey, nor what he had now done, out of love to him, but all for the good of the commonwealth: that in private, if he asked him, he would freely give his advice; but in public, though he asked him not, he would always speak his opinion. And he did accordingly: for first, when Pompey made severe laws for punishing and laying great fines on those who had corrupted the people with gifts, Cato advised him to let alone what was already passed, and to provide for the future; for if he should seek into past crimes, it would be difficult to know where to stop; and if he would ordain new penalties, it would be unreasonable to punish men by a law which they had never broken. Afterward, when many considerable men, and some of Pompey's own relations, were accused, he grew remiss, and let fall the prosecution; but Cato sharply reproved him, and urged him to proceed.

Cato's Death

After supper, the wine produced a great deal of wit and learned discourse; many philosophical questions were discussed. At length they came to the strange opinions of the Stoics, called Paradoxes; and to this in particular, That the good man only is free, and that all wicked men are slaves. The Peripatetic (as 'tis likely) opposing this, Cato fell upon him very warmly; and somewhat raising his voice, he argued the matter in a discourse of some length, which he urged with such wonderful vehemence that 'twas apparent to everybody he was resolved to put an end to his life, and set himself at liberty. Hereupon, when he had done speaking, there was a great silence, and the company much dejected. But Cato, to divert them from any suspicion of his design, turned the discourse, and fell again to talk of the present affairs . . .

When the company was broke up, Cato walked with his friends as he used to do after supper, gave the necessary orders to the officers of the watch; and going into his chamber, he embraced his son, and every one of his friends, with more than usual ardor, which again renewed their suspicion of his design. Then laying himself down, he took into his hand Plato's dialogue concerning the soul. Having read more than half the book, he looked up, and missing his sword (which his son had taken away, while he was at supper), he called his servant and asked who had taken away his sword. . . .

Then the sword being brought in by a little boy, Cato took it, drew it out, and looked on it; and when he saw the point was good, Now (said he), I am master of myself; and laying down the sword, he took his book again, which, it is reported, he read twice over. After this he slept so soundly that he was heard snore by those that were without. . . .

At length Butas came back and told him all was quiet in the haven. Then Cato, laying himself down, as if he would sleep out the rest of the night, bid him shut the door after him. But as soon as Butas was gone out, he took his sword, and stabbed it into his breast. . . .

When he [Caesar] heard of Cato's death, it is reported, he said these words: "Cato, I envy thee thy death, for thou hast envied me the preservation of thy life." And indeed if Cato would have suffered himself to be preserved by Caesar, 'tis like he would not so much have impaired his own honor, as augmented the other's glory.

Tiberius Gracchus (162–133 B.C.)

When the wealthy men began to raise the rents and turn the poor people out of their possessions, it was enacted by law that no person whatever should enjoy more than 500 acres of ground. This act did for some time restrain the avarice of the richer, and was no small supply to the poorer people, who possessed their respective proportions of ground, as they had been formerly rented by them. Afterwards the rich men of the neighborhood contrived to get these lands again into their possessions, under other people's names, and at last would not stick to claim most of them publicly in their own. The poor, who were thus deprived of their farms, would neither list themselves in the militia, nor take any care of the education of their children: insomuch that in a short time there were few free-men remaining in all Italy, which swarmed with a numerous company of barbarous slaves. These the rich men employed about the cultivating their ground, dispossessing the citizens. . . .

When Tiberius went through Tuscany into Numantia, and found the country almost depopulated, there being hardly any free husbandmen or shepherds, and for the most part only barbarous foreign slaves, he from that time took into his serious consideration the management of this affair, which in the sequel proved so fatal to his family. . . .

However, he did not make this law without the advice and assistance of those citizens that were then most eminent for their virtue and authority . . . Never did any law appear more moderate and gentle, especially being enacted against so great opposition and avarice. For they who ought to have been severely punished for transgressing the former laws, and should at least have lost all their titles to such lands, which they had unjustly usurped; yet they were ordered notwithstanding to receive a gratuity, for quitting their unlawful claims, and restoring their lands to those right owners . . . The moneyed men, and those of great estates, were exasperated, through covetousness, against the law itself, and against the lawgiver, through anger and obstinacy; they therefore endeavored to seduce the people, insinuating to them that Tiberius had introduced such a division of the lands, with a design only to disturb the government, and put all things into confusion.

But they succeeded not in this project; for Tiberius . . . made a speech on the behalf of the poor people to this effect. "The savage beasts," says he, "in Italy, have their particular dens, they have their places of repose and refuge; but the men who bore arms and exposed their lives for the safety of their country, enjoyed in the meantime nothing more in it but the fresh air and sunshine, and having no houses or settlements of their own, were constrained to wander from place to place with their wives and children."

[Tiberius's law was confirmed and commissioners appointed to survey the lands; nevertheless, resentment led to his murder, and that of his brother with him.]

Marcus Brutus (85–42 B.C.)

Brutus, whose life we now write, having to the goodness of his disposition added the improvements of learning and study of philosophy, and having stirred up his natural parts, of themselves grave and gentle, by applying himself to business and public affairs, seems to have been of a temper exactly framed for virtue; insomuch that they who were most his enemies, upon the account of his conspiracy against Caesar, if in that whole affair there was any honorable or generous action done, refer it wholly to Brutus. . . .

Brutus, for the sake of his virtue, was esteemed by the people, beloved by his friends, admired by the best men, and hated by none, no, not his enemies themselves. For he was a man of an extraordinary mild nature, of a great spirit, insensible of the passions of anger or pleasure or covetousness; steady and inflexible in his opinion, and zealous for whatever he thought right and honest. And that which gained him the greatest credit and reputation among the people, was their belief that his designs in this whole undertaking were honorable and just. . . . Nay, many have heard Antony himself say that Brutus was the only man that conspired against Caesar out of a sense of the glory and justice of the action; but that all the rest rose up against the MAN, and not the TYRANT. . . .

The very enemies of Brutus would say that he had no other end or aim, from first to last, save only to restore to the Roman people their ancient government.

St. Augustine

354–430 A.D.

◄§ The old Rome was dying, already dead, when Augustine wrote his *De Civitate Dei* ("City of God") in 412–427 A.D. In 410 the Goths under Alaric had entered Rome itself and scattered its leading citizens by death or flight. There were those who blamed the new religion for the catastrophe, and Augustine wrote his book in part to answer them. It is not a book of politics, though he reviews the history of Rome (as found in Varro, it is said). He speaks of the old city not without respect: "Rome, by which God was pleased to conquer the whole world and subdue it far and wide by bringing it into one fellowship of government and laws" (Book XVIII, Chapter 22). He even echoes Cicero: "How much more powerfully do the laws of man's nature move him to hold fellowship and maintain peace with all men, as far as in him lies" (XIX, 12). Even the old philosophers had some merit, especially Plato, though they are still the "devil's ambushes." Yet his picture of pagan Rome, its obscene rites and plays, its many gods and false miracles and astrologers, its idols and images, is unsparing and evidently first hand. Even though he rehearses Scipio's argument from *De Re Publica* that "only where justice and honesty have full execution" is there a good commonwealth, he follows it with Cicero's confession that the old Rome is no more, and corruption has set in. Only in the City of God will true justice be found.

With Augustine we stand on the edge of the Middle Ages, the age of the Church supreme, the abandonment of the perfect society except in the realm beyond. Quoted below is Augustine's criterion for the good emperor. But it is clear that the emperor is accepted as the form of government, and faith and hope are to be placed in his benevolence and justice; for Christians are to obey, the only exception being when commands directly oppose faith. The translation is that of J(ohn) H(ealey) of 1610, second edition, as amended in 1620. Spelling has been modernized. ॐ

The Good Emperor

[V, 24]. For we Christians do not say that Christian emperors are happy because they have a long reign; or die, leaving their sons in quiet possession of their empires; or have been ever victorious, or powerful against all their opposers. These are but gifts and solaces of this laborious, joyless life. Idolators, and such as belong not to God (as these emperors do) may enjoy them: because God in his mercy will not have these that know him to believe that such things are the best goods he giveth. But happy they are (say we) if they reign justly, free from being puffed up with the glozing exaltations of their attendants, or the cringes of their subjects, if they know themselves to be but men, and remember that, if they make their power their trumpeter to divulge the true adoration of God's majesty; if they love, fear and honor him; if they long the most for that empire where they need not fear to have partners; if they be slack to revenge, quick to forgive; if they use correction for the public good, and not for private hate; if their pardons promise not liberty of offending, but indeed only hope of reformation; if they counterpoise their enforced acts of severity with the like weight of bounty and clemency; if their lusts be the lesser because they have the larger licence; if they desire to rule their own affects, rather than others' estates; and if they do all things not for glory, but for charity, and with all, and before all, give God the due sacrifice of prayer for their imperfections: Such Christian emperors we call happy, here in hope, and hereafter, when the time we look for cometh indeed.

Justinian

483–565 A.D.

ॐ In 528 the Emperor Justinian of Byzantium (Constantinople) ordered the compilation of a new code of laws and a Digest or Pandect of the Roman law. Completed in 533, Justinian's *Institutes*, in Greek, though lost to the western world for fully eight centuries, were studied from the time of the Renaissance. The *Institutes* were based on Roman law, the codification of Hadrian, and other such sources. Much space is given to property, including slaves, marriage laws, inheritance, and so forth. Long forgotten, however, were the old days of the Greek city-states or the Roman Republic; Justinian's rule was absolutist and military, and his attempt to unite the East and West, around 553, was destined to failure. Of interest, nevertheless, are the echoes below of the familiar phrases of "law of nations," "law of nature," and the distinction between man-made "contracts" and the immutable law of the Stoics. John Adams studied Justinian's *Institutes* assiduously for a time, but Justinian seems remote from most of the concerns of the day.

Excerpts are from the translation of George Harris (London, 1756), the second edition of 1761. Harris' introduction traced the story of Roman law from the Twelve Tables of 303 B.C. to Flavian's law of 448 A.D.

For a study of Justinian, see P. N. Ure, *Justinian and his Age* (Penguin Books, 1951).

On the Law of Nations

[Bk. I, Title I, Sec. 3]. The precepts of the law are these: to live honestly, not to hurt any man, and to give everyone that which is his due.

[I, II, 1]. Civil law is distinguished from the law of nations, because every community uses partly its own particular laws, and partly the general laws which are common to all mankind. That law which a people enacts for the government of itself is called the civil law of that people. But that law which natural reason appoints for all mankind is called the law of nations, because all nations make use of it. The people of Rome are governed partly by their own laws, and partly by the laws which are common to all men.

[I, II, 2]. The law of nations is common to mankind in general, and all nations have framed laws through human necessity; for wars arose, and the consequences were captivity and servitude; both which are contrary to the law of nature; for by that law all men are free. But almost all contracts were at first introduced by the law of nations; as for instance, buying, selling, letting, hireing, society, a deposit, a *mutuum* [contract to return in same value], and others without number.

[I, II, 11]. The laws of nature, which are observed by all nations, inasmuch as they are the appointment of divine providence, remain constantly fixed and immutable. But those laws which every city has enacted for the government of itself suffer frequent changes, either by tacit consent or by some subsequent law, repealing a former.

PART II · THE ENGLISH TRADITION TO 1700

"Yield due reverence and obedience to the common laws of England: of all laws these are most equal and most certain, of greatest antiquity and least delay, and most beneficial and easy to be observed." Edward Coke (1552–1634) *Institutes*

"And here it is worthy of consideration, how the laws of England are not derived from any foreign law, either canon or other; but a special law appropriated to this kingdom, and most accomodate and apt for the good government thereof, under which it hath wonderfully flourished." Edward Coke, *Institutes*, Part III

"Fear not to do right to all, and to deliver your opinion justly according to the laws; for fear is nothing but a betraying of the succors which reason should afford." Edward Coke, admonition to judges (quoted as conclusion of Sir John Hawles' *The Englishman's Rights*, 1680)

"You will observe that from Magna Charta to the Declaration of Right, it has been the uniform policy of our constitution to claim and assert our liberties, as an entailed inheritance derived to us from our forefathers, and to be transmitted to our posterity; as an estate specially belonging to the people of the kingdom, without any reference whatever to any other more general or prior right." Edmund Burke, *Reflections on the Revolution in France*, 1790

"Coke's Littleton was the universal lawbook of students, and a sounder Whig never wrote nor of profounder learning in the orthodox doctrines of the British constitution; or in what was called British liberties." Thomas Jefferson, *Writings*, IV

"This slow co-operation of free men, this liberty in democracy—the only sort that America possesses or believes in—is wholly English in its personal basis, its reserve, its tenacity, its empiricism, its public spirit, and its assurance of its own rightness; and it deserves to be called English always, to whatever countries it may spread." George Santayana, *Character and Opinion in the United States*, pp. 194–195. Copyright 1920 by Charles Scribner's Sons. Reprinted by permission of the publisher.

THE ENGLISH TRADITION TO 1700

It MAY BE argued that this study should have started with the British story; for American political history is rooted first of all in English history. The prolonged struggle within the British seventeenth century between a medieval concept of inviolable authority in a sovereign monarch and a deeply ingrained national tradition of common law had ended in the triumph of common sense, rationalized by John Locke. Long before their own Revolution, then, British colonials in America had absorbed the language of "our late glorious revolution" of 1688, and shared a common belief in English liberties. In both countries, too, the appeal to the classical heritage and to the "law of nature" had emerged later. It is no betrayal, then, of the frontier thesis for American history to insist also on this solid British inheritance. Why, otherwise, did not other European colonies arrive at a similar liberalism?

The great reverence paid the Magna Carta today was a thing of slow development. Perhaps most influential in this shift was Sir Edward Coke, a fighting conservative, tough and resolute, "the greatest common lawyer of all time," a lawyer's classic; none sounder, said Jefferson, on British liberties.[1] Coke, before his death, had amassed an impressive body of legal precedent not easily set aside, even by royal claims to divine prerogatives.

Edward I (1239–1307), Coke found, had urged the training of selected laymen exclusively in English common law, in places and with teachers provided for that purpose. Here was the origin of "students and practicers of the law of England," the Inns of Court to which more than a hundred Americans had gone for study between 1750 and the American Revolution. Coke's researches led him to Anglo-Saxon law, to Ranulph de Glanville's Treatises on the *Laws and Customs of England* (1187–89), antedating the Magna Carta; to Bracton's treatise of the same title (1250); to the quaint *Mirrour of Justices* (1290?), of questionable authenticity, yet listing 155 "abusions" of English justice, in themselves an imposing precedent; to many statutes of early kings; and to the *De Laudibus Legum Angliae* (In Praise of the Laws of England) of Fortescue, Chief Justice from 1442 to 1461. Chief of Coke's admirations was the *Tenures* (1482–83) of Thomas Littleton, which by Coke's time had gone through seventy editions.

Thus by the mid-seventeenth century an imposing literature of precedent and argument had arisen. Coke's own works alone constituted a ponderous and exacting repository of English law for all time to come. To American law he is said to have given not only this historical substructure, but also the principle of judicial review, and the concept of a fundamental law or constitution above the whim of king or parliament. By such argument many a resolute man was sustained in the struggle for British rights, often men of dignity and status, yet men imprisoned, deprived of estates, even beheaded. They were the ancestors of the American cause.

Slowly writers and reasoners like Hobbes, Milton, Sidney, Harrington and Locke shifted the analogy of government from the old paternalistic one to the new one of a practical agency through which the demands of citizens might be accomplished. Such an internal conflict could not take place without abuses. Charges and countercharges of treason, blasphemy and impiety were hurled about, for the age was still theological, with scholastic and authoritarian habits. Yet the basic issues remained economic, social and political. A new economic order, a rising merchant and middle class, vast colonial enterprises, a corresponding expansion of opportunity for even the humblest, a new science to challenge old infallibilities, a clamorous nationalism, and a new religious individualism — all these demanded solution and adjustment.

The Anglo-Saxon kings, it was argued, had had their *Witenagemot* (council of elders); and William the Conqueror had summoned councils of nobles and churchmen, and, in the manner of his predecessors, issued a code of laws. His brother, Henry I (1100–1135), drew up a charter, finding precedent in Edward the Confessor (1042–1066). Of special significance is Henry II (1154–1189), who labored to bring unity out of the confusion of three languages and three kinds of courts—Anglo-Saxon, Norman-French, and ecclesiastical—by establishing king's judges to make circuits in the land, and to take sworn testimony (*juror*—I am sworn) from local citizens on land and other cases. Thus the old habit of trial by ordeal or battle was gradually replaced. Records kept of these local judgments accumulated to be known as common law, and to furnish a growing body of precedent for a native tradition. On what were they dependent, these precedents? Increasingly, at least, not on the whims of a king nor the bias of a judge, but on a growing body of local experience.

Eventually there arose the question of church courts. These, too, had grown gradually to meet and replace old abuses. The twelfth century had been peculiarly a period of renewed study of the Roman inheritance in law, and a recodification of canon law amid feudal diversities. Collected around 1140 and administered by canons, it became known as Canon Law. Since this law was, in a sense, a reassertion of the Italian inheritance over Germanic customs in northern Europe, and was often strengthened at the expense of local law, some clashes were inevitable; especially as nationalisms and local churches arose to assert their institutions against the single supremacy of the medieval church. Citizens might choose between appeal to local civil courts or the ecclesiastical courts, which meant canon law, whose officials were confirmed and paid by Rome.

Thus, long before the Reformation, there had been a history of English common law writs, called *praemunire*, "forbidding" church courts to handle certain cases ruled as outside their jurisdiction; for example, cases dealing with non-church property, or the value of tithes paid in kind (produce). Parishioners brought to court for being remiss in tithes might appeal to a common law court, made up of neighbors, and hope for a favorable verdict. Could ecclesiastical courts, Roman or Anglican, fine or imprison in local jurisdictions? One Nicholas Fuller, barrister, spent a summer in jail for defending a protester.

Magna Carta had been confirmed by both Henry III (1216–1272) and

Edward I (1272–1307), under whom Parliament began to assert its power. Each new confirmation was likely to be accompanied by documents extending the laws of the land (See Edward I, below). Long before the rule of James I (1603–1625), then, English lawyers could argue a long heritage of freedoms. Nevertheless, James I, preparing to assume the throne, had concluded in his *True Law of Free Monarchs* that a king ruled by divine prerogatives, which permitted him to make or break judges as he saw fit. Here is where Coke entered; and before the struggle was over, one king had been beheaded, another forced into exile, and a third into abdication, until English kings were once more willing to affirm the heritage of common law. By the time of Blackstone, the story was a part of every lawyer's training and every citizen's knowledge, in America as in England.

From Coke's time on we may observe two main streams of development: one the legalistic, the other the metaphysical; the one leading through petition and legal debate to the Declaration of Rights of 1688; the other, more abstract, reviving an ancient concept of "natural law," the "law of reason," and the "law of nations." In the first stream we may put Fortescue, Coke, Selden, Somers, even Milton; in the second, Richard Hooker, Harrington, Hobbes, Sidney, and Locke. The last named brought the two streams together in a well-timed defense of an accomplished reform, and became so a major source of the American political argument.

It had been Coke's contribution to clarify British common law, and to insist that Parliament alone had the right to alter the fundamental law of the land. The issue was the realistic one of the rights of Englishmen to be free from arbitrary arrest and punishment without clear accusation and trial; and the right of Parliament to conduct open debate on national issues without fear of interference or reprisal. Long before, the petition of 1301 had urged that the "charters of liberty and of the Forest" be observed from that time forward. The Petition of 1628 reviewed history and cited current abuses; the Agreement of the People insisted on *native* rights; and the Declaration of 1688 reaffirmed basic and native rights. Roman law, it has been said, feared anarchy; common law feared tyranny. The Americans drew from the second tradition.

As time went on, however, the larger questions of authority and right in the abstract had to be faced. In a less literate and less determined people they might never have got into the political arena. We might begin the account with Richard Hooker; for Hooker, making use of the classical and medieval language of reason and nature, and drawing heavily on Aristotle, Cicero, Aquinas and the Scriptures, introduced the ancient language of "law of reason," "law of society," and "consent of governed." Scholastic in learning and language, he wished, nevertheless, by his moderate reasonableness to effect a reconciliation for his nation between an uncompromising Catholicism and a rising Puritanism. He prepared the way for a more liberal political language to follow.

Milton's prose, in the interim between the Stuart kings, constituted a more immediate participation in the political debate, a concrete defense of freedom from censorship, and a government without arbitrary encroachments. He was silenced by the Restoration, but not forgotten.

Harrington, Hobbes, Sidney and Locke show the expanding thesis. Hobbes seized upon the new geometry in an effort to project a mathematically ordered view of man as basically warlike, who therefore demanded an inviolable sovereign. Hobbes was not what English or Americans sought in their need. Harrington more ponderously but more realistically envisaged the economic factors behind shifts in government, and foresaw that expanding freedoms must follow on economic opportunities. He died broken by long imprisonment. Sidney vigorously advanced the thesis that monarchs and magistrates alike were responsible to the people. He was beheaded. Locke, more cautiously, waiting until the revolution was accomplished, utilized the work of his predecessors to make the final and supreme justification for the whole revolution of government as paternalistic fiat to government as a trust. For American liberals and French radicals alike he became the symbol of British common sense and balance in an age of upheavals.

The religious ferment of this period is too complex for present elaboration. Catholic and Protestant alike might challenge the divine right of a king when he was of another faith; and each, given the circumstance, could insist that civil laws must be disobeyed when they ran counter to the "laws of God." Appeal to the sovereignty of the state could have but temporary usefulness for Protestant sects. "The religion of the prince is the religion of the people" merited only brief popularity. The problem, then, became: should people of *any* faith have a right to defend their faith against arbitrary threat? Only slowly could the influence of men like Grotius or Locke prevail to assert an essential and larger justice to which all men and all states should give assent.*

Appeals to Scriptural and religious sanctions were heard on all sides. Most frequently quoted, for example, was Romans 13:1: "Let every soul be subject to the higher powers. For there is no power but of God; the powers that be are ordained of God." This Biblical injunction seemed made to order for monarchs, and it was so used. Yet Cromwell's armies, paralleling it with "We ought to obey God rather than men," routed the armies of obedience. Jonathan Mayhew and Jonathan Boucher in America use the identical verse on opposite sides: "Stand fast, therefore, in the liberty wherewith Christ hath made us free." (Gal. 5:1). Or listen to Roger Williams, one-time student of law under Coke: "The Church of Christ is the ship wherein the prince—if a member—is a passenger. . . . If in matters of religion the king command what is contrary to Christ's rule . . . who sees not that . . . he ought not to be obeyed: Yea, and (in case) boldly, with spiritual force and power, he ought to be resisted?"[2]

Separatist groups in England or on the continent fostered a kind of pietist democracy. To the affirmation of Anglican canons in 1640 that the king is accountable to God alone, they replied that all men were alike accountable to God alone. The Levellers insisted on the natural right of resistance and the sovereignty of the people; the Brownists placed power in the congregations by covenant and mutual consent; and Independents taught a natural equality and consent of the people. Yet their total appeal was less to realistic politics than to religious conviction. Nevertheless, a sincere subject, in a single lifetime, might live under an Anglican king, a Presbyterian commonwealth, and a Catholic monarch. Wherein, then, lay duty?

The sensible solution, though slow in coming, could only be toleration of variant faiths, within a unity on a common body of civil law which even king or ecclesiastic could not abrogate. Not unreasonably, then, did Americans, reviewing the past, decide upon a thoroughgoing separation of church and state, the first such act in modern history, and a basic decision in the American way.

Yet the long-established habit of seeking religious sanctions for all things was not easily set aside, even in the midst of religious diversity

* See Appendix B, footnote 3. Conclusion, p. 283.

and a new empirical science. Should a king rest his authority on the old divine rights, or on an appeal to the law of the land? The latter had the advantage of being more inclusive and more obviously rational. It responded to the new view of governments as practical devices founded on human necessity and rooted in the way of nature; and, as George Santayana said of English liberties, they were "in harmony with the nature of things; and when living things have managed to adapt their habits to the nature of things, they have entered the path of health and wisdom."

There were, then, obvious advantages in the widespread appeal to the law of Nature. For one thing, it loomed eternal, abstract, unchanging, and thus could absorb something of the old metaphysical sanctions, even while it permitted a secular appeal to the common sense of all men of reason everywhere. Again, it made room for useful analogies borrowed from the new mathematics and the new physical sciences. Furthermore, it reopened classical literature and the old Stoic concepts of government, making of them a kind of political Scriptures, also applicable to the experience of men everywhere. For a secularization of politics had to accompany a rising new class of men, middle-class men with business interests on a global scale, whose loyalties were tempered by their ambitions and their need for a stable society in which to expand. Science meant practical knowledge, as it did for Benjamin Franklin; and religion gravitated toward Deism, as it did for most of the founding fathers. Thus these men wisely forbore appeal to sectarian differences and underlined the new language of science and a rational practicality. No wonder the "law of nature" was heard on all sides.

Such, then, were some of the precedents within English history upon which Americans were vocal and well informed, until they came to defend common law and common rights against new corruptions, and finally to advance the law of nature and consent of governed as fundamental principles. Not even in their independence was there denial of the common heritage, but rather an insistence on the old Bill of Rights as imperative. And in their appeal to nature and nature's God, they were drawing, it is clear, less upon Aquinas and Hooker than upon the later modifications of Sidney and Locke, Newton and the prevailing Deism, plus a practical necessity to find an argument more inclusive than loyalty to British law and the British crown.

This brief outline, too condensed to be more than a sketchy view, may nevertheless suggest a few of the central issues sampled in the pages that follow.[2]

Sir Thomas More

1478–1535

◆§ Sir Thomas More, Lord Chancellor of England in 1529, was like his friend Erasmus a lover of classic learning and reason. His *Utopia* ("Nowhere") was published in Latin in 1516, but was not Englished until 1551 (revised 1556) by one Ralph Robynson. Clearly influenced by Plato's *Republic*, it was nevertheless modern in its social criticism and its tolerance. Important, too, is the fact that, impressed by the reports of Americus Vespucius, More placed his imaginary world in the Americas, and thereby started the trend of associating promise and reform with the New World, that is, in the realizable world inhabited by earthly creatures.* Yet it is doubtful whether *Utopia* had much direct influence on political history.

Its popularity in America is shown by its publication in Philadelphia in 1753, in the Robynson text of 1556. Excerpts below are taken from this first American edition. It was again translated in 1684 by Gilbert Burnet, and given new life in 1751 by a further revision by Thomas Williamson.[3]

In Book I the author meets through a friend in Antwerp a learned mariner who tells a strange tale of Utopia, where the prince is elected for life or for good behavior, and the council is elected yearly by representation. As to virtue, says the author, "They agree with the Stoicians." Before the mariner embarks upon his description of Utopia, however, the three gentlemen engage in a criticism of England, in which country the rich are idle and the poor are deprived of their lands or hanged for thievery. The mariner argues that fines for theft should go to the losers, not to the king, and that thieves, instead of being hanged, should be employed for cheap labor. ⸸∾

Virtue and Nature

[Bk. II]. Therefore, the matter diligently weighed and considered, thus, they think, that all our actions and in them the virtues themselves be referred at the last to pleasure, as their end and felicity. Pleasure they call every motion and state of body or mind wherein man hath

* Compare Sir Thomas Browne's "The America and untraveled parts of truth."

naturally delectation. Appetite they join to Nature, and that not without a good cause. For like as not only the senses, but also right reason, coveteth whatsoever is naturally pleasant, so that it may be gotten without wrong or injury, not letting or debarring a greater pleasure nor causing painful labor, even so those things that men, by vain imagination, do feign against Nature to be pleasant (as though it lay in their power to change the things as they do the names of things), all such pleasures they believe to be of so small help and furtherance to felicity that they count them a great let or hindrance. Because that in whom they have once taken place, all his mind they possess with a false sense of pleasure; so that there is no place left for true and natural delectations.

Religion in Utopia

[Nowhere does More show his Humanism more than in his tolerant view of religion.]

There be divers kinds of religion, not only in sundry parts of the Island but also in divers places of every city. Some worship for God the sun; some the moon; others the planets. There be that give worship to a man that was of excellent virtue or of famous glory, not only as God but also as chiefest and highest God. But the most and wisest part, rejecting all these, believe that there is a certain godly power unknown, everlasting, incomprehensible, inexplicable, far above the capacity and reach of man's wit, dispersed throughout all the whole world, not in bigness but in virtue and power, Him they call the Father of All. . . .

For every one of them, whatsoever that is which he taketh for the chief God, thinketh it be of the very same nature to whose only divine might and majesty the sum and sovereignty of all things, by the consent of the people, is attributed and given. However, they all begin by little and little to forsake and fall from this variety of superstitions and to agree together in that religion which seemeth by reason to pass and excel the residue. . . . [However, says the mariner, they gladly accepted Christianity.]

They also which do not agree to Christ's religion fright no man from it, nor speak against any man that have received it; saving that one of our company, in my presence, was sharply punished. He, as soon as he was baptised, began against our wills with more earnest affection than wisdom to reason of Christ's religion; and began to be so hot in this matter that he did not only prefer our religion before all others, but also did utterly despise and condemn all others, calling them prophane, and the followers of them wicked and devilish, and the children of everlasting damnation. When he had thus long reasoned the matter, they laid hold of him and condemned him into exile, not as a despiser of religion but as a seditious person, and a raiser-up of dissention among the people. For this is one of the ancientest laws among them, that no man shall be blamed for reasoning in the maintenance of his own religion. For King Utopus . . . first of all made a decree that it should be lawful for every man to favor and follow what religion he would, and that he might do the best he could to bring others to his opinion, so that he did it peaceably, gently, quietly and soberly, without haste and contentious rebuking and inveighing against others. . . . And this surely he thought a very unmeet and foolish thing, and a point of arrogant presumption, to compel all others by violence and threatenings to agree to the same thou believest to be true. . . .

They be persuaded that it is in no man's power to believe what he list. No, nor they constrain him not with threatenings to dissemble his mind, and shew countenance contrary to his thought. For deceit and falsehood and all manner of lies, as next unto fraud, they do marvelously reject and abhor.

The Commonwealth

Now I have declared and prescribed unto you, as truly as I could, the form and order of that commonwealth, which verily in my judgment is not only the best, but also that which alone of good right may claim and take upon it the name of a Common-wealth or Public Weal. For in other places they speak still of a Commonwealth; but every man procureth his own private gain. Here, where nothing is private, the common affairs be earnestly looked upon. And truly on both parts they have good cause to do so. For in other countries, who knoweth not but he shall starve for hunger, unless he make some several provision for himself, though the Commonwealth flourish never so much riches? And therefore he is compelled of very necessity to have regard to himself rather than to the people, that is to say, to others.

Contrary-wise, there where all things be common to every man, it is not to be doubted that any man shall lack any thing necessary for his private uses, so that the common storehouse and barns be sufficiently stored. For there nothing is distributed after a niggish sort, neither is there any poor man or beggar. And though no man hath any thing, yet every man is rich. For what can be more rich than to live joyful and merrily, without all grief and pensiveness; not caring for his own living, nor vexed or troubled with his wife's importunate complaints, nor dreading poverty to his son, nor sorrow for his daughter's dowry. . . .

Here now would I see if any man dare be so bold as to compare with this equity the justice of other nations; among whom, in truth, I can find no sight or token of equity or justice. For what justice is this, that a rich goldsmith or an usurer or, to be short, any of them which either do nothing at all, or else that which they do is such that it is not very necessary to the Commonwealth, should have a pleasant and a wealthy living, either by idleness or by unnecessary business; when in the meantime poor laborers, carters, ironsmiths, carpenters, ploughmen, by so great and continual toil as drawing and bearing beasts be scarce able to sustain, and again so necessary toil that without it no Commonwealth were able to continue and endure one year, should get so hard and poor a living, and live so wretched and miserable a life that the state and condition of a laboring beast may seem much better and wealthier? For they be not put to so continual labor, nor their living is not much worse; yea, to them much pleasanter, taking no thought in the mean season for the time to come. But these silly poor wretches be for the present tormented with barren and unfruitful labor, and the remembrance of their poor, indigent and beggarly old age killeth them quite. For their daily wages is so little that it will not suffice for the same day, much less yieldeth it any overplus that may daily be laid up for the relief of old age.

Is not that an unjust and an unkind public weal which giveth great fees and rewards to gentlemen, as they call them, and to goldsmiths and to such others which be either idle persons, or else only flatterers and devisers of vain pleasures; and on the contrary part, maketh no gentle provision for poor ploughmen, colliers, laborers, ironsmiths and carpenters, without whom no Commonwealth can continue? But after it hath abused the laborers and their lusty and flourishing age, at the last, when they be oppressed with old age and sickness, being needy, poor and indigent of all things, then, forgetting their so many benefits, recompenceth and acquitteth them most unkindly with miserable death. And yet, besides this, the rich men not only by private fraud, but also by common laws, do every day pluck and snatch away from the poor some part of their daily living. So, whereas it seemed before unjust to recompense with unkindness their pains, that they have been beneficial to the Common-weal, now they have to their wrong and unjust dealing (which is yet a much worse point) given the name of Justice, yea, and that by force of a law. Therefore, when I consider and weigh in my mind all these Commonwealths which now-a-days anywhere do flourish so, God help me, I can perceive nothing but a certain conspiracy of rich men procuring their own commodities, under the name and title of the Commonwealth.

Magna Carta: Confirmation of Edward I

◆§ Around 1700, the laws and documents of English liberties up to that date were compiled and published by one Henry Care, under the title of *English Liberties: or the Free-born Subject's Inheritance*. Care, a rather unimportant figure who had previously gathered the laws on religion and had known arrest and a scandalous trial under Charles II, insisted in this compilation that these laws were in no sense *concessions*, but the birthright of Englishmen, "not to be exempt from the law, but to be freed in person and estate from arbitrary violence." His book went through five editions by 1720, with additions, and was printed in Boston in 1721, and in Providence in 1774. Hence its usefulness for some of the documentation below. The Confirmation of Edward I in 1297 repeated the Magna Carta, notably the excerpts below, quoted from Care, fifth edition of 1721. ℬ

Confirmation of Edward I

Know ye . . . that the Charter of Liberties, and Charter of the Forest,* which were made by common assent of all the realm, in the time of King Henry our father, shall be kept in every point without breach . . . that is to wit, the Great Charter as the Common Law, and the

* The Forestry Laws referred to the King's habit of taking forests from subjects for game or for minerals without satisfaction to the owner. Owners could cut no timber, even to repair their own houses, without license, and the King's Foresters exacted tolls and bribes, and punished poaching severely, even to maiming and execution. The Forest Charter made provisions for the rights of owners to pasture, retain rights to products, ask restitution for wrongs done, and be given well-defined laws on the subject. Edward I's Confirmation was strengthened by the curse of excommunication, which was printed with these statutes down to the mid-sixteenth century.

Charter of the Forest for the wealth of the realm . . . and shall be read before the People two times by the year.

[Ch. V]. And foreasmuch as divers people of our realm are in fear that the aids and taxes which they have given us before time towards our wars, and other businesses, of their own grant or good-will, however they were made, might turn to bondage to them and their heirs, because they might be at another time found in the Rolls, and likewise for the prices taken throughout the realm by our Ministers; We have granted for Us and our Heirs that we shall not draw no such aids, tasks nor prices into a Custom, for any that hath been done heretofore, be it by Roll, or any other precedent that may be founden.

[Ch. VI]. Moreover, We have granted for us and our Heirs . . . That for no business from henceforth we shall take such manner of aids, tasks, or prices, but by the common Assent of the Realm, and for the common profit thereof.

Excerpts from the Magna Carta

[Ch. I]. We have granted also, and given to all the Free-men of our realm, for Us and for our Heirs forever, those Liberties under-written; to have and to hold, to them and their Heirs for ever.

[Ch. IX]. The City of London shall have all the old Liberties and Customs which it hath been used to have. Moreover, we will and grant that all other Cities and Boroughs, Towns, and the Barons of the Five Ports, and all other Ports, shall have all their Liberties and Free Customs.

[Ch. XI]. Common Pleas shall not follow our Court, but shall be holden in some place certain.

[Ch. XXIX]. No Freeman shall be taken or imprisoned, or disseised of his Freehold, or Liberties, or Free Customs, or be outlawed, or exiled, or any otherwise destroyed, nor will we pass upon him, nor condemn him, but by lawful Judgment of his Peers, or by the Law of the Land. We will sell to no man, we will not deny or defer to any man, either Justice or Right. [Said Henry Care of XXIX, "These words deserve to be written in letters of gold."]

On Fortescue [4]

[Preface of Henry Care]. For all our Kings take a solemn Oath at their coronation "To observe and cause all the laws to be kept . . ."

Likewise all our Judges take an Oath, wherein, amongst other points, they swear "To do equal Law and Right to all the King's subjects, rich and poor, and not to delay any person of common right for the Letters of the King, or of any other person, or for any cause: But if any such Letters come to them, they shall proceed to do the Law, the same Letters nothwithstanding." Therefore, saith Fortescue (who was first Chief Justice, and afterwards Lord Chancellor to King Henry 6th) in his book *De Laudibus Legum Angliae,* cap. 9, "The King of England can not alter nor change the Laws of his Realm at his pleasure: for why, he governeth his people by power not only royal but also politic. . . . For he can neither change laws without the consent of his subjects nor yet charge them with impositions against their wills: Wherefore his people do frankly and freely enjoy and occupy their own goods, being ruled by such laws as they themselves desire." [Care further quotes Bracton: "The King in his Realm hath two superiors, God and the Law."]

The Great Protestation

◄§ James I, as we have noted, assumed that his power was not subject to question. Coke and others, protesting arbitrary church courts which rendered judgments not subject to appeal, were met by the argument that the king might take any cause from the common-law judges and decide as he himself pleased. The Archbishop of Canterbury upheld him in this. Coke replied that by the laws of the land all cases, civil and criminal, were to be determined by the courts of justice, and that the king was also under the law. To James this was treason. James was opposed by lawyers, Puritans, and lovers of just government. This was the period of the first Pilgrim and Puritan emigrations to America.

In the argument over the king's right to raise customs duties without consultation with Parliament, the Commons eventually drew up the so-called Great Protestation of December 21, 1621, from which the following excerpt is taken, recalling that James had summoned no Parliament since 1614. James tore the Protestation from the entry book and sent Coke, Pym, and Selden to the Tower. ►

The Great Protestation

The Commons now assembled in Parliament, being justly concerned thereunto concerning sundry liberties, franchises and privileges of Parliament, amongst others not herein mentioned do make this protestation following: That the liberties, franchises, privileges, and jurisdictions of Parliament are the ancient and undoubted birthright and inheritance of the subjects of England; and that the arduous and urgent affairs concerning the King, State, and defense of the realm and of the Church of England, and the making and maintenance of laws, and redress of grievances, which daily happen within this realm, are proper subjects of counsel and debate in Parliament; and that in the handling and proceeding of those businesses every member of the House hath, and of right ought to have, freedom of speech to propound, treat, reason, and bring to conclusion the same: That the Commons in Parliament have like liberty and freedom to treat of those matters, in such order as in their judgment shall seem fittest, and that every member of the said House hath like freedom from all impeachment, imprisonment, and molestation other than by the censure of the House itself, for or concerning any bill, speaking, reasoning, or declaring of any matter or matters touching the Parliament or Parliament business; and that, if any of the said members be complained of and questioned for anything said or done in Parliament, the same is to be shewed the King by the advice and assent of all the Commons assembled in Parliament before the King give credence to any private information.

Petition of Right

◆§ James I died in 1625. His son Charles had learned little, and soon dissolved his first Parliament because of its refusal to grant moneys for extravagance and foreign wars. Charles put pressure on citizens to *lend* him money, imprisoning some who declined. Aroused, Parliament drew up in 1628 the famous *Petition of Right*, a document of importance in English history. Charles I reluctantly acceded to its demands, but summoned no Parliament from 1629 to 1640. ﹩◆

The Petition of Right

The Petition exhibited to his Majesty, by the Lords Spiritual and Temporal and Commons, in this present Parliament assembled, concerning the Rights and Liberties of the Subjects:

To the King's most excellent Majesty,

Humbly shew unto our Sovereign Lord the King, the Lords Spiritual and Temporal and Commons, in Parliament assembled. That whereas it is declared and enacted, by a Statute made in the time of the reign of King Edward the First, commonly called *Statutum de Tallagio non concedendo*, that no Tallage * or Aid shall be laid or levied by the King or his Heirs, in this Realm, without the good will and assent of the Archbishops, Bishops, Earls, Barons, Knights, Burgesses, and other the Freemen of the Commonalty of this Realm. (2) And by authority of Parliament, holden in the five and twentieth year of the reign of King Edward the Third, it is declared and enacted that from henceforth no person shall be compelled to make any loans to the King against his will, because such loans were against reason and the franchise of the land. (3) And by other laws of the Realm it is provided that none should be charged by any Charges or Imposition called a Benevolence, nor by such like charge. (4) By which the Statute before mentioned, and other the good laws and statutes of this Realm, your subjects have inherited this Freedom, that they should not be compelled to contribute to any tax, tallage, aid, or other like charges not set by common consent in Parliament.

2. Yet nevertheless of late, divers Commissions directed to sundry Commissioners in several Counties, with Instructions have issued, by means whereof a People have been in divers places assembled, and required to lend certain sums of money unto your Majesty; and many of them, upon their refusal so to do, have had an Oath administered unto them, not warrantable by the laws or statutes of this Realm, and have been constrained to become bound to make appearance and attendance before your Privy Council, and in other places; and others of them have been therefore imprisoned, confined, and sundry other ways molested and disquieted. (2) And divers other charges have been laid and levied upon your people in several Counties by Lord Lieutenants and Deputy Lieutenants, Commissioners for Musters, Justices of Peace, and others, by command or direction from your Majesty to your Privy Council, against the laws and free customs of this Realm.

3. And where also by the Statute called the Great Charter of the Liberties of England, it is declared and enacted, That no Freeman may be taken or imprisoned, or disseised of his freehold or liberties, or of his free customs, or be outlawed or exiled, nor in any manner destroyed, but by the lawful judgment of his Peers, or by the Law of the Land.

* Includes subsidies, taxes, aids, impositions, tenths, etc., taken or cut from (French *tailler*) a man's estate, by the King.

4. And in the eight and twentieth year of the reign of King Edward the Third it was declared and enacted by authority of Parliament, That no man, of what estate or condition that he be, should be put out of his lands or tenaments, nor taken, nor imprisoned, nor disinherited, nor put to death, without being brought to answer by due Process of Law.

5. Nevertheless, against the tenor of the said Statutes and other the good Laws and Statutes of your Realm, to that end provided, divers of your subjects of late have been imprisoned without any cause shewed. (2) And when for deliverance they were brought before Justices by your Majesty's Writs of *Habeas Corpus*, there to undergo and receive as the Court should order, and their keepers commanded to certify the causes of their detainor, no cause was certified, but that they were detained by your Majesty's *Special Command*, signified by the Lords of your Privy Council, and yet were returned back to several prisons without being charged with anything to which they might make answer according to the Law.

6. Whereas of late great *Companies of Soldiers* and Mariners have been dispersed into divers Counties of the Realm, and the inhabitants against their wills have been compelled to receive them in their houses, and there to suffer them to sojourn against the Laws and Customs of this Realm, and to the great grievance and vexation of the people.

7. And whereas also by authority of Parliament, and in the five and twentieth year of the reign of King Edward the Third, it is declared and enacted, That no man shall be forejudged of life and limb against the form of the Great Charter and Law of the Land. (2) And by the said Great Charter, and other the Laws and Statutes of this your Realm, no man ought to be judged to death but by the Laws established in this your Realm, either by the customs of the Realm or by Acts of Parliament. (3) And whereas no offender of what kind soever is exempted from the Proceedings to be used, and punishment to be inflicted by the Laws and Statutes of this your Realm; nevertheless, of late divers Commissions under your Majesty's Great Seal have issued forth, by which certain persons have been assigned and appointed Commissioners with power and authority to proceed within the land, according to the justice of *Martial Law*, against such soldiers and mariners or other dissolute persons joining with them as should commit any murder, robbery, felony, mutiny, or other outrage or misdemeanor

whatsoever, and by such summary course and order as is agreeable to Martial Law, and as is used in armies in time of war, to proceed to the trial and condemnation of such offenders, and them cause to be executed and put to death, according to the Law Martial.

8. By pretext whereof some of your Majesty's subjects have been by some of the said Commissioners *put to death*, when and where, if by the Laws and Statutes of the Land they had deserved death, by the same Laws and Statutes also they might, and by no other ought to have been judged and executed.

9. And also sundry grievous offenders, by color thereof claiming an exemption, have escaped punishments due to them by the Laws and Statutes of this your Realm, by reason that divers of your Officers and Ministers of Justice have unjustly refused or forborn to proceed against such offenders, according to the same Laws and Statutes, upon pretence that the said offenders were punishable only by Martial Law, and by authority of such Commission as aforesaid. (2) Which Commissions, and all other of like nature, are wholly and directly contrary to the said Laws and Statutes of this your Realm.

10. They do therefore humbly pray your most Excellent Majesty, that no man hereafter be compelled to make or yield any Gift, Loan, Benevolence, Tax, or such like charge without common consent by Act of Parliament; (2) And that none be called to make answer or take such Oath, or to give attendance, or be confined, or otherwise molested or disquieted concerning the same, or for refusal thereof; (3) And that no Freeman in any such manner as is before mentioned be imprisoned or detained. (4) And that your Majesty would be pleased to remove the said soldiers and mariners, and that your people may not be so burdened in time to come; (5) And that the foresaid Commissions for proceeding by Martial Law may be revoked and annulled; and that hereafter no Commissions of like nature may issue forth to any person or persons whatsoever to be executed as aforesaid, lest by color of them any of your Majesty's subjects be destroyed or put to death contrary to the Laws and Franchises of the Land.

11. All which they most humbly pray of your most Excellent Majesty, *as their Rights and Liberties*, according to the Laws and Statutes of this Realm, and that your Majesty would also vouchsafe to declare that the awards, doings and proceedings to the prejudice of your people in any of the premises, shall not be drawn hereafter into consequence

or example. (2) And that your Majesty would be also graciously pleased for the further comfort and safety of your people, to declare your own Royal Will and Pleasure that in the things aforesaid, all your Officers and Ministers shall serve according to the Laws and Statutes of this Realm, as they tender the Honor of your Majesty, and the prosperity of this kingdom.

[Which petition being read, the King's answer was thus delivered unto it: but this answer not giving satisfaction, the King was again petitioned unto, that he would give a full and satisfactory answer to their petition in full Parliament, which he did.]

Thomas Hooker

1586?–1647

◄§ The first settlers in the British American colonies were Englishmen born under Elizabeth and carrying with them to the New World the knowledge of English customs and laws. The fact that in New England they were religious dissenters makes them no less Englishmen; and the famous Mayflower Compact of 1620 was almost by accident at once a document beginning with an assertion of loyalty and a forerunner of the enforced self-determination of groups cast on the wilderness. More significant are Roger Williams' deliberate defense of religious toleration and self-rule by "arbitration" and Thomas Hooker's plan for the earliest Connecticut colony. Though more will be said below of some American documents, Hooker rightfully belongs here, because he and his colony were all English born, and his Fundamental Orders precede in date the "Agreement of the People," the execution of Charles I, and the whole literature of Milton, Sidney, Harrington, Locke, and the Declaration of Rights.

Hooker led a congregation in 1636 from Cambridge (then Newtown) to the Connecticut River country; and in January 1638, the original settlement of Hartford and its offshoots gathered and drew up what has been claimed as the first written constitution in history, a document without reference in it to royal or parliamentarian authority, but a covenant of the peoples concerned, under an ecclesiastic who willingly planned a democracy, remote from England's rising war clouds but not unaware of their meaning. The text here is that of the *Old South Leaflets*, Vol. I, No. 8 (Boston, n.d.). Spelling is modernized. ៩◄

The Fundamental Orders of Connecticut

We the inhabitants and residents of Windsor, Hartford and Wethersfield . . . do therefore associate and conjoin ourselves to be as one

Public State or Commonwealth; and do, for ourselves and our successors and such as shall be adjoined to us at any time hereafter, enter into Combination and Confederation together, to maintain and preserve the liberty and purity of the gospel of our Lord Jesus which we now profess . . . as also in our Civil Affairs to be guided and governed according to such Laws, Rules, Orders and decrees as shall be made, ordered and decreed, as followeth:—

1. It is ordered, sentenced and decreed, that there shall be yearly two general Assemblies or Courts . . . the first shall be called the Court of Election, wherein shall be yearly chosen from time to time so many Magistrates and other public Officers as shall be found requisite: Whereof one to be chosen Governor for the year ensuing and until another be chosen, and no other Magistrate to be chosen for more than one year; provided always there be six chosen besides the Governor; which being chosen and sworn according to an Oath recorded for that purpose shall have power to administer justice according to Laws here established, and for want thereof according to the rule of the word of God; which choice shall be made by all that are admitted freemen and have taken the Oath of Fidelity, and do cohabit within this jurisdiction. . . .

4. It is ordered . . . that no person be chosen Governor above once in two years, and that the Governor be always a member of some approved congregation, and formerly of the Magistracy within this jurisdiction; and all the Magistrates Freemen of this Commonwealth. . . .

6. . . . If the Governor and Major part of Magistrates shall either neglect or refuse to call the two General standing Courts or either of them . . . the Freemen thereof, or the major part of them, shall petition to them so to do: if then it be either denied or neglected the said Freemen or the major part of them shall have power to give order to the Constables of the several towns to do the same, and so may meet together and chose to themselves a Moderator, and may proceed to do any Act of power which any other General Court may. . . .

10. It is ordered . . . that every General Court, except such as through neglect of the Governor and the greatest part of the Magistrates the Freemen themselves do call, shall consist of the Governor, or some one chosen to moderate the Court, and four other Magistrates at least, with the major part of the deputies of the several Towns legally

chosen; and in case the Freemen or major part of them, through neglect or refusal of the Governor and major part of the magistrates, shall call a Court, it shall consist of the major part of Freemen that are present or their deputies, with a Moderator chosen by them: In which said General Courts shall consist the supreme power of the Commonwealth, and they only shall have power to make laws or repeal them, to grant levies, to admit of Freemen, dispose of lands undisposed of, to several Towns or persons, and also shall have power to call either Court or Magistrate or any other person whatsoever into question for any misdemeanor, and may for just causes displace or deal otherwise according to the nature of the offence; and also may deal in any other matter that concerns the good of this commonwealth, except election of Magistrates, which shall be done by the whole body of Freemen. . . . But none of these Courts shall be adjourned or dissolved without the consent of the major part of the Court.

An Agreement of the People

◄§ The Parliament which convened in 1640, made up of many of the same men disbanded in 1629, was in a resolute mood, and in 1641 passed Acts to abolish the Star Chamber and other special courts, the ship moneys and other moneys not granted by Parliament, and asked other reforms. The Star Chamber, anciently an instrument for review of court cases affecting the Crown or even the welfare of citizens oppressed by powerful nobles, had become subject to abuse, because it was of no specified personnel and possessed unlimited jurisdiction at the king's will, trying by rumor and without jury, and making use of torture. It was never revived, though James II was accused of imitating its procedure.

When Charles I attempted to arrest members of this Parliament and failed, he turned to his army and refused to compromise with various proposals advanced by the House. After 1644, his army was routed by Cromwell's Ironsides, and he was captured.

Now a quarrel arose between Parliament and the army, the one being increasingly Presbyterian, the other increasingly Independent and demanding complete toleration and a more democratic government. Parliament voted a smaller army, but the army refused to disband and its committee drew up *An Agreement of the People*, a document chiefly remarkable for its foreshadowing of the later American system, though in 1647 it was given no clear machinery. War was renewed, Charles again arrested and, by a picked and hence probably illegal commission, condemned to die (1649). There followed the decade of Cromwell's Protectorate. During these trying periods many English emigrated to America, Puritans before 1649 and after 1660, Royalists in the 1650s.

The text below is that of *An Agreement of the People for a firm and present Peace*, printed in London in 1647. ⮞

An Agreement of the People (October 28, 1647)

Having by our late labors and hazards made it appear to the world at how high a rate we value our just freedom, and God having so far owned our cause as to deliver the enemies thereof into our hands: We do now hold ourselves bound in mutual duty to each other, to avoid both the danger of returning into a slavish condition, and the chargeable remedy of another war. . . . In order whereof we declare,

I. That the people of England being at this day very unequally distributed by Counties, Cities, and Boroughs, for the election of their deputies in Parliament, ought to be more indifferently proportioned, according to the number of the Inhabitants . . .

II. That, to prevent the many inconveniences apparently arising from the long continuance of the same persons in authority, this present Parliament be dissolved upon the last day of September, which shall be in the year of our Lord 1648.

III. That the people do of course choose themselves a Parliament once in two years, viz. upon the first Thursday in every 2nd March . . . to begin to sit upon the first Thursday in April following . . . and to continue till the last day of September then next ensuing, and no longer.

IV. That the power of this, and all future Representatives of this Nation, is inferior only to theirs who choose them, and doth extend, without the consent or concurrence of any other person or persons to the enacting, altering, and repealing of laws; to the erecting and abolishing of offices and courts; to the appointing, removing, and calling to account magistrates, and officers of all degrees; to the making war and peace, to the treating with foreign States: And generally, to whatsoever is not expressly, or impliedly reserved by the represented to themselves.

Which are as followeth, 1. That matters of religion, and the ways of God's worship, are not at all entrusted by us to any human power, because therein we cannot remit or exceed a tittle of what our consciences dictate to be the mind of God, without wilful sin: nevertheless the public way of instructing the nation (so it be not compulsive) is referred to their discretion.

2. That the matter of impresting [*sic*] and constraining any of us to serve in the wars is against our freedom; and therefore we do not allow it in our Representatives; the rather, because money (the sinews of war) being always at that disposal, they can never want numbers of men apt enough to engage in any just cause.

3. That after the dissolution of this present Parliament, no person be at any time questioned for anything said or done, in reference to the late public differences, otherwise than in execution of the judgments of the present Representatives, or House of Commons.

4. That in all laws made, or to be made, every person may be bound alike, and that no Tenure, estate, charter, degree, birth or place, do confer any exemption from the ordinary course of legal proceedings, whereunto others are subjected.

5. That as the laws ought to be equal, so they must be good, and not evidently destructive to the safety and well-being of the people.

These things we declare to be our *native Rights*, and therefore are agreed and resolved to maintain them with our utmost possibilities against all opposition whatsoever, being compelled thereunto, not only by the examples of our ancestors, whose blood was often spent in vain for the recovery of their freedom, suffering themselves, through fraudulent accomodations, to be still deluded of the fruit of their victories, but also by our own woeful experience, who, having long expected and dearly earned the establishment of these certain rules of government, are yet made to depend for the settlement of our peace and freedom upon him that intended our bondage, and brought a cruel war upon us.

The Hampdens, Vanes, Seldens, etc.

"The Brookses, Hampdens, Vanes, Seldens, Miltons, Nedhams, Harringtons, Nevilles, Sidneys, Lockes," wrote John Adams in 1765 in his *Dissertation on Canon and Feudal Law* ". . . have owed their eminence in political knowledge to the tyrannies of those reigns." In 1776 in his *Thoughts on Government*, he lists them again: "Sidney, Harrington, Locke, Milton, Nedham, Neville, Burnet and Hoadly . . . The wretched condition of this country . . . has frequently reminded me of their principles and reasonings."

Who were these subjects of American admiration? Milton, Sidney, Harrington, and Locke appear below. A word about a few others may serve to remind us of names familiar to the revolutionary period.

John Selden (1584–1654), jurist and scholar, began early to write on English law, publishing in 1610 his *English Law down to Henry II* and in 1616 his Notes on Fortescue's *De Laudibus Legum Angliae*. A *History of Tithes* in 1618 aroused the ecclesiastics and was suppressed by the king's council, and all discussion on the subject forbidden. A co-author of the Protestation of 1621, Selden went to the Tower with Coke. Nevertheless, he was in the Parliament of 1626 and helped draw up the Petition of Right in 1628, and was off to the Tower again. A studious, retiring man by nature, he withdrew from public life, yet in 1642 published his *Discourse concerning the Rights and Privileges of Subjects*. Like Coke, he contributed much to the history of English common law.

John Hampden (1594–1643), a country squire who refused to pay the ship money tax because it was diverted from the navy to the king's uses, became a symbol of firmness and courage. Though a quiet and studious man, he was accused in his trial of 1640 of being "a pernicious and seditious man, and a person of a wicked mind, and of an impious, unquiet and turbulent disposition, and seditiously intending the peace of our Sovereign Lord King Charles." Though he was convicted, the arguments of his defense made valuable reading. Hampden was killed in battle in 1643 at the age of forty-nine, leading one of Cromwell's regiments.

Thomas Brooks (1608–1680), now all but forgotten, was a Puritan divine who preached to the House of Commons around 1648–1650, and whose sermons were once widely read.

Marchmont Nedham (1620–1678), sometimes called the Anti-Machiavelli, published a number of pamphlets now rare, such as *The Case of the Kingdom Stated* (1647), and *The Excellence of a Free State* (1656, republished in 1767).

Harry Vane (1612–1662) was a popular name in America because he was briefly, at the age of twenty-four, a governor of Massachusetts, and was one of the first victims of the Restoration. Knighted in 1640, he was a member of the Parliament of 1641. He helped Roger Williams found Rhode Island, and like him argued for full liberty of conscience in religious matters. He held also that the people were the source of just power, but in the name of moderation opposed the extremes of Cromwell as of Charles I. Charged with treason by the courts of Charles II, he defended himself, arguing that the sovereign power of Parliament was traditional in England, and expressing like Sidney and Locke the compact theory, that if a king failed in his duties, the people might resume their original rights and freedom. He was executed in 1662. His friends published in 1662 a pamphlet entitled, "*The Substance of what Sir Harry Vane intended to have spoken upon the Scaffold on Tower-Hill at the time of his Execution.* Two excerpts read:

"All parts together do assert that this Cause which was owned by Parliament was the cause of God . . .

"And I must still assert that I remain wholly unsatisfied that the course of proceedings against me at my trial were according to the Law, but that I was run upon and destroyed contrary to right, and the Liberties of Magna Charta under the form of justice."

Henry Neville (1620–1694), friend of James Harrington and member of the Council of State in 1651, was banished by Cromwell from London for his extremism, but returned to Parliament in 1658. He was thrown into the Tower in 1663 by Charles II on charges of atheism, blasphemy, and probable participation in an uprising in Yorkshire, but released after a year for lack of evidence. He was the author of some rather coarse humor, and of *Plato Redivivus, or a Dialogue Concerning Government* in 1681, republished in 1698 as *Discourses Concerning Government*, in which he advocated a council of state responsible to Parliament, one third of whose members should retire each year. He also translated Machiavelli into English.

Sir John Hawles (1645–1716), Whig lawyer, and solicitor-general in 1695, sided with Parliament in the civil struggle, and in 1680 published *The Englishman's Rights*, a booklet often republished, including a Boston edition of 1772. It was subtitled: "A dialogue between a barrister-at-law and a juryman; plainly setting forth I. The Antiquity, II. The excellent designed use, III. The office and just privileges of juries, by the law of England."

A London issue of 1732 was prefaced by an "unknown" old gentleman, whose excuse for this reissue was that he was "not only an eye-witness of the illegal and arbitrary proceedings in the reigns of King Charles and King James the Second, and by myself a sufferer by them," but also now disturbed by the "memory, which I still retain of the dread and terror we were continually under in those times not only from packed and corrupted juries, but from the influence of the Courts upon weak and timorous juries."

Hawles' juryman tries to avoid jury duty on a plea of lack of time and knowledge, and a fear of the displeasure of the Court. The barrister argues the traditional protection of juries, "contemporary with the nation itself," and compares English conditions with the "miserable condition of the poor people in most other nations," under arbitrary rulers and methods of torture. He further explains to the juryman the nature of the jury system, the responsibility to decide not only on "guilt of Fact," but also on the deeper questions of conscience against injustice. "Fining or imprisoning of jurors for giving their verdicts is illegal," he quotes from the Parliamentary Proceedings of 1667, and assures the citizen that it is his duty to protect the jury system by service. He concludes with the third quotation from Coke which appears on page 94.

Gilbert Burnet (1643–1715) turned from Scotch Presbyterianism and the study of law to become an Anglican bishop. Onetime professor of divinity at Glasgow, he became a royal chaplain in London, but at the coming of James II took himself to Paris and Holland, where he became a Dutch subject and a friend of William of Orange. In 1689 he became Bishop of Salisbury, a position in which he served with latitudinarian liberalism. He was best remembered for two books, a *History of the Reformation*, from original documents, and an *Inquiry into Measures of Submission to the Supreme Authority* (1688), in which he defended the bloodless revolution.

Benjamin Hoadly (1676–1761), also a divine and a royal chaplain, nevertheless in 1717 attacked the divine authority of both king and clergy and denied the power of church over conscience, thereby starting a tremendous war of pamphlets, which reached the number of seventy-four in one year. His writings were entitled *Measures of Submission to Civil Magistrates*, and *The Origin and Institution of Civil Government*.

Such were the men whom Adams and other Americans selected for special mention as sources and symbols of resistance to arbitrary power. ह्ॐ

Richard Hooker

1554–1600

ह्ॐ Frequent American mention of the "judicious Hooker" in the eighteenth century sends us back to Elizabethan days, before the difficult era of the Stuarts. Hooker, a clergyman and Oxford graduate, had a profound influence upon the polity of the rising English church toward a compromise between the extremes of supernaturalism and rationalism, between the literal Scriptures of the Puritans and the rigid authoritarianism of dogma. His way out through reason as a law of nature influenced Locke's theory of government. No doubt much of his own argument derived from Cicero, Aristotle's *Ethics*, Saint Augustine, and Thomas Aquinas. From his studies came his *Laws of Ecclesiastical Polity*, the first four books of which were printed without date around 1592–1594; four others appeared after his death. His *Works* were printed with a *Life* by Isaak Walton in 1666 and thereafter. Present excerpts are from the London edition of 1705 of Hooker's *Works*. Spelling has been slightly modernized. ह्ॐ

The Law of Reason

[I, 8]. Laws of Reason have these marks to be known by: Such as keep them resemble most lively in their voluntary actions that very manner of working which Nature herself doth necessarily observe in the course of the whole world. The works of Nature are all behoveful, beautiful, without superfluity or defect; even so theirs, if they be framed according to that which the Law of Reason teacheth. Secondly, those Laws are investigable by Reason, without the help of Revelation, supernatural and divine. Finally, in such sort they are investigable, that the knowledge of them is general, the world hath always been acquainted with them; according to that which one in Sophocles observeth concerning a branch of this Law: "It is no child of today's or yesterday's birth, but hath been no man knoweth how long sithence." It is not agreed upon by one, or two, or a few, but by all. Which we may not so understand, as if every particular man in the whole world did know and confess whatsoever the Law of Reason doth contain: but this Law is such that being proposed no man can reject it as unreasonable and unjust. Again, there is nothing in it but any man (having natural perfection of wit and ripeness of judgment) may by labor and travel [travail] find out. And to conclude, the general principles thereof are such, as it is not easy to find men ignorant of them. Law rational therefore, which men commonly use to call the Law of Nature, meaning thereby the Law which human nature knoweth itself in reason universally bound unto, which also for that cause may be termed most fitly the Law of Reason; this Law, I say, comprehendeth all those things which men by the light of their natural understanding evidently know, or at leastwise may know, to be beseeming or unbeseeming, virtuous or vicious, good or evil for them to do.

Law of Society

[I, 10]. But forasmuch as we are not by ourselves sufficient to furnish ourselves with competent store of things needful for such a life as our nature doth desire, a life fit for the dignity of man; therefore to supply those defects and imperfections which are in us living single and solely by ourselves, we are naturally induced to seek communion and fellowship with others. This was the cause of men's uniting themselves at the first in politic societies, which societies could not be without government, nor government without a distinct kind of Law from that which hath been already declared. Two foundations there are which bear up public societies; the one, a natural inclination whereby all men desire sociable life and fellowship; the other, an order expressly or secretly agreed upon touching the manner of their union in living together. The latter is that which we call the Law of a Commonweal, the very soul of a politic body, the parts whereof are by law animated, held together, and set on work in such actions as the common good requireth.

Consent of Governed

[I, 10]. To take away all such mutual grievances, injuries and wrongs, there was no way but only by growing unto composition and agreement amongst themselves, by ordaining some kind of government public, and by yielding themselves subject thereunto; that unto whom they granted authority to rule and govern, by them the peace, tranquility, and happy estate of the rest might be procured. Men always knew that when force and injury was offered they might be defenders of themselves; they knew that howsoever men may seek their own commodity, yet if this were done with injury unto others it was not to be suffered, but by all men and by all good means to be withstood; finally, they knew that no man might in reason take upon him to determine his own right, and according to his own determination proceed in maintenance thereof, inasmuch as every man is towards himself and them whom he greatly affecteth partial: and therefore that strifes and troubles would be endless, except they gave their common consent all to be ordered by some whom they should agree upon. Without which consent there were no reason that one man should take upon him to be lord or judge over another; because, although there be according to the opinion of some very great and judicious men a kind of natural right in the noble, wise and virtuous to govern them which are of servile disposition; nevertheless, for manifestation of this right, and men's more peaceable contentment on both sides, the assent of them who are to be governed seemeth necessary. . . .

So that, in a word, all public regiment, of what kind soever, seemeth evidently to have risen from deliberate advice, consultation and composition between men. . . .

Howbeit, laws do not take their constraining force from the quality of such as devise them, but from that power which doth give them the strength of laws. That which we spake before concerning the power of government, must here be applied unto the power of making laws whereby to govern, which power God hath over all; and by the natural law, whereunto he hath made all subject, the lawful power of making laws to command whole politic societies of men belongeth so properly unto the same entire societies, that for any prince or potentate of what kind soever upon earth to exercise the same of himself, and not either by express commission immediately and personally received from God, or else by authority derived at the first from their consent upon whose persons they impose laws, it is no better than mere tyranny.

Laws they are not therefore which public approbation hath not made so. But approbation not only they give who personally declare their assent by voice, sign, or act; but also when others do it in their names, by right originally at the least derived from them. As in parliaments, councils, and the like assemblies, although we be not personally ourselves present, notwithstanding our assent is by reason of other agents there in our behalf. And what we do by others, no reason but that it should stand as our deed, no less effectually to bind us than if ourselves had done it in person.

The King James Bible of 1611

◅§ It was inevitable in the days of the Puritan revolt against arbitrary kings that there should be a searching of the Scriptures. Most often quoted as "proof" that God did not favor kings was I Samuel 8:4–22. See, for example, Milton's *Ready and Easy Way to Establish a Free Commonwealth*, 1659, or Tom Paine's *Common Sense*. §▻

I Samuel 8

4. Then all the elders of Israel gathered themselves together, and came to Samuel unto Ramah.

5. And said unto him, Behold, thou art old, and thy sons walk not in thy ways: now make us a king to judge us like all the nations.

6. But the thing displeased Samuel, when they said, Give us a king to judge. And Samuel prayed unto the Lord.

7. And the Lord said unto Samuel, Hearken unto the voice of the people in all that they say unto thee: for they have not rejected thee, but they have rejected me, that I should not reign over them.

8. According to all the works which they have done since the day that I brought them up out of Egypt even unto this day, wherewith they have forsaken me, and served other gods; so do they also unto thee.

9. Now, therefore, hearken unto their voice: howbeit yet protest solemnly unto them, and shew them the manner of the king that shall reign over them.

10. And Samuel told all the words of the Lord unto the people that asked of him a king.

11. And he said, This will be the manner of the king that shall reign over you: He will take your sons, and appoint them for himself, for his chariots, and to be his horsemen: and some shall run before his chariots.

12. And he will appoint him captains over thousands, and captains over fifties, and will set them to ear [i.e., plow] his ground, and to reap his harvest, and to make his instruments of war, and instruments of his chariots.

13. And he will take your daughters to be confectionaries, and to be cooks, and to be bakers.

14. And he will take your fields, and your vineyards, and your oliveyards, even the best of them, and give them to his servants.

15. And he will take the tenth of your seed, and of your vineyards, and give to his officers, and to his servants.

16. And he will take your menservants, and your maidservants, and your goodliest young men, and your asses, and put them to his work.

17. He will take the tenth of your sheep: and ye shall be his servants.

18. And ye shall cry out in that day because of your king which ye shall have chosen you; and the Lord will not hear you in that day.

19. Nevertheless, the people refused to obey the voice of Samuel: and they said, Nay; but we will have a king over us;

20. That we also may be like all the nations; and that our king may judge us, and go out before us, and fight our battles.

21. And Samuel heard all the words of the people, and he rehearsed them in the ears of the Lord.

22. And the Lord said to Samuel, Hearken unto their voice, and make them a king.

John Milton

1608–1674

◄§ Among the great essays of English literature is Milton's *Areopagitica*, provoked by an Act of Parliament in 1643 to reestablish censorship over the press (i.e., printing), but rising above the local to a timeless expression of the right of the free mind to read, to have access to the thoughts of others, to speak one's own reflections. The essay should be read in its entirety.

Milton was caught up in the tide of the times and became secretary to Cromwell, carrying on a heavy correspondence with foreign nations, often in Latin. Yet he found time to write in 1649 his *Eikonoklastes* ("image-breaker"), defending the action against Charles I, and his *Tenure of Kings and Magistrates*, perhaps the best known in America of his political writings, and frequently referred to. Even in 1659, having become blind in the service of the Commonwealth, Milton made a last bold attempt in his *Ready and Easy Way to Establish a Free Commonwealth* to urge a government without a king. Perhaps it was his blindness and his reputation as a poet that saved him from no greater retaliation than exile from London upon the accession of Charles II.

Milton's works were early known in America and exercised their influence upon New England election sermons and political papers. "They are indeed," wrote Jonathan Mayhew in a letter, "the principles which, God be thanked, generally prevail in New England." [5]

Milton's prose works were edited in 1697-1698 by Toland in three volumes and reprinted in 1738 and 1753. Quotations below are from the Toland edition of 1753, London, 7 volumes. ᘔ✺

Areopagitica

If ye be thus resolved, as it were injury to think ye were not, I know not what should withhold me from presenting ye with a fit instance wherein to shew both that love of truth which ye eminently profess, and that uprightness of your judgment which is not wont to be partial to yourselves; by judging over again that order which ye have ordained "to regulate Printing: that no book, pamphlet, or paper shall be henceforth printed, unless the same be first approved and licensed by such, or at least one of such, as shall be thereto appointed. . . ."

I deny not but that it is of greatest concernment in the church and Commonwealth to have a vigilant eye how books demean themselves as well as men; and thereafter to confine, imprison, and do sharpest justice on them as malefactors: For books are not absolutely dead things, but do contain a potency of life in them to be as active as that soul was whose progeny they are; nay, they do preserve as in a vial the purest efficacy and extraction of that living intellect that bred them. I know they are as lively, and as vigorously productive, as those fabulous dragon's teeth; and being sown up and down, may chance to spring up armed men. And yet, on the other hand, unless wariness be used, as good almost kill a man as kill a good book; who kills a man kills a reasonable creature, God's image; but he who destroys a good book, kills reason itself, kills the image of God, as it were in the eye. Many a man lives a burden to the earth; but a good book is the precious life-blood of a master spirit, embalmed and treasured up on purpose to a life beyond life. . . .

Another reason, whereby to make it plain that this order will miss the end it seeks, consider by the quality which ought to be in every licenser. It cannot be denied but that he who is made judge to sit upon the birth or death of books, whether they may be wafted into this world or not, had need to be a man above the common measure, both studious, learned, and judicious; there may be else no mean mistakes in the censure of what is passable or not; which is also no mean injury. If he be of such worth as behoves him, there cannot be a more tedious and unpleasing journey-work, a greater loss of time levied upon his head, than to be made the perpetual reader of unchosen books and pamphlets, ofttimes huge volumes. . . .

If therefore ye be loth to dishearten heartily and discontent, not the mercenary crew of false pretenders to learning, but the free and ingenuous sort of such as evidently were born to study and love learning for itself, not for lucre, or any other end, but the service of God and of truth . . . then know, that so far to distrust the judgment and the honesty of one who hath but a common repute in learning, and never yet offended, as not to count him fit to print his mind without a tutor and examiner, lest he should drop a schism, or something of corruption, is the greatest displeasure and indignity to a free and knowing spirit that can be put upon him.

What advantage is it to be a man, over it is to be a boy at school, if we have only escaped the ferular to come under the fescue of an Imprimatur? If serious and elaborate writings, as if they were no more than the theme of a grammar-lad under his pedagogue, must not be uttered without the cursory eyes of a temporizing and extemporizing licenser? He who is not trusted with his own actions, his drift not being known to be evil . . . has no great argument to think himself reputed in the commonwealth wherein he was born, for other than a fool or a foreigner. When a man writes to the world, he summons up all his reason and deliberation to assist him; he searches, meditates, is industrious, and likely consults and confers with his judicious friends . . . If in this the most consummate act of his fidelity and ripeness, no years, no industry, no former proof of his abilities can bring him to that state of maturity, as not to be still mistrusted and suspected, unless he carry all his considerate diligence . . . to the hasty view of an unleisured licenser, perhaps much his younger, perhaps far his inferior in judgment, perhaps one who never knew the labor of book-writing . . . it cannot be but a dishonor and derogation to the author, to the book, to the privilege and dignity of learning. . . .

And how can a man teach with authority, which is the life of teaching, how can he be a doctor in his book as he ought to be, or else had better be silent, whenas all he teaches, all he delivers, is but under the tuition, under the correction of his patriarchal licenser, to blot or to alter what precisely accords not with the hidebound humor which he calls his judgment? . . . I hate a pupil teacher, I endure not an instructor that comes to me under the wardship of an overseeing fist. I know nothing of the licenser, but that I have his own hand for his arrogance; who shall warrant me his judgment? the state, Sir, replies the stationer: but has a quick return, the state shall be my governors, but not my critics; they may be mistaken in the choice of a licenser, as easily as the licenser may be mistaken in an author . . . For though a licenser should happen to be judicious more than ordinary . . . yet his very office and his commission enjoins him to let pass nothing but what is vulgarly received already. . . .

And as it is a particular disesteem of every knowing person alive, and most injurious to the written labors and monuments of the dead, so to me it seems an undervaluing and vilifying of the whole nation. I cannot set so light by all the invention, the art, the wit, the grave and solid judgment which is in England, as that it can be comprehended in any twenty capacities how good soever; much less that it should not pass except their superintendence be over it, except it be sifted and strained with their strainers, that it should be undercurrent without their manual stamp. Truth and understanding are not such wares as to be monopolised and traded in by tickets, and statutes, and standards. . . .

And lest some should persuade ye, Lords and Commons, that these arguments of learned men's discouragement at this your order, are mere flourishes and not real, I could recount what I have seen and heard in other countries, where this kind of inquisition tyrannizes; when I have sat among their learned men (for that honor I had) and been counted happy to be born in such a place of philosophic freedom as they supposed England was, while themselves did nothing but bemoan the servile condition into which learning amongst them was brought; that this was it which had damped the glory of Italian wits; that nothing had been there written now these many years but flattery and fustian. There it was that I found and visited the famous Galileo grown old, a prisoner to the Inquisition, for thinking in astronomy otherwise than the Franciscan and Dominican licensers thought. . . .

What should ye do then, should ye suppress all this flowery crop of knowledge and new light sprung up and yet springing daily in this city? should ye set an oligarchy of twenty engrossers over it, to bring a famine upon our minds again, when we shall know nothing but what is measured to us by their bushel? Believe it, Lords and Commons, they who counsel ye to such a suppressing, do as good as bid ye suppress yourselves; and I will soon show how. If it be desired to know the immediate cause of all this free writing and free speaking, there cannot be assigned a truer than your own mild and free and humane government: it is the liberty, Lords and Commons, which your own valorous and happy counsels have purchased us; liberty which is the nurse of all great wits . . . Ye cannot make us now less capable, less knowing, less eagerly pursuing of the truth, unless ye first make yourselves, that made us so, less the lovers, less the founders of our true liberty. We can grow ignorant again, brutish, formal and slavish, as ye found us; but you then must first become that which ye cannot be, oppressive, arbitrary and tyrannous, as they were from whom ye have freed us. . . . Although I dispraise not the defence of just immunities, yet love my peace better, if that were all. Give me the liberty to know, to utter, and to argue freely according to conscience, above all liberties. . . .

And now the time in special is by privilege to write and speak what may help to the further discussing of matters in agitation. The temple of Janus, with his two controversal faces, might now not unsignificantly be set open. And though all the winds of doctrine were let loose to play upon the earth, so truth be in the field, we do injuriously by licensing and prohibiting to misdoubt her strength. Let her and Falsehood grapple; who ever knew truth put to the worse, in a free and open encounter? Her confuting is the best and surest suppressing. . . .

For who knows not that truth is strong, next to the Almighty; she needs no policies, nor stratagems, nor licensings to make her victorious; those are the shifts and the defences that error uses against another power: give her but room, and do not bind her when she sleeps, for then she speaks not true, as the old Proteus did, who spake oracles only when he was caught and bound, but then rather she turns herself into all shapes, except her own, and perhaps tunes her voice according to the time, as Micaiah did before Ahab, until she be adjured into her own likeness. Yet is it not impossible that she may have more shapes than one? What else is all that rank of things indifferent, wherein truth may be on this side, or on the other, without being unlike herself? What but a vain shadow else is the abolition of "those ordinances, that handwriting nailed to the cross?" What great purchase is this Christian liberty which Paul so often boasts of? His doctrine is, that he who eats or eats not, regards a day or regards it not, may do either to the Lord. How many other things might be tolerated in peace, and left to conscience, had we but charity, and were it not the chief stronghold of our hypocrisy to be ever judging one another?

The Tenure of Kings and Magistrates

Proving that it is lawful, and hath been held so through all ages, for any who have the power, to call to account a Tyrant, or wicked King, and after due conviction, to depose, and put him to death; if the ordinary magistrate have neglected or denied to do it. And that they who of late so much blame deposing, are the men that did it themselves.

If men within themselves would be governed by reason, and not generally give their understanding to a double tyranny of custom from without, and blind affections within, they would discern better what it is to favor and uphold the tyrant of a Nation. But being slaves within doors, no wonder that they strive so much to have the public state conformably governed to the inward vicious rule, by which they govern themselves. For indeed none can love freedom heartily but good men; the rest love not freedom, but licence; which never hath more scope or more indulgence than under tyrants. Hence is it that tyrants are not oft offended, nor stand much in doubt of bad men, as being all naturally servile; but in whom virtue and true worth most is eminent, them they fear in earnest, as by right their master; against them lies all their hatred and suspicion. Consequently neither do bad men hate tyrants, but have always been readiest, with the falsified names of Loyalty and Obedience, to color over their base compliances. . . .

No man who knows aught can be so stupid to deny that all men naturally were born free, being the image and resemblance of God himself, and were by privilege above all the creatures born to command and not to obey: and that they lived so, till from the root of Adam's transgression, falling among themselves to do wrong and violence, and foreseeing that such courses must needs tend to the destruction of them all, they agreed by common league to bind each other from mutual injury, and jointly to defend themselves against any that give disturbance or opposition to such agreement. Hence came cities, towns and commonwealths. And because no faith at all was found sufficiently binding, they saw it needful to ordain some authority, that might restrain by force and punishment what was violated against peace and common right.

This authority and power of self-defence and preservation being originally and naturally in every one of them, and unitedly in them all; for ease, for order, and lest each man should be his own partial judge, they communicated and derived either to one, whom for the eminence of his wisdom and integrity they chose above the rest, or to more than one whom they thought of equal deserving: the first was called a king; the other magistrates: not to be their lords and masters (though afterward those names in some places were given voluntarily to such as have been authors of inestimable good to the people) but to be their deputies and commissioners, to execute, by virtue of their entrusted power, that justice which else every man by the bond of nature and of covenant must have executed for himself, and for one another. And to him that shall consider well why among free persons, one man by civil right should bear authority and jurisdiction over another, no other end or reason can be imaginable.

These for a while governed well, and with much equity decided all things at their own arbitrement: till the temptation of such a power left absolute in their hands, perverted them at length to injustice and partiality. Then did they who now by trial had found the danger and inconveniences of committing arbitrary power to any, invent laws either framed, or consented to by all, that should confine and limit the authority of whom they choose to govern them: that so man, of whose failing they had proof, might no more rule over them, but law and reason abstracted as much as might be from personal errors and frailties. While as the magistrate was set above the people, so the law was set above the magistrate. When this would not serve, but that the law was either not executed, or misapplied, they were constrained from that time, the only remedy left them, to put conditions and take oaths from all kings and magistrates at their first instalment to do impartial justice by law: who upon those terms and no other, received allegiance from the people, that is to say, bond or covenant to obey them in execution of those laws which they the people had themselves made or assented to. And this ofttimes with express warning, that if the king or magistrate proved unfaithful to his trust, the people would be disengaged. . . .

To say kings were accountable to none but God, is the overturning of all law and government. For if they may refuse to give account, then all covenants made with them at coronation, all oaths are in vain and mere mockeries; all laws which they swear to keep, made to no purpose, for if the king fear not God (as how many of them do not?) we hold then our lives and estates by the tenure of his mere grace and mercy, as from a God, not a mortal magistrate; a position that none but court-parasites or men besotted would maintain! Aristotle therefore, whom we commonly allow for one of the best interpreters of nature and morality, writes in the fourth of his politics, chap. X, that "monarchy unaccountable is the worst sort of tyranny; and least of all to be endured by freeborn men."

The Ready and Easy Way to Establish a Free Commonwealth

[The above idea, familiar yet here most clearly expressed, leads Milton to hope against hope in 1659 that it might not yet be too late to establish a free commonwealth; and for such he argued in *The Ready and Easy Way to Establish a Free Commonwealth*. The Restoration, 1660, silenced him, but not his ideas. Note the proposal of a "delegated" congress.]

If we return to kingship, and soon repent (as undoubtedly we shall, when we begin to find the old encroachments coming on by little and little upon our consciences, which must necessarily proceed from king and bishop united inseparably in one interest), we may be forced perhaps to fight over again all that we have fought, and spend over again all that we have spent, but are never like to attain thus far as we are now advanced to the recovery of our freedom, never to have it in possession as we now have it. . . .

Now is the opportunity, now the very season wherein we may obtain a free commonwealth, and establish it for ever in the land, without difficulty or much delay. Writs are sent out for elections, and which is worth observing, in the name not of any king, but of the keepers of our liberty, to summon a free parliament; which then only will indeed be free, and deserve the true honor of that supreme title, if they preserve us a free people. Which never parliament was more free to do; being now called, not as heretofore, by the summons of a king, but by the voice of liberty; and if the people, laying aside prejudice and impatience, will seriously and calmly now consider their own good, both religious and civil, their own liberty and the only means thereof, as shall be here laid down before them, and will elect their knights and burgesses able men, and according to the just and necessary qualifications . . . men not addicted to a single person or house of lords, the work is done; at least the foundation firmly laid of a free commonwealth, and good part also erected of the main structure. For the ground and basis of every just and free government (since men have smarted so oft for committing all to one person) is a general council of ablest men, chosen by the people to consult of public affairs from time to time for the common good. In this grand council must the sovereignty, not transferred, but delegated only, and as it were deposited, reside; with this caution, they must have the forces by sea and land committed to them for preservation of the common peace and liberty; must raise and manage the public revenue, at least with some inspectors deputed for satisfaction of the people, how it is employed; must make or propose, as more expressly shall be said anon, civil laws, treat of commerce, peace, or war with foreign nations, and for the carrying on some particular affairs with more secrecy and expedition, must elect, as they have already out of their own number and others, a council of state.

James Harrington

1611–1677

◦§ Had Harrington ("the incomparable Harrington," James Otis called him) been able to conquer a love of minute detail and a confusing disguise of historical names, he might have written the political classic of his time. Even so, he stands apart in having observed before all others the fact that economic shifts in England explained more than did all the theorizing about divine rights. His *Oceana* was a kind of utopia, but vastly closer to practical realities. An increasing distribution of land, he saw, made the narrow absolutism of a monarch or a few nobles less and less tenable, for independent men will demand a voice and will wield military power (as, indeed, Cromwell had demonstrated). Hence England moved quite naturally toward a commonwealth with popular assemblies. One can imagine that Harrington would have clearly seen that an America of free land would move toward a democracy; for Harrington endeared himself to Americans by his advocacy of characteristic reforms: better agrarian distribution, a liberal constitution, a government of laws, not men, rotation of public offices, the ballot, separation of powers, religious freedoms, compulsory free public education, self-governing colonies within empires.

Harrington's *Oceana* was published in 1656 and addressed to Cromwell, who nearly had it destroyed. Harrington later went to the Tower under Charles II and there languished into mental and physical decay. His works were published in 1699. Present excerpts are from the London edition of 1771, with the original preface by John Hall. Hall said (Preface, page xv): "That empire follows the balance of property, whether lodged in one, in a few, or in many hands, he was the first that ever made out: and is a noble discovery, whereof the honor solely belongs to him, as much as those of the circulation of the blood, or printing, of guns, or the compass or of optic glasses to the several authors." The quotation shows the empiric temper of the late seventeenth century; it also reveals Harrington as a forerunner of the physiocrats.[6]

Harrington reviewed government from ancient times, quoting much from classics and from Machiavelli. ஓ◦

Definitions

Government (to define it *de jure*, or according to ancient prudence) is an art whereby a civil society of men is instituted and preserved upon the foundation of common right or interest; or (to follow Aristotle and Livy) it is the empire of laws, not of men.

And government (to define it *de facto*, or according to modern prudence) is an art whereby some man, or some few men, subject a city or a nation, and rule it according to his or their private interest: which, because the laws in such cases are made according to the interest of a man, or of some few families, may be said to be the empire of men, and not of laws.

The former kind is that which Machiavel (whose books are neglected) is the only politician that has gone about to retrieve; that Leviathan (who would have his book imposed upon the universities) goes about to destroy. For "It is (says he) another error of Aristotle's politics that in a well-ordered commonwealth not men should govern, but the laws. What man that has his natural senses, though he can neither write nor read, does not find himself governed by them he fears, and believes can kill or hurt him when he obeys not? Or who believes that the law can hurt him, which is but words and paper, without the hands and swords of men?"* . . .

But legislators having found these three governments [i.e., Aristotle's monarchy, aristocracy, democracy] at the best to be naught, have invented another consisting of a mixture of them all, which only is good. This is the doctrine of the ancients. . . .

To begin with riches, in regard that men are hung upon these, not of choice . . . but of necessity and by the teeth; for as much as he who wants bread is his servant that will feed him; if a man thus feeds a whole people, they are under his empire. . . .

If the whole people be landlords, or hold the lands so divided among them that no one man, or number of men, within the compass of the *few* or *aristocracy*, overbalance them, the empire (without the interposition of force) is a commonwealth.

If force be interposed in any of these three cases, it must either frame the government to the foundation, or the foundation to the government; or holding the government not according to the balance, it is not natural but violent; and therefore if it be at the devotion of a prince, it is tyranny; if at the devotion of the few, oligarchy; or if in the power of the people, anarchy. Each of which confusions, the balance standing otherwise, is but of short continuance, because against the nature of the balance, which not destroyed, destroys that which opposes it.

But there be other confusions which, being rooted in the balance, are of longer continuance, and of worse consequence: as, at first, where

* Harrington answers this quotation from Hobbes by pointing out that it is men whose hands hold the sword and who may govern by laws.

a nobility holds half the property or about that proportion, and the people the other half; in which case, without altering the balance, there is no remedy but the one must eat out the other: as the people did the nobility in Athens, and the nobility the people in Rome. Secondly, when a prince holds about half a dominion, and the people the other half (which was the case of the Roman emperors, planted partly upon their military colonies, and partly upon the senate and the people) the government becomes a very shambles both of the princes and the people. Somewhat of this nature are certain governments at this day, which are said to subsist by confusion. In this case, to fix the balance is to entail misery: but in the three former, not to fix it is to lose the government. . . . This kind of law, fixing the balance in lands, is called *Agrarian* . . . Without an Agrarian law, government, whether monarchical, aristocratical, or popular, has no long lease. . . .

There is a private reason, which is the interest of the private man.

Secondly, there is reason of state, which is the interest of the ruler or rulers, that is to say, of the prince, of the nobility, or of the people.

Thirdly, there is that reason which is the interest of mankind, or of the whole. . . . There is a common right, law of nature, or interest of the whole; which is more excellent, and so acknowledged to be by the agents themselves, than the rights or interest of the parts only. . . .

Mankind then must . . . acknowledge his common interest to be common right. And if reason be nothing else but interest, and the interest of mankind be the right interest, then the reason of mankind must be right reason. Now compute well: for if the interest of popular government come the nearest to the interest of mankind, then the reason of popular government must come the nearest to right reason.

[Harrington argued for a senate to propose, people acting through representatives to consent to, and magistracy to execute, laws.]

"The Prerogative of Popular Government"

[Under this heading Harrington replied to some of the critics of *Oceana*.]

Whosoever sheds man's blood, by man shall his blood be shed, for in the image of God made he man. If the rule holds as well in shedding the blood of a Turk as of a Christian, then *that wherein man is the image of God is Reason*. Of all controversies those of the pen are most honorable: for in those of force there is more of the image of the beast, but in those of the pen there is more of the image of God. In the controversies of the sword, there is but too often no other reason than force; but the controversy of the pen has never any force but that of reason. Of all controveries of the pen next those of religion, those of government are the most honorable and the most useful . . . Of all controversies of government, those in the vindication of government are the most noble, as being that constitution alone from whence all we have that is good is descended to us; and, if it had not existed, mankind at this day had been but a herd of beasts. The prerogative of popular government must either be in an ill hand, or else it is a game against which there is not a card in the whole pack. . . .

A man may be possessed of a piece of ground by force, but to make use or profit of it, he must build upon it and till it by reason; *for whatever is not founded upon reason cannot be permanent.* In reason there are two parts, invention and judgment: as to the latter, *in a multitude of counsellors* (say both Solomon and Machiavel) there is strength. Nay as for judgment, there is not that order in art or nature that can compare with a popular assembly. *The voice of the people is the voice of God.* Hence it is that in all well-ordered policies the people have the ultimate result: but unless there is some other to invent, a popular assembly can be of no effect at all but confusion. Invention is a solitary thing. All the physicians in the world put together invented not the circulation of the blood, nor can invent any such thing, though in their own art: yet this was invented by one alone, and being invented is unanimously voted and embraced by the generality of physicians. . . . *Let one speak and the rest judge.* On whatever any one man can say or do, mankind is the natural and competent judge.

Sir Algernon Sidney

1622–1683

Sidney had a very considerable reputation.in the American colonies, for few British writers on government were mentioned oftener. Even thirty years after the American Revolution, Jefferson linked Sidney with Locke as a prime source of ideas on government. Second son of the Earl of Leicester, Sidney had traveled on the continent, served as a soldier, and opposed both the royal Charles and the usurper Cromwell, for he favored civil law above all arbitrary power. Though a member of the council of state in 1659, he went into exile after the Restoration, but returned in 1677, and between 1680 and 1683 wrote his *Discourses Concerning Government*.

Sidney was arrested on a charge of complicity in the Rye House plot, tried, and executed in 1683. The accusation was that of seditious and traitorous utterances, such as that a king is subject to the law and responsible to the people, and may be deposed. At his death he expressed himself again that "magistrates were set up for the good of nations, not nations for the honor and glory of magistrates."

One of the first acts of Parliament in 1689 was to declare that "Algernon Sidney, Esq., was most unjustly and wrongfully convicted and attainted . . . and that all records and proceedings relating to the said attainder be wholly cancelled and taken off the file."

His *Discourses Concerning Government*, entrusted to a friend, was published in 1698, from which edition the excerpts below are taken. The work was provoked in part by Filmer's *Patriarcha*, which argued that "the desire of liberty was the first cause of the fall of man." *The Essence of* [Sidney's] *Work on Government* was published in 1795, with a statement that though much deserving of attention, this work had been neglected because of its length and because of the odium cast on it by a corrupt ruling class.[7] ⟨⟩

Reply to Filmer

[Ch. I, Sec. V]. Whilst he [Filmer] denies they [the rights of the people] can proceed from the laws of natural liberty, or any other root than the Grace and Bounty of the Prince, he declares they can have none at all. For as liberty solely consists in an independency upon the will of another, and by the name of slave we understand a man who can neither dispose of his person or goods, but enjoys all at the will of his master; there is no such thing in nature as a slave if those men or nations are not slaves who have no other title to what they enjoy than the grace of the Prince, which he may revoke whensoever he pleaseth.

But there is more than ordinary extravagance in his assertion that "the greatest liberty in the world is for a people to live under a monarch," when his whole book is to prove that this monarch has his right from God and nature, is endowed with an unlimited power of doing what he pleases, and can be restrained by no law. If it be liberty to live under such a government, I desire to know what is slavery. It has hitherto been believed in the world that the Assyrians, Medes, Arabs, Egyptians, Turks, and others like them, lived in slavery, because their princes were masters of their lives and goods: whereas the Grecians, Italians, Gauls, Germans, Spaniards and Carthaginians, so long as they had any strength, virtue or courage amongst them, were esteemed free nations, because they abhorred such a subjection. They were and would be governed only by laws of their own making: *potentiora erant legum quam hominum imperia* [rule of laws was more powerful than the rule of men]. Even their princes had the authority or credit of persuading, rather than the power of commanding.

But all that was mistaken: these men were slaves, and the Asiatics were free men. By the same rule the Venetians, Switzers, Grisons and Hollanders are not free nations: but liberty in its perfection is enjoyed in France and Turkey. The intention of our ancestors was, without doubt, to establish this amongst us by Magna Charta, and other preceding or subsequent laws; but they ought to have added one clause, that the contents of them should be in force only so long as it should please the King. Alfred, upon whose laws Magna Charta was grounded, when he said the English nation was as free as the internal thoughts of a man, did only mean that it should be so as long as it pleased their master. This it seems was the end of our law, and we who are born under it, and are descended from such as have so valiantly defended their rights against the encroachments of Kings, have followed after vain shadows, and without the expense of sweat, treasure or blood, might have secured our beloved liberty by casting all into the King's hands. . . . He that oppugns the public liberty overthrows his own, and is guilty of the most brutish of follies, whilst he arrogates to himself that which he denies to all men. . . .

[I, VI]. First, he [Filmer] very wittily concludes that "if, by the law of God, the power be immediately in the people, God is the author of a democracy." And why not, as well as of a tyranny? Is there any thing in it repugnant to the being of God? Is there more reason to impute to God Caligula's monarchy than the democracy of Athens? Or is it more for the glory of God to assert his presence with the Ottoman or French monarchs than with the popular governments of the Switzers and Grisons? Is pride, malice, luxury and violence so suitable to his being that they who exercise them are to be reputed his ministers? And is modesty, humility, equality and justice so contrary to his nature that they who live in them should be thought his enemies? . . .

[I, X]. It were a folly hereupon to say that the liberty for which we contend is of no use to us, since we cannot endure the solitude, barbarity, weakness, want, misery and dangers that accompany it whilst we live alone, nor can enter into a society without resigning it, for the choice of that society, and the liberty of framing it according to our own wills, for our own good, is all we seek. This remains to us whilst we form governments, that we ourselves are judges how far 'tis good for us to recede from our natural liberty; 'tis of so great importance that from thence only can we know whether we are freemen or slaves; and the difference between the best government and the worst doth wholly depend upon a right or wrong exercise of that power. If men are naturally free, such as have wisdom and understanding will always frame good governments: but if they are born under the necessity of perpetual slavery, no wisdom can be of use to them; but all must forever depend on the will of their lords, how cruel, mad, proud or wicked soever they be. . . . 'Tis hard to comprehend how one man can come to be master of many, equal to himself in right, unless it be by consent or by force. If by consent, we are at an end of our controversies: Governments, and the magistrates that execute them, are created by man. They who give a being to them cannot but have a right of regulating, limiting and directing them as best pleaseth themselves; and all our author's [Filmer's] assertions concerning the absolute power of one man fall to the ground. If by force, we are to examine how it can be possible or justifiable . . . but as he that forceth must be stronger than those that are forced, to talk of one man who in strength exceeds many millions of men, is to go beyond the extravagances of fables and romances. . . .

[II, III]. Common sense teaches, and all good men acknowledge, that governments are not set up for the advantage, profit, pleasure or glory of one or a few men, but for the good of the society. For this reason Plato and Aristotle find no more certain way of distinguishing between a lawful King and a tyrant, than that the first seeks to procure the common good, and the other his own pleasure or profit; and doubt not to declare that he who according to his institution was the first, destroys his own being and degenerates into the latter, if he deflect from that rule: he that was the best of men becomes the worst; and the father or shepherd of the people makes himself their enemy. And we may hence collect that in all controversies concerning the power of magistrates, we are not to examine what conduces to their profit or glory, but what is good for the public.

Appeal to Reason

[II, XX]. Man being a rational creature, nothing can be universally natural to him that is not rational. But this liberty without restraint being inconsistent with any government, and the good which man naturally desires for himself, children and friends, we find no place in the world where the inhabitants do not enter into some kind of society or government to restrain it: and to say that all men desire liberty without restraint and yet that all do not restrain it, is ridiculous. The truth is, man is hereunto led by reason which is his nature. Every one sees they can not well live asunder, nor many together, without some rule to which all must submit. This submission is a restraint of liberty, but could be of no effect as to the good intended, unless it were general; nor general unless it were natural. When all are born to the same freedom, some will not resign that which is their own unless others do the like. This general consent of all to resign such a part of their liberty as seems to be for the good of all is the voice of nature, and the act of men (according to natural reason) seeking their own good. . . .

Again, if man were by nature so tenacious of his liberty without restraint, he must be rationally so. The creation of absolute monarchies, which entirely extinguishes it, must necessarily be most contrary to it, though the people were willing; for they thereby abjure their own nature. The usurpation of them can be no less than the most abominable and outrageous violence of the laws of nature that can be imagined: The laws of God must be in the like measure broken; and of all governments, democracy, in which every man's liberty is least restrained, because every man hath an equal part, would certainly prove to be the most just, rational and natural. . . . He that inquires more exactly into the matter may find that reason enjoins every man not to arrogate to himself more than he allows to others, nor to retain that liberty which will prove hurtful to him; nor to expect that others will suffer themselves to be restrained while he, to their prejudice, remains in the exercise of that freedom which nature allows. He who would be exempted from this common rule must shew for what reason he should be raised above his brethren; and if he do not do it, he is an enemy to them. This is not popularity but tyranny; and tyrants are said *exuisse hominem*, to throw off the nature of men, because they do unjustly and unreasonably assume to themselves that which agrees not with the frailty of human nature, and set up an interest in themselves contrary to their equals, which they ought to defend as their own.

Chapter Headings

[The headings of this last and subsequent chapters will well indicate the tenor of Sidney's *Discourses*.]

[II, XX]. Man's natural love to liberty is tempered by reason, which originally is his nature.

[II, XXI]. Mixed and popular governments preserve peace and manage wars better than absolute monarchies.

[II, XXIV]. Popular governments are less subject to civil disorders than monarchies, manage them more ably, and more easily recover out of them.

[II, XXVII]. Mischiefs and cruelties proceeding from tyranny are greater than any that can come from popular or mixed governments.

[II, XXX]. A monarchy can not be well regulated, unless the powers of the monarch are limited by law.

[II, XXXI]. The liberties of nations are from God and nature, not from Kings.

[II, XXXII]. The contracts made between magistrates and the nations that created them were real, solemn, and obligatory.

[III, XI]. That which is not just is not law; and that which is not law ought not to be obeyed.

[III, XIII]. Laws were made to direct and instruct magistrates, and if they will not be directed, to restrain them.

[III, XV]. A general presumption that Kings will govern well is not a sufficient security to the people.

[III, XXI]. It cannot be for the good of the people that the magistrate have a power above the law; and he is not a magistrate who has not his power by law.

[III, XXVII]. The Magna Charta was not the original, but a declaration of the English liberties. The King's power is not restrained but created, by that and other laws; and the Nation that made them can only correct the defects of them.

[III, XXVIII]. The English nation has always been governed by itself, or its representatives.

[III, XXXI]. Free nations have a right of meeting, when and where they please, unless they deprive themselves of it.

[III, XXXIV]. No veneration paid, or honor conferred upon a just and lawful magistrate can diminish the liberty of a nation.

[III, XXXVI]. The general revolt of a nation cannot be called a rebellion.

[III, XXXVII]. The English government was not ill constituted, the defects more lately observed proceeding from the change of manners and corruption of the times.

[III, XXXVIII]. The power of calling and dissolving Parliaments is not simply in the King.

[Quotation from the chapter:] The question is not whether the parliament be impeccable or infallible, but whether an assembly of nobility, with a house of commons composed of those who are best esteemed by their neighbors in all the towns and counties of England, are more or less subject to error or corruption than such a man, woman or child as happens to be next in blood to the last King.

[III, XLI]. The people for whom and by whom the magistrate is created can only judge whether he rightly perform his office or not.

[III, XLIII]. Proclamations are not laws.

[III, XLIV]. No people that is not free can substitute delegates.

[Quotation from the chapter:] Proclamations and other significations of the King's pleasure are not laws to us. They are to be regulated by the law, not the law by them. They are to be considered only so far as they are conformable to the law from which they receive all the strength that is in them, and can confer none upon it. We know no laws but our own statutes, and those immemorial customs established by the consent of the nation: which may be, and often are, changed by us. The legislative power, therefore, that is exercised by the Parliament cannot be conferred by the Writ of Summons, but must be essentially and radically in the people, from whom their delegates and representatives have all that they have.

(Quotation from the chapter:) Though every private man singly taken be subject to the commands of the Magistrate; the whole body of the people is not so; for he is by and for the people, and the people is neither by nor for him.

[III, XLV]. The legislative power is always arbitrary, and not to be trusted in the hands of any who are not bound to obey the laws they make.

Thomas Hobbes

1588–1679

༆ No one ever accused Hobbes of being a friend of representative government; yet his impact upon political philosophy was very great, since he instituted a behavioristic approach to man and society, and challenged traditional views.

According to Hobbes, man begins in basic sensory experience, and his primary motivations are fear of death by violence and a search for satisfactions. This man lives in nature in a state of fear (war) and anarchy, from which the sole escape (self-preservation) lies in a total surrender of his rights to government, a single sovereign, a "mortal God" whose authority is complete, even over belief. Thus man by reason and necessity creates the huge Leviathan state; yet grants the artificial monster unquestioned power over him.

Hobbes, it may be imagined, was not popular with those whose freedom he presented as an irreversible gift to an absolute monarch; nor yet with ecclesiastics or statesmen, whom he subordinated as utilitarian tools only under this monarch; nor even with monarchs, whose "divine" rights he ignored. Skeptical of scholastic logic, indifferent to the new science, he built his argument on the analogy of geometry's axioms and demonstrations, since mathematics alone seemed exempt from undermining by skepticism. His psychology owes something to the ancients; and his third book foreshadows the Biblical criticism of Tom Paine.

Locke likewise assumed an original "state of nature" for man; but he emerged quite differently, finding man capable of self-government by consent, and control of government for his own welfare. Hobbes appears infrequently in American political thought, though Hamilton protested Bishop Seabury's Hobbsian argument.

Hobbes published two essays on government, then in 1651 his completed *Leviathan*. The original text, and the Oxford edition of the same in 1909, were consulted for excerpts below.

The Condition of Men

[I, XI]. In the first place, I put for a general inclination of all mankind a perpetual and restless desire for power after power, that ceaseth only in death. . . . Competition of riches, honor, command, or other power, inclineth to contention, enmity, and war. . . . Desire of ease, and sensual delight, disposeth men to obey a common power. . . . Fear of death and wounds disposeth to the same.

[I, XIII]. Men have no pleasure (but on the contrary a great deal of grief) in keeping company, where there is no power able to over-awe them all. . . .

Hereby it is manifest that during the time men live without a common power to keep them all in awe, they are in that condition which is called War; and such a war as if of every man against every man. . . . The nature of war consisteth not in actual fighting; but in the known disposition thereto, during all the time there is no assurance to the contrary. All other time is Peace.

Whatsoever therefore is consequent to a time of war, where every man is enemy to every man, the same is consequent to the time wherein men live without other security than what their own strength, and their own invention shall furnish them withall . . . And which is worst of all, continual fear, and danger of violent death; and the life of man, solitary, poor, nasty, brutish, and short.

[II, XVII]. The only way to erect such a Common Power . . . is to confer all their power and strength upon one man, or upon one assembly of men, that may reduce all their wills, by plurality of voices, unto one will . . . and therein to submit their wills everyone to his will, and their judgments to his judgment. . . . This is the generation [i.e., origin] of that great *Leviathan*, or rather (to speak more reverently) of that Mortal God, to which we owe under the Immortal God our peace and defence.

[II, XXIX]. As to rebellion in particular against Monarchy; one of the most frequent causes of it is the reading of the books of Policy, and Histories of the ancient Greeks and Romans. . . . In sum, I cannot imagine how anything can be more prejudicial to a Monarchy that the allowing of such books to be publicly read. [Also prejudicial, Hobbes finds, is permitting two authorities, Temporal and "Ghostly," "which is a kingdom divided in itself, and cannot stand." "Mixed" government, too, breeds factions. The only remedy is absolute sovereignty.]

[For a comment on Hobbes' sensory psychology, see Appendix C, Note 3.]

Lord John Somers

1651–1716

◄§ Lord Somers was Lord High Chancellor of England in 1697. At an earlier date he had presided over the committee that framed the

Declaration of Rights, and had written an argument to prove that James II had abdicated. Swift dedicated to him his *Tale of a Tub* (1704).

Somers was the author of various political papers, including in 1681 his *Just and Modest Vindication of the Proceedings of the Last Two Parliaments*, and his *Judgment of Whole Kingdoms and Nations*, frequently reprinted. A number of his papers were collected and published as Somers' *Tracts* (London, 1748–1752).

Best known, perhaps, was his *The Security of Englishmen's Lives* ("or the Trust, Power and Duty of the Grand Juries of England, explained according to the fundamentals of the English government, and the Declarations of the same made in Parliament by many statutes"). Published in 1681, it was, like Hawles' *The Englishman's Rights*, a defense of the British jury system. "The principal ends of all civil governments," he says, "and of human society, were the security of men's lives, liberties and properties, mutual assistance and help, from each unto other, and provision for their common benefit and advantage." For this reason, "it is made a fundamental in our government that . . . no man's life shall be touched for any crime whatsoever save by the judgment of at least twenty-four men, that is, twelve or more, to find the Bill of Indictment." Excerpts below are from the edition of 1681, a book of 168 pages, republished in Boston, 1720, New York, 1773. ❧

Why Juries?

It was absolutely necessary for the support of the government and the safety of every man's life and interest, that some should be trusted to inquire after all such as by treasons, fellonies [*sic*], or lesser crimes, disturbed the peace, that they might be prosecuted, and brought to condign punishment; and it was no less needful for every man's quiet and safety that the trust of such inquisitions should be put into the hands of persons of understanding, and integrity, indifferent and impartial, that might suffer no man to be falsely accused, or defamed, nor the lives of any to be put in jeopardy, by the malicious conspiracies of great or small, or the perjuries of any profligate wretches: for these necessary, honest ends was the institution of grand juries.

Our ancestors thought it not best to trust this great concern of their lives and interests in the hands of any officer of the King's, or in any judges named by him, nor in any certain number of men during life, lest they should be awed or inflamed by great men, corrupted by bribes, flatteries or love of power, or become negligent, or partial to friends and relations, or pursue their own quarrels or private revenges, or connive at the conspiracies of others, and indict thereupon. But this trust of enquiring out, and indicting all the criminals in a county, is placed in men of the same county, more at least than twelve of the most honest and most sufficient for knowledge, and ability of mind and estate. . . .

[Somers then explains oaths taken by jurors, their duties, procedures, and the problems of accusations for treason.]

Duties of Jurors

If it be asked how, or in what manner, the juries shall enquire, the answer is ready, according to the best of their understandings. They only, not the judges, are sworn to search diligently to find out all treasons, etc., within their charge, and they must and ought to use their own discretion in the way and manner of their enquiry: no directions can legally be imposed upon them by any Court or judges; an honest jury will thankfully accept good advice from judges, as they are assistant of; but they are bound by their oaths to present the truth, the whole truth and nothing but the truth, to the best of their own, not the judge's, knowledge: neither can they, without breach of that oath, resign their consciences, or blindly submit to the dictates of others; and therefore ought to receive or reject such advices as they judge them good or bad.

If the jury suspect a combination of witnesses against any man's life (which perhaps the judges do not discern), and think it needful to examine them privately and separately, the discretion of the juries in such a case is their only best and lawful guide, though the example of all ages and countries, in examining suspected witnesses privately and separately, may be a good direction to them.

Nothing can be more plain and express than the words of the oath are to this purpose. The jurors need not search the law books, nor tumble over heaps of old records for the explanation of them. Our greatest lawyers may from hence learn more certainly our ancient law in this case than from all the books in their studies. The language wherein the oath is penned is known and understood by every man, and the words in it have the same signification as they have wheresoever else they are used. The judges (without assuming to themselves a legislative power) cannot put a new sense upon them, other than according to their genuine, common meaning. They cannot magisterially im-

pose their opinions upon the jury and make them forsake the direct
words of their oath, to pursue their glosses.

Freedom from Pressures

If it should be said that whatsoever reasons there are for this oath of
secrecy, yet it cannot deprive the King of the benefit of having the
evidence made public, if he desires it, and that the grand jury do not
break their oaths when the King or the Prosecutor for him will have
it so: 'Tis not hard to show that such notions have no foundation in
Law or Reason, and seem to come from men who have not well studied
the first principles of the English government or of true religion.

Whosoever hath learnt that the Kings of England were ordained for
the good government of the kingdom and the execution of the laws,
must needs know that the King cannot lawfully seek any other benefit
in judicial proceedings than that common right and justice be done to
the people according to their laws and customs.

[Quoting Tacitus, Fortescue, Coke, etc., Somers reviews the history
and procedures of juries.]

John Locke

1632–1704

"Locke's little book on government is perfect as far as it goes." Thomas
Jefferson, Letter to William Short, April 30, 1790.

◄§ The influence of John Locke, though much debated, has never
been denied. University students used his *Essay on Human Understanding* as late as the nineteenth century. His argument for tolerance was
effective in America and France. And his *Two Treatises on Civil Government* (especially the second) became the bible of political liberalism
at home and abroad. On *Toleration*, see Appendix B, Note 3.

Yet John Locke was essentially a conservative man, bent first of all
on justifying an accomplished political and social readjustment. If he
dominated a grateful age, it was because he so thoroughly summarized
its direction and its desires, its weariness with civil war and with political and religious bickering, its demand for common sense and sanity,
and particularly its wish to get about the main business of the day, the
exploitation of a great colonial and economic opportunity, in which a
rising group of merchants and colonizers were to play a leading part.
The age, it is true, was alert to worldly and materialistic concerns. Is
it the implication of this admission that England should have abandoned

the exploitation of the New World to more altruistic rivals? Since such likelihood was small, the age worked out its philosophy and politics accordingly.

Locke, though possibly already somewhat "dated" by 1776, remained still the greatest single exponent of government by contract and consent. The old appeal of natural law as encompassing men's duties had shifted to natural law as natural rights; governments, from being viewed on the analogy of the father, benevolent or despotic, became governments viewed as agents, responsible to those who used them for specific ends. Americans, on the front line of the new age, were not slow to learn this new language and its logic.

Locke, it is clear, had first to validate the "bloodless revolution" of 1688. Borrowing freely from Richard Hooker, Harrington, perhaps Grotius and other figures, perhaps even from Hobbes, whom he scarcely mentioned, Locke modified to his own uses the concept of a "law" above rulers, which imposed on them obligations toward their subjects. He assumed a "law of nature" by which men possess certain inalienable rights, to protect which they have organized government by mutual consent or contract, and by which they test the right of government to survive. Departing from Hobbes' cynical view of man as basically warlike and antisocial, Locke assumed that men are by nature social creatures; hence their society is less a product of fear than of common sense and a common experience. Government, thus, is "fiduciary," a kind of trusteeship, depending less on unquestioning obedience than on the consent and confidence of the people, and forfeiting allegiance if it abuses the terms of the contract. Human society, said Locke, can exist, at least temporarily, without formal government, and until it has time to frame a more satisfactory one. This, indeed, was exactly what England had experienced after the flight of James II, and what America was to know in the interim before its own framing. To this terminology Patrick Henry referred by his: "Sir, we are in a state of Nature."

Such theories opened the door to new views of government—government, as both John Locke and John Adams said, without recourse to supernatural arguments or mysticism. Locke's refusal to entangle himself in the arguments of the past was inevitable; it was precisely such entanglement that he had to avoid, if all were not to be thrown once more into the old cauldron of civil war. If he followed Hobbes, it was in saying: Study man as he is; but Locke's study came out with a vastly more optimistic encouragement for the future of the common man under government. The Americans could hardly be expected to turn to Hobbes.

It matters little, then, in one sense, whether Locke's premises were wholly sound or not. The significant thing is that men had just acted on these premises with signal success, and were to act on them again;

and that they became eminently useful for the American cause. The very words "ruler" and "subject" became anachronisms, and government became a sensible and necessary function within the social whole, subject to pragmatic adjustments, and divorced from confusions about divine rights, blind obedience, and vested prerogatives.

So simple a concept was a long time in coming; but once given form, it had far-reaching results. It was opposed, naturally, by those in positions of special privilege and power who were guarded by hierarchical sanctions; it was supported, as was also natural, by the rising commercial and industrial interests that turned increasingly to the vast New World. The concept of government as a job for responsible men, who forfeited their advantages as they became irresponsible, was a corollary with infinite possibilities of extension to all kinds of society.

Locke's *Treatises* came in 1690, close on the Declaration of Rights. His collected *Works* appeared in three volumes in 1714 and thereafter; and in four in 1768, nine in 1801, and ten in 1812. Quotations below are from the third London edition of 1727, Volume II, the second *Treatise* only. Excessive capitalization and italicizing have been reduced.[8] ⚬⚬

Man in the State of Nature

[Ch. 2]. To understand political power right, and derive it from its original, we must consider what state all men are naturally in, and that is, a state of perfect freedom to order their actions, and dispose of their possessions and persons as they think fit, within the bounds of the law of nature, without asking leave, or depending upon the will of any other man.

A state also of equality, wherein all the power and jurisdiction is reciprocal, no one having more than another; there being nothing more evident than that creatures of the same species and rank, promiscuously born to all the same advantages of nature, and the use of the same faculties, should also be equal one amongst another without subordination or subjection, unless the lord and master of them all, should by any manifest declaration of his will set one above another, and confer on him, by an evident and clear appointment, an undoubted right to dominion and sovereignty.

This *equality* of men by nature the judicious Hooker looks upon as so evident in itself and beyond all question, that he makes it the foundation of that obligation to mutual love amongst men, on which he builds the duties they owe one another, and from whence he derives the great maxims of justice and charity. . . . [Here follows a quotation from Hooker.]

But though this be a state of liberty, yet it is not a state of licence . . . The state of nature has a law of nature to govern it, which obliges every one: and reason, which is that law, teaches all mankind who will but consult it, that being all equal and independent, no one ought to harm another in his life, liberty, or possessions. . . .

And that all men may be restrained from invading others' rights, and from doing hurt to one another, and the law of nature be observed, which willeth the peace and preservation of all mankind, the execution of the law of nature is in that state put into every man's hand, whereby every one has a right to punish the transgressors of that law to such a degree as may hinder its violation. For the law of nature would, as all other laws that concern men in this world, be in vain, if there were nobody that in the state of nature had a power to execute that law, and thereby preserve the innocent and restrain offenders. And if any one in the state of nature may punish another, for any evil he has done, every one may do so: for in that state of perfect equality, where naturally there is no superiority or jurisdiction of one over another, what any man may do in prosecution of that law, every one must needs have a right to do.

And thus in the state of nature one man comes by a power over another; but yet no absolute or arbitrary power to use a criminal, when he has got him in his hands, according to the passionate heats or boundless extravagancy of his own will; but only to retribute to him, so far as calm reason and conscience dictate, what is proportionate to his transgression, which is so much as may serve for reparation and restraint. For these two are the only reasons why one man may lawfully do harm to another, which is that we call punishment. In transgressing the law of nature, the offender declares himself to live by another rule than that of common reason and equity, which is that measure God has set to the actions of men for their mutual security; and so he becomes dangerous to mankind, the tie which is to secure them from injury and violence being slighted and broken by him. . . .

'Tis often asked as a mighty objection, "where are, or ever were there any men in such a state of nature?" To which it may suffice as an answer at present, that since all princes and rulers of independent governments all through the world, are in a state of nature, it is plain the world never was, nor ever will be, without numbers of men in that state. . . . for it is not every compact that puts an end to the state of nature between men, but only this one of agreeing together mutually to enter into one community and make one body politic; other promises and compacts men may make one with another, and yet still be in the state of nature. . . .

[Hooker (I, 10) is again quoted here; see Hooker above, pages 121-123, for same passage.]

But I moreover affirm, that all men are naturally in that state, and remain so, till by their own consents they make themselves members of some politic society; and I doubt not in the sequel of this discourse to make it very clear.

[Ch. 3]. The state of war is a state of enmity and destruction: and therefore declaring by word or action, not a passionate and hasty, but a sedate settled design upon another man's life, puts him in a state of war with him against whom he has declared such an intention, and so has exposed his life to the other's power to be taken away by him, or any one that joins with him in his defense and espouses his quarrel; it being reasonable and just. I should have a right to destroy that which threatens me with destruction. For by the fundamental law of nature, man being to be preserved as much as possible, when all cannot be preserved, the safety of the innocent is to be preferred. . . .

And hence it is, that he who attempts to get another man into his absolute power, does thereby put himself into a state of war with him; it being to be understood as a declaration of a design upon his life. For I have reason to conclude that he who would get me into his power without my consent, would use me as he pleased when he had got me there, and destroy me too when he had a fancy to it; for nobody can desire to have me in his absolute power, unless it be to compel me by force to that which is against the right of my freedom, i.e., make me a slave. To be free from such force is the only security of my preservation; and reason bids me look on him as an enemy to my preservation who would take away that freedom which is the fence to it: so that he who makes an attempt to enslave me, thereby puts himself into a state of war with me. He that in the state of nature would take away the freedom that belongs to any one in that state, must necessarily be supposed to have a design to take away everything else, that freedom being the foundation of all the rest: as he that in the state of society would take away the freedom belonging to those of that society or commonwealth, must be supposed to design to take away from them everything else, and so be looked on as in a state of war. . . .

And here we have the plain difference between the state of nature and the state of war, which however some men have confounded, are as far distant as a state of peace, good will, mutual assistance and preservation, and a state of enmity, malice, violence and mutual destruction are one from another. Men living together according to reason, without a common superior on earth with authority to judge between them, is properly the state of nature. But force, or a declared design of force upon the person of another, where there is no common superior on earth to appeal to for relief, is the state of war: and it is the want of such an appeal gives a man the right of war even against an aggressor, though he be in society and a fellow-subject. Thus a thief, whom I cannot harm but by an appeal to the law for having stolen all that I am worth, I may kill when he sets on to rob me but of my horse or coat; because the law which was made for my preservation, where it cannot interpose to secure my life from present force, which if lost is capable of no reparation, permits me my own defense and the right of war, a liberty to kill the aggressor, because the aggressor allows not time to appeal to our common judge, nor the decision of the law, for remedy in a case where the mischief may be irreparable. Want of a common judge with authority puts all men in a state of nature: force without right upon a man's person makes a state of war, both where there is and is not a common judge.

But when the actual force is over, the state of war ceases between those that are in society, and are equally on both sides subjected to the fair determination of the law . . . but where no such appeal is, as in the state of nature, for want of positive laws and judges with authority to appeal to, the state of war once begun continues with a right to the innocent party to destroy the other whenever he can, until the aggressor offers peace. . . .

[Ch. 4]. The natural liberty of man is to be free from any superior power on earth, and not to be under the will or legislative authority of man, but to have only the law of nature for his rule. The liberty of man, in society, is to be under no other legislative power but that established by consent in the commonwealth; nor under the dominion of any will, or restraint of any law, but what that legislative shall enact, according to the trust put in it. Freedom then is not what Sir Robert

Filmer tells us, "a liberty for every one to do what he lists, to live as he pleases, and not to be tied by any laws"; but freedom of men under government is to have a standing rule to live by, common to every one of that society, and made by the legislative power erected in it; a liberty to follow my own will in all things where that rule prescribes not; and not to be subject to the inconstant, uncertain, unknown, arbitrary will of another man: as freedom of nature is to be under no other restraint but the law of nature.

This freedom from absolute arbitrary power is so necessary to, and closely joined with a man's preservation that he cannot part with it but by what forfeits his preservation and life together. For a man not having the power of his own life, cannot by compact or his own consent, enslave himself to any one, nor put himself under the absolute, arbitrary power of another to take away his life when he pleases. Nobody can give more power than he has himself; and he that cannot take away his own life, cannot give another power over it. Indeed having by his fault forfeited his own life, by some act that deserves death, he to whom he has forfeited it may (when he has him in his power) delay to take it. For whenever he finds the hardship of his slavery outweigh the value of his life, 'tis in his power, by resisting the will of his master, to draw on himself the death he desires.

This is the perfect condition of slavery, which is nothing else but the state of war continued between a lawful conqueror and a captive. For if once compact enter between them and make an agreement for a limited power on the one side, and obedience on the other, the state of war and slavery ceases, as long as the compact endures.

On Property

[Ch. 5]. Though the earth and all inferior creatures be common to all men, yet every man has a property in his own person: this nobody has any right to but himself. The labor of his body and the work of his hands we may say are properly his. Whatsoever then he removes out of the state that nature hath provided and left it in, he hath mixed his labor with, and joined to it something that is his own, and thereby makes it his property. It being by him removed from the common state nature hath placed it in, it hath by this labor something annexed to it that excludes the common right of other men. For this labor being the unquestionable property of the laborer, no man but he can have a right to what that is once joined to, at least where there is enough and as good left in common for others.

He that is nourished by the acorns he picked up under an oak, or the apples he gathered from the trees in the wood, has certainly appropriated them to himself. Nobody can deny but the nourishment is his. I ask then, when did they begin to be his? When he digested? Or when he ate? Or when he boiled? Or when he brought them home? Or when he picked them up? And it is plain, if the first gathering made them not his, nothing else could. That labor put a distinction between them and common: that added something to them more than nature, the common mother of all, had done, and so they became his private right. And will any one say he had no right to those acorns or apples he thus appropriated, because he had not the consent of all mankind to make them his? Was it a robbery thus to assume to himself what belonged to all in common? If such a consent as that was necessary, man had starved, notwithstanding the plenty God had given him. We see in commons, which remain so by compact, that it is the taking any part of what is common, and removing it out of the state nature leaves it in, which begins the property without which the common is of no use. And the taking of this or that part does not depend on the express consent of all the commoners. . . . The labor that was mine, removing them out of that common state they were in, hath fixed my property in them. . . .

It will perhaps be objected to this, that if gathering the acorns or other fruits of the earth, etc. makes a right to them, then any one may engross as much as he will. To which I answer, Not so. The same law of nature that does by this means give us property, does also bound that property too. "God has given us all things richly," is the voice of reason confirmed by inspiration. But how far has He given it us? To enjoy. As much as any one can make use of to any advantage of life before it spoils, so much he may by his labor fix a property in: Whatever is beyond this is more than his share, and belongs to others. . . . As much land as a man tills, plants, improves, cultivates, and can use the product of, so much is his property. . . .

God gave the world to men in common; but since He gave it them for their benefit and the greatest conveniences of life they were capable to draw from it, it cannot be supposed He meant it should always remain common and uncultivated. He gave it to the use of the industrious and rational (and labor was to be his title to it); not to the fancy or covetousness of the quarrelsome and contentious. . . .

Nature has well set the measure of property by the extent of men's labor and the conveniences of life: No man's labor could subdue or appropriate all, nor could his enjoyment consume more than a small part; so that it was impossible for any man, this way, to entrench upon the right of another, or acquire to himself a property to the prejudice of his neighbor, who would still have room for as good and as large a possession (after the other had taken out his) as before it was appropriated. This measure did confine every man's possession to a very moderate proportion, and such as he might appropriate to himself, without injury to anybody, in the first ages of the world . . . And the same measure may be allowed still, without prejudice to anybody, as full as the world seems. For supposing a man or family, in the state they were at first peopling of the world by the children of Adam or Noah; let him plant in some inland vacant places of America, we shall find that the possessions he could make himself, upon the measures we have given, would not be very large, nor, even to this day, prejudice the rest of mankind, or give them reason to complain. . . .

Thus in the beginning all the world was America, and more so than that is now; for no such thing as money was anywhere known. . . . But since gold and silver, being little useful to the life of man in proportion to food, raiment and carriage, has its value only from the consent of men, whereof labor yet makes in great part the measure, it is plain that men have agreed to a disproportionate and unequal possession of the earth; they having by a tacit and voluntary consent found out a way how a man may fairly possess more land than he himself can use the product of, by receiving in exchange for the overplus gold and silver.

On Law and Freedom

[Ch. 6]. For law, in its true notion, is not so much the limitation as the direction of a free and intelligent agent to his proper interest, and prescribes no farther than is for the general good of those under that law. Could they be happier without it, the law, as a useless thing, would of itself vanish . . . So that, however it may be mistaken, the end of law is not to abolish or restrain, but to preserve and enlarge freedom. For in all the states of created beings capable of laws, where there is no law there is no freedom. For liberty is to be free from restraint and violence from others, which cannot be where there is not law. . . .

Thus we are born free, as we are born rational; not that we have actually the exercise of either: age, that brings one, brings with it the other too. . . .

The freedom then of man, and liberty of acting according to his own will, is grounded on his having reason, which is able to instruct him in that law he is to govern himself by, and make him know how far he is left to the freedom of his own will.

On the Beginning of Political Societies

[Ch. 8]. Men being, as has been said, by nature all free, equal, and independent, no one can be put out of this estate and subjected to the political power of another, without his own consent. The only way whereby any one divests himself of his natural liberty and puts on the bonds of civil society, is by agreeing with other men to join and unite into a community, for their comfortable, safe, and peaceable living one amongst another, in a secure enjoyment of their properties, and a greater security against any that are not of it. This any number of men may do, because it injures not the freedom of the rest; they are left as they were in the liberty of the state of nature. When any number of men have so consented to make one community or government, they are thereby presently incorporated, and make one body politic, wherein the majority have a right to act and conclude the rest.

For when any number of men have, by the consent of every individual, made a community, they have thereby made that community one body, with a power to act as one body, which is only by the will and determination of the majority. For that which acts any community, being only the consent of the individuals of it, and it being necessary to that which is one body to move one way, it is necessary the body should move that way whither the greater force carries it, which is the consent of the majority. . . .

And thus every man, by consenting with others to make one body politic under one government, puts himself under an obligation to every one of that society to submit to the determination of the majority, and to be concluded by it; or else this original compact, whereby he with others incorporates into one society, would signify nothing, and be no compact, if he be left free, and under no other ties than he was in before in the state of nature. For what appearance would there be of any compact? What new engagement, if he were no farther tied by any decrees of the society than he himself thought fit, and did actually consent to? This would be still as great a liberty as he himself had before his compact, or any one else in the state of nature hath, who may submit himself and consent to any acts of it, if he thinks fit. . . .

Whosoever therefore out of a state of nature unite into a community, must be understood to give up all the power necessary to the ends for which they unite into society to the majority of the community, unless they expressly agreed in any number greater than the majority. And this is done by barely agreeing to unite into one political society, which is all the compact that is, or needs be, between the individuals that enter into or make up a commonwealth. And thus that which begins and actually constitutes any political society is nothing but the consent of any number of freemen capable of majority, to unite and incorporate into such a society. And this is that, and that only, which did or could give beginning to any lawful government in the world.

To this I find two objections made. First, that there are no instances to be found in story, of a company of men independent and equal one amongst another, that met together, and in this way began and set up a government.* Secondly, it is impossible of right that men should do so, because all men being born under government, they are to submit to that, and are not at liberty to begin a new one.

To the first there is this to answer, That it is not at all to be wondered that history gives us but a very little account of men that lived together in the state of Nature. The inconveniences of that condition, and the love and want of society, no sooner brought any number of them together, but they presently united and incorporated, if they designed to continue together. . . . Government is everywhere antecedent to records, and letters seldom come in amongst a people till a long continuation of civil society has, by other more necessary arts, provided for their safety, ease and plenty. And then they begin to look after the history of their founders, and search into their original, when they have outlived the memory of it. . . .

Every man being, as has been showed, naturally free, and nothing being able to put him into subjection to any earthly power but only his own consent, it is to be considered what shall be understood to be

* The United States of America were one day to furnish an example.

a sufficient declaration of a man's consent, to make him subject to the law of any government. There is a common distinction of an express and a tacit consent, which will concern our present case. Nobody doubts but an express consent of any man entering into any society makes him a perfect member of that society, a subject of that government. The difficulty is, what ought to be looked upon as a tacit consent, and how far it binds, i.e. how far any one shall be looked on to have consented and thereby submitted to any government, where he has made no expressions of it at all. And to this I say that every man that hath any possessions or enjoyment of any part of the dominions of any government, doth thereby give his tacit consent, and is as far forth obliged to obedience to the laws of that government during such enjoyment, as any one under it; whether this his possession be of land, to him and his heirs forever, or a lodging only for a week. . . . For it would be a direct contradiction for any one to enter into society with others for the securing and regulating of property, and yet to suppose his land whose property is to be regulated by the laws of the society, should be exempt from the jurisdiction of that government to which he himself, the proprietor of the land, is a subject.

Ends of Political Society

[Ch. 9]. If man in the state of nature be so free as has been said; if he be absolute lord of his own person and possessions, equal to the greatest and subject to nobody, why will he part with his freedom? Why will he give up his empire, and subject himself to the dominion and control of any other power? To which it is obvious to answer that though in the state of nature he hath such a right, yet the enjoyment of it is very uncertain, and constantly exposed to the invasion of others . . . This makes him willing to quit this condition, which however free, is full of fears and continual dangers; and it is not without reason that he seeks out and is willing to join in society with others who are already united, or have a mind to unite, for the mutual preservation of their lives, liberties and estates, which I call by the general name, property.

The great and chief end, therefore, of men's uniting into commonwealths and putting themselves under government, is the preservation of their property. To which in the state of nature there are many things wanting.

First, there wants an established, settled, known law, received and allowed by common consent to be the standard of right and wrong, and the common measure to decide all controversies between them. . . .

Secondly, in the state of nature there wants a known and indifferent [i.e., impartial] judge, with authority to determine all differences according to the established law. . . .

Thirdly, in the state of nature, there often wants power to back and support the sentence when right, and to give it due execution. They who by any injustice offend will seldom fail, where they are able, by force to make good their injustice. . . .

Thus mankind, notwithstanding all the privileges of the state of nature, being but in an ill condition while they remain in it, are quickly driven into society. . . .

The first power, viz., of doing whatsoever he thought fit for the preservation of himself and the rest of mankind, he gives up to be regulated by laws made by the society, so far forth as the preservation of himself and the rest of that society shall require; which laws of the society in many things confine the liberty he had by the law of nature.

Secondly, the power of punishing he wholly gives up, and engages his natural force . . . to assist the executive power of the society, as the law thereof shall require. . . . And all this to be directed to no other end but the peace, safety, and public good of the people.

Legislative and Executive Powers

[Ch. 11]. These are the bounds which the trust that is put in them by the society, and the law of God and nature have set to the legislative power of every commonwealth, in all forms of government.

First, they are to govern by promulgated established laws, not to be varied in particular cases, but to have one rule for rich and poor, for the favorite at court and the countryman at plough.

Secondly, these laws ought to be designed for no other end ultimately but the good of the people.

Thirdly, they must not raise taxes on the property of the people without the consent of the people, given by themselves or their deputies. And this properly concerns only such governments where the legislative is always in being, or at least where the people have not reserved any part of the legislative to deputies, to be from time to time chosen by themselves.

Fourthly, the legislative neither must nor can transfer the power of making laws to any body else, or place it any where but where the people have. . . .

[Ch. 12]. And because it may be too great a temptation to human frailty, apt to grasp at power, for the same persons who have the power of making laws to have also in their hands the power to execute them, whereby they may exempt themselves from obedience to the laws they make, and suit the law both in its making and execution to their own private advantage, and thereby come to have a distinct interest from the rest of the community, contrary to the end of society and government: therefore in well-ordered commonwealths, where the good of the whole is so considered as it ought, the legislative power is put into the hands of divers persons, who duly assembled, have by themselves or jointly with others, a power to make laws, which when they have done, being separated again, they are themselves subject to the laws they have made; which is a new and near tie upon them to take care that they make them for the public good.

But because the laws that are at once and in a short time made, have a constant and lasting force, and need a perpetual execution, or an attendance thereto: therefore it is necessary there should be a power always in being, which should see to the execution of the laws that are made, and remain in force. And thus the legislative and executive power come often to be separated.

How May a Government Be Dissolved?

[Ch. 19]. There is one way more whereby such a government may be dissolved, and that is, when he who has the supreme executive power neglects and abandons that charge, so that the laws already made can no longer be put in execution. This is demonstratively to reduce all to anarchy, and so effectually to dissolve the government. For laws not being made for themselves, but to be by their execution the bonds of the society, to keep every part of the body politic in its due place and function, when that totally ceases, the government visibly ceases, and the people become a confused multitude without order or connection. Where there is no longer the administration of justice, for the securing of men's rights, nor any remaining power within the community to direct the force, or provide for the necessities of the public, there certainly is no government left. Where the laws cannot be executed, it is

all one, as if there were no laws; and a government without laws is I
suppose a mystery in politics unconceivable to human capacity, and inconsistent with human society.

In these and the like cases, when the government is dissolved, the
people are at liberty to provide for themselves by erecting a new legislative, differing from the other by the change of persons, or form, or
both, as they shall find it most for their safety and good. For the society can never by the fault of another lose the native and original right
it has to preserve itself; which can only be done by a settled legislative,
and a fair and impartial execution of the laws made by it. But the state
of mankind is not so miserable that they are not capable of using this
remedy till it be too late to look for any. To tell people they may provide for themselves by erecting a new legislative, when by oppression,
artifice, or being delivered over to a foreign power, their old one is
gone, is only to tell them they may expect relief when it is too late, and
the evil is past cure. This is in effect no more than to bid them first be
slaves, and then to take care of their liberty; and when their chains are
on, tell them they may act like freemen. This, if barely so, is rather
mockery than relief; and men can never be secure from tyranny, if
there be no means to escape it till they are perfectly under it: and
therefore it is that they have not only a right to get out of it, but to
prevent it.

Declaration of Rights, 1688

◄§ When Charles II returned to the throne in 1660 (the Restoration),
there was a general expectation of peace and stability. He was declared
king as of 1649 and all interim acts repealed. However, certain reforms
were retained, such as the abolitions of the Star Chamber, of taxation
without consent of Parliament, and of legislation by proclamation. But
Charles II was a pleasure-loving monarch and not overly concerned
about public opinion. He did little to check the wave of retaliation
against leaders in the commonwealth, or the enforced oaths of allegiance to one church only, which drove hundreds of pastors to resign
and whole minority groups to emigration to America. He even intrigued
with foreign monarchs and accepted secretly subsidies from Louis XIV
of France.

Nevertheless, Charles II played an important part in the destinies of
America by a vigorous policy of consolidating British holdings from
Nova Scotia to Carolina, seizing the Dutch colony in New York and

urging settlement of Pennsylvania and other vacant areas. Under a mercantile theory of colonies as furnishers of raw materials for home consumption, settlement was necessary; and inducements were held out like free land, minimum taxes, and religious toleration. Thus the character of the American colonies was early determined as practical, middle and lower class, and religiously diversified. Economic and intellectual individualism were also encouraged by a policy of relative noninterference. Even the later religious development in England of the "religion of nature" (Deism) made possible American figures like Franklin, Paine, Jefferson, Madison, Freneau, and even Lincoln. Without these men and others of their persuasion, America's characteristic religious freedom might not have occurred.[9]

The terms Whig and Tory arose under Charles II, the Tories being landed gentry and Anglican clergy who favored royal prerogatives, the Whigs being a mixture of nobility, commercial class, artisans, and religious dissenters who favored parliamentarian control.

When James II, who ruled from 1685 to 1688, succeeded his brother, he managed to antagonize whole segments of England by his arbitrary acts and his open encouragement of foreign interference in English affairs, notably that of making English once more Catholic by French aid. Patriots and parliamentarians, dissenters and Anglicans joined against him, the last-named being caught in a dilemma of their own making—namely, the theory of passive obedience to the divinely appointed monarch. Once again, rule by constitution seemed threatened in England. United action turned to William of Holland, husband of James' daughter Mary, and he was invited to visit England. There was no battle, for James' own troops deserted him and he fled to France, where Louis XIV continued to promise aid. England was without a government; but a parliament was convened and decided that James had broken his "contract," and that a compact might lawfully be made by Parliament with a new king, of their own choosing. A Declaration of Rights was drawn up, accepted in 1689 as a Bill of Rights by the new monarch.

This Declaration is not new, being clearly similar to the Petition of Rights of 1628. A part of it appears almost verbatim in the American Bill of Rights (Amendments I–X, Constitution) of a century later, except that British "ought" becomes American "shall." But this Declaration did affirm the British theory of government by consent of the governed, rights entrusted to a government, not surrendered to it. Divine rights of kings was dead in England, though it survived a century in France, and in Germany and Russia into the twentieth century. British tradition had proved too tough, however, for the once sacred prerogatives.

Not that England had no problems thereafter. There were recurrences of intolerance and governmental corruption, which served only to strengthen America's position as a symbol of escape and freedom. Nevertheless, few political stories are more ·significant than that of England in the long struggle of the seventeenth century.

The text below is from Henry Care, *English Liberties: or the Free-born Subject's Inheritance* (fifth ed., 1719). &

The Declaration of Rights

Declaration presented to their Majesties by the Lords Spiritual and Temporal, and the Commons, assembled in Parliament, upon their Accession to the Throne. 1688.

[After reciting the abuses of James II:]

And therefore the said Lords Spiritual and Temporal, and Commons, pursuant to their respective letters and elections, being now assembled in a full and free Representative of this Nation, taking into their most serious consideration the best means for attaining the ends aforesaid: Do, in the first place (as their ancestors in like case have usually done), for the vindicating and asserting their ancient rights and liberties, Declare that the pretended power of suspending the Laws, or the execution of laws by Regal Authority, without consent of Parliament, is illegal. That the pretended power of dispensing with Laws, or the execution of laws by Regal Authority, as it hath been assumed and exercised of late, is illegal. That the Commission for erecting the late Court of Commissioners and Ecclesiastical Causes, and all other Commissions and Courts of like nature are illegal and pernicious. That levying money for or to the use of the Crown, by pretence of Prerogative, without Grant of Parliament, for longer time or in other manner than the same is, or shall be granted, is illegal. That it is the Right of subjects to petition the King, and all commitments and prosecution for such petitioning are illegal. That the raising qr keeping a Standing Army within this Kingdom in time of peace, unless it be with consent of Parliament, is against Law. That the subjects which are Protestants may have arms for their defence, suitable to their conditions, and as allowed by law. That election of Members of Parliament ought to be free. That the freedom of speech, and debates or proceedings in Parliament, ought not to be impeached or questioned in any Court or Place out of Parliament. That excessive bail ought not to be required, nor excessive fines imposed, nor cruel and unusual punishments inflicted. That Jurors ought to be duly impanelled and returned, and Jurors which pass upon men in trials for high treason ought to be Freeholders. That all Grants and Promises of fines and forfeitures of particular persons, before convicted, are illegal and void. And that for redress of all grievances, and for the amending, strengthening, and preserving of the Laws, Parliaments ought to be held frequently.

And they do claim, demand and insist upon all and singular the premises, as their undoubted Rights and Liberties; and that no declarations, judgments, doings or proceedings, to the prejudice of the people in any of the said premises, ought in any wise to be drawn hereafter into consequence or example. To which demand of their Right, they are particularly encouraged by the Declaration of His Highness the Prince of Orange, as being the only means of obtaining a full redress and remedy therein.

Having therefore an entire confidence that his said Highness the Prince of Orange will perfect the deliverance so far advanced by him, and will still preserve them from the violation of their Rights, which they have here asserted, and from all other attempts upon their Religion, Rights and Liberties, the said Lords Spiritual and Temporal and Commons assembled at Westminster do resolve, That William and Mary, Prince and Princess of Orange, be, and be declared King and Queen of England, France and Ireland, and the Dominions thereunto belonging, to hold the Crown and Dignity of said Kingdoms and Dominions to them the said Prince and Princess during their lives, and the life of the survivor of them.

[To this later was attached an oath required of all subjects:]

1. I do sincerely promise and swear, That I will be faithful and bear true allegiance to their Majesties King William and Mary. So help me God.

2. I do swear, That I do from my heart abhor, detest and abjure, as impious and heretical, this damnable doctrine and position that Princes excommunicated or deprived by the Pope, or any authority of the See of Rome, may be deposed or murthered by their subjects, or any other whatsoever.

And I do declare, That no Foreign Prince, Person, Prelate, State or Potentate, hath, or ought to have, any jurisdiction, power, superiority, pre-eminence or authority, ecclesiastical or spiritual, within this Realm. So help me God.

PART III · THE CONTINENTAL STREAM

"No French tradition is more alive than that of the century of Enlightenment. . . . It is Voltaire and Rousseau, and sometimes Montesquieu and Condorcet, that one finds almost always behind the living influence of France on the masses and the ideologies of South America, of the United States itself, of central and eastern Europe, and that one will find tomorrow in Africa and Asia." Henri Peyre, "Influence of Eighteenth Century Ideas on the French Revolution," *Journal of the History of Ideas*, January 1949, p. 85. Quoted by permission of the editors.

"The expressed faiths of the Enlightenment are sometimes naive and never self-evident; yet I hold that they are noble and necessary faiths. They are the more necessary because the dignity and the rights of man are not an inalienable birthright, but a hard-earned acquisition." Herbert Muller, *The Uses of the Past*, p. 278.

THE CONTINENTAL STREAM

THOUGH colonial Americans were more intimately concerned with the literature of England than with that of the continent, certain important works in Latin and French stimulated their interests and their energies. For convenience we may suggest three tentative groupings:

1. Earlier writers in the Renaissance tradition, concerned with man and his place in nature and in the body politic. Such were Machiavelli, Jean Bodin, Grotius, and Pufendorf, all of whom were known to the American reader, though the last two contributed more directly to his thinking.

2. Eighteenth-century writers, especially French, in the same tradition, though influenced by the history of the seventeenth century. Such were Montesquieu, Burlamaqui, and Emmerich de Vattel. Vattel, whose *Law of Nations*, 1758, was translated into English in 1759, and published in London in 1760, and in New York in 1796, 1805, etc., is not represented below, though he was frequently consulted on international law. He won approval by quoting Puritan maxims on liberty, and by his argument that the aim of the state was the happiness of the people, not of the prince; and chiefly because he sought to mitigate the horrors of war. The other two figures precede Vattel by a decade.

3. The rising tide of the French Age of Enlightenment, the *philosophes*, encyclopedists, and ideologists, before, during, and after the French Revolution. Of these, Voltaire and Rousseau alone precede the American Revolution; others, such as Mably, Condorcet, Condillac, de Tracy, Helvetius, Raynal, or Volney, are contemporary with it or follow it. Some of these men were friends of Franklin or Jefferson, and

known to the less approving Adams. All were read in some degree in America.

The period of French ferment coincided very closely with that in the American colonies, and French observers watched closely the developments abroad. Again, French radical thought was influenced by what had happened across the Channel, and by the visits of Montesquieu, Voltaire, and Rousseau to England. French apologists for the old regime were inclined to blame the French Revolution on English influence (especially Locke's), on French Protestants, on secret societies, on the Encyclopedists and *philosophes*, or on the general depravity of the lower orders. These may all have been factors at work, but not the least as causes were plain human misery on one level, and ideas that filtered down from the intellectuals on another. It was sometimes said that French intellectuals taught the people to see themselves as unhappy. There was Rousseau's famous "Man is born free and everywhere he is in chains." There was Saint Just's "Royalty is an eternal crime . . . One cannot reign in innocence," and Voltaire's *Ecrasez l'infame* ("Crush the infamy.") Surely the philosophers weakened old loyalties, taught a secular religion of service to humanity, and reviewed history as evidence against entrenched privilege, at times with a violence and extremism that contrasted with English moderation.

Howard Mumford Jones, in a study of French influence in America from 1750 to 1848, admits that French literature was likely to be somewhat limited to the intellectuals, and yet points out a very considerable importation of French books, especially to Philadelphia.[1] He finds mention of Buffon, Fénelon, Molière and Racine, Le Sage, Montesquieu, Voltaire, Raynal, Rousseau, and Condorcet. Nor had the French themselves been absent from our early history. Quite apart from French penetration, before English settlements, into the St. Lawrence and the Mississippi valleys, French Huguenots were fairly numerous in the English colonies. For years public documents in New York were in Dutch, French, and English; and Walloons, Swiss, and French appeared in the Hudson valley, in Charleston, and in intervening spots. *Emigrés* at a later date sought out Philadelphia; and French teachers were not uncommon in the larger centers.

That Americans read European, and especially French, authors is not surprising. Hamilton's private library contained over 240 French titles. John Adams frequently mentions grammars of modern European languages, and Franklin, Jefferson, and Madison had by foreign residence imbibed something of French culture. Jefferson cherished a personal correspondence with more than one *idéologue*. John Adams at one time made some study of the Italian Renaissance republics, but, concluding that they were scarcely models for New England, preferred the Swiss cantons, the Dutch United States, or the English political literature.

Voltaire was rather widely read in America from the 1740s on, at least in excerpts, and especially in his histories. His *Treatise on Toleration*, which advocated separation of church and state, was well known; and his edition of Beccaria's *On Crime and Punishment* was published in 1770 in Philadelphia and thereafter. His *Philosophical Dictionary*, like Bayle's, was certainly known, being mentioned, says Mary M. Barr, more than forty times in library lists.[2] Timothy Dwight complained bitterly of Voltaire's influence on the youth of Yale, and ironically dedicated to Voltaire his own *Triumph of Infidelity* (1788).

Thus we may safely assume that certain continental figures, chiefly French, made their contribution to American thinking, either as they had been absorbed into English literature and so imported to America, or had been received more directly in Latin, French, or English. In turn, some influence of American political documents upon the French Declaration of the Rights of Man may be assumed. Certainly Lafayette, who introduced a first draft into the French Assembly, was a friend of Jefferson, as was Condorcet; and a French translation of the American documents, including a number of state constitutions, is known to have been dedicated to Franklin, approved by him, and presented by him to foreign ministers and sovereigns.

As the English seventeenth-century revolution ran its course, settling into a conservative holding of its gains, the battle for rights shifted to France. Here an absolutism of long standing, supported by an aristocracy and a clerical hierarchy voting their own revenues, under which the States General had not convened since 1614, and ruled by a monarch with unchecked powers of taxation and vast expenditures without accounting, had made of France a symbol of despotic monarchy, with lessons not unheeded across the channel.

The French *philosophes* therefore represented a new and radical breed of men. Behind them they had the new mathematical and empirical sciences, the weight of Descartes and Newton, the reasoning of Locke and Shaftesbury, the heavier tomes of Grotius and Pufendorf, and the flowering of the Enlightenment. Abandoning the Renaissance abstractions of a Grotius, even the cautious liberalism of Montesquieu, they attacked with wit and innuendo, circumventing censorship thus to plant the seeds of a radical restatement that grew less and less from a desire for reconciliation.

Nevertheless, the new "grand principles" were promulgated with the expectation that they would flower into "progress," guided by reason and nature. Hence arises much of the optimism which characterizes the eighteenth century, as well as the critical review of past history, the fresh use of the classics, and the humanitarianism and tolerance toward new ideas. American thought never wholly accepted this French enlightenment, perhaps because its own obstacles were less formidable. Only a few minds like those of Jefferson, Franklin, Madison, or Tom Paine, can be said to be truly representative of the Enlightenment in the continental sense.[3] Yet there was a considerable infiltration of eighteenth century opinion into America; and from continental figures, from Grotius to Burlamaqui, the Americans drew not a little.

Hugo Grotius
1583–1645

◆§ In a strictly chronological ordering, Hugo van de Groot (Grotius) should precede Milton, Harrington, Sidney, Hobbes, and Locke, all of whom felt his influence. The works of Grotius, too, appear frequently in American libraries after 1700. Hence a glance at his significance will not be amiss.

Grotius was born in Delft, Holland. A precocious youth, holding a degree in law at sixteen, he became historian of the Spanish in the Netherlands at nineteen, and advocate-general at twenty-one. His studies and observations of war developed in him a passionate desire to find a cure within human possibilities, that is, within the legal structure and the institutions known to man. Conscious of the seeds of conflict in warring sects and jealous nations, he sought the answer in something that should transcend the limitations of these obstacles, that is, some common denominator admitted by all sensible men everywhere. Thus he turned to the classical expression of natural law and the law of nations. But he extended the ancient abstraction to something like the modern science of international law, the creation by men of some workable agreements among sovereign and equal nations, functioning as single men might function within civil laws in the smaller community.

Grotius was quite aware of the difficulties of his proposal. Yet he never ceased trying to urge peace as the natural state, war as the unnatural. He was not a pacifist, but admitted the existence of "just" wars; for example, wars of self-preservation or of protection of common rights. Yet he urged the reasonableness of lessening wars of caprice, of promoting arbitration, and of encouraging the habit of international discussion.

Grotius shared the predilection of his day for "logical" argument. Thus he sought a base for his philosophy in man in nature, the natural man as "sociable." "Thou art not alone in the world," he wrote. Contrary to Hobbes' vision of man as living in mutual fear and warfare, Grotius sees man as moving naturally toward communal living, toward property contracts, civil law, and governments for his own peace and stability. In man's natural instincts he finds the grounds for agreements, civil contracts, oaths, property rights, laws (which are agreements man with man, community with individual, even potentially nation with nation).

Grotius' work *De Jure Belli et Pacis* ("On the Rights of War and Peace"), published in 1625, went through many editions and translations. It appeared in English in 1682, translated by William Evats; and in French in 1729 with notes by Barbeyrac, issued in English in 1738. A copy of this work appears in the library of Harvard University with George Washington's bookplate. An abridgment of this large work was made later by George Whewell, the quotations below being from the 1853 edition in London.

Book I of this great work discusses the present state of war and defines terms. Book II examines the causes of wars, and the development in society of common property rights and civil contracts. Book III proposes some general rules for wars, declarations of war, the treatment of the conquered, the need for good faith among nations. Neutrals, he argues, should not supply munitions to belligerents. Grotius admits the lack of precedent for some of his proposals, but says he referred the solutions to "natural law."

Though a man of peace and tolerance, he knew flight and exile, imprisonment and charges of heresy. Some said he quoted the Bible too much, others, not enough. Some said he gave the state too much power, others, too little; some, that he was a materialist, denying revealed truth. Yet it is possible that Grotius sensed a very modern problem—the fact that world peace and stability cannot wait on political or religious uniformity, but must, as Grotius urged, seek a common and human denominator that transcends the narrower bounds of nationalisms and religious differences. We are no longer talking of neighbor nations, sharing some common heritage, but of many peoples, colors, and heritages that must somehow live together, bound by some common need and mutual respect, unable longer to stake all on some supernationalism or some universal conversion to one dogma, even if that were desirable. That Grotius was not without influence is shown by his final appointment at Heidelberg as professor of his new subject, the first professorship in international law in the world. Gustavus Adolphus of Sweden is said to have carried Grotius' book with him, and Cardinal Richelieu to have modified in consequence of it some of the cruelties of war upon conquered peoples. Sabine, modern student of political history, says that Grotius finally detached law from the traditional religious entanglements, and gave the first significant expression to law as regulating the relations between sovereign states.[4] 〰

Reason for Writing

[From the Preface]. I, for the reasons which I have stated, holding it to be most certain that there is among nations a common law of Rights which is of force with regard to war, and in war, saw many and grave causes why I should write a work on that subject. For I saw prevailing throughout the Christian world a license in making war of which even barbarous nations should have been ashamed; recourse being had to arms for slight reasons or no reasons; and when arms were once taken up, all reverence for divine and human law was thrown away, just as if men were thenceforth authorized to commit all crimes without restraint.

And the sight of these atrocities has led many men, and these estimable persons, to declare arms forbidden to the Christian, whose rule of life mainly consists in love to all men . . . But this attempt to drive things too far is often so far from succeeding that it does harm . . . We are to provide a remedy for both disorders; both for thinking that nothing is allowable, and that everything is.

Source of Natural Law

[From the Preface. Grotius begins with the statement that no one has treated of a law between peoples (international law), and only utility has ruled where wars are concerned; yet "our discussion of Rights is worthless if there are no Rights." Thus he starts with man as a social animal, unable to seek his own individual good alone.]

This tendency to the conservation of society, which we now expressed in a rude manner, and which tendency is in agreement with the nature of the human intellect, is the source of *Jus*, or Natural Law, properly so called. To this *Jus* belongs the rule of abstaining from that which belongs to other persons; and if we have in our possession anything of others, the restitution of it, or of any gain which we have made from it; the fulfilling of promises, and the reparation of damage done by fault; and the recognition of certain things as meriting punishment among men.

From this signification has flowed another larger sense of *Jus*: for inasmuch as man is superior to the animals, not only in the social impulse of which we have spoken, but in his judgment and power of estimating advantages and disadvantages; and in these, not only present good and ill, but also future good and ill, and what may lead to each; we may understand that it is congruous to human nature to follow, in such matters also, a judgment rightly framed; not to be misled by fear or by the temptation of present pleasure, not to be carried away by blind and thoughtless impulse; and that what is plainly repugnant to such judgment is also contrary to *Jus*, that is, to Natural Human Law. . . .

In the next place, since it is conformable to Natural Law to observe compacts (for some mode of obliging themselves was necessary among men, and no other natural mode could be imagined) Civil rights were derived from this source, mutual compact.

Definitions of Terms

[Bk. I, Pt. I, Ch. I, Sec. 10]. Natural Law is the dictate of Right Reason . . . Acts concerning which there is such a dictate are obligatory, or are unlawful, in themselves, and are therefore understood as necessarily commanded or forbidden by God; and in this character, Natural Law differs not only from Human Law, but from positive Divine Law, which does not forbid or condemn acts which in themselves and by their own nature are either obligatory or unlawful; but by forbidding them makes them unlawful, by commanding them makes them obligatory. . . .

Natural Law is so immutable that it cannot be changed by God himself. For though the power of God be immense, there are some things to which it does not extend: because if we speak of those things being done, the words are mere words and have no meaning, being self-contradictory. Thus God himself cannot make twice two not be four; and in like manner, he cannot make that which is intrinsically bad, not be bad. For as the essence of things, when they exist and by which they exist, does not depend on anything else, so is it with the properties which follow that essence: and such a property is the baseness of certain actions, when compared with the nature of rational beings. And God himself allows himself to be judged of by this rule (as see Gen. 18, 25)* . . .

That there is such a thing as Natural Law is commonly proved both *a priori* and *a posteriori*; the former the more subtle, the latter the more popular proof. It is proved *a priori* by shewing the agreement or disagreement of anything with the rational and social nature of man. It is proved *a posteriori* when by certain or very probable accounts we find anything accepted as Natural Law among all nations, or at least the more civilized. For a universal effect requires a universal cause. Now such a universal belief can hardly have any cause except the common sense of mankind.

Resistance toward Superiors

[Bk. I, Pt. IV, Ch. I, Sec. 3]. It is beyond controversy among all good men that if the persons in authority command anything contrary to Natural Law or the divine precepts, it is not to be done. For the apostles, in saying that we must obey God rather than man, appealed to an undoubted rule, written in the minds of all, which you may find almost in the same words in Plato. But if we receive any injury from such a cause, or in any other way from the will of the Supreme Power, we are to bear it rather than resist by force.

By Natural Law, all have the right of repelling wrong. But civil society being instituted to secure public tranquillity, the State acquires a superior right over us and ours, as far as it is necessary for that end. Therefore the State may prohibit the promiscuous right of resisting, for the sake of public peace and order; and it is to be presumed to have intended that, since it cannot otherwise attain its end. If this prohibition does not exist, there is no State, but a multitude without the tie of society.† . . .

[Bk. I, Pt. IV, Ch. VIII, Sec. 1]. First, those rulers who are subject

---

* "Shall not the judge of all the earth do right?"
† Elsewhere Grotius says: "But still, I do not venture indiscriminately to condemn either individuals or a minority of the people who thus have recourse to the ultimate means of necessity, provided they do not desert a respect for the common good."

to the people, whether by original institution or by subsequent convention, if they transgress against the laws of the State, may not only be resisted, but put to death.[4] . . .

Sixthly, if the King have only a part of the sovereignty, another part being in the Senate or the people, and if the King invade the part which is not his, he may justly be opposed by force, because in that part he has not authority. And this I conceive may be, although the law directs that the power of making war be in the King. For this must be understood of external war. And since each party has its portion of the sovereignty, it must also have the right of defending that part. When this is the case, the King may lose his portion of the Sovereignty by the right of war.

Seventhly, if in conferring the royal authority, it be stated that in a certain event, the King may be resisted, although by that means there is not a part of the sovereignty withheld, yet a certain natural liberty is retained by the subjects and exempted from the royal authority. He who alienates his right may limit by compact the right so alienated.

Samuel Pufendorf
1632–1694

◄§ Samuel Pufendorf was the son of a German Lutheran pastor, but early shifted from theology to law and became a disciple of Grotius, whose work he attempted to complete by a grand system of law which should be universal and everywhere applicable, because founded on reason. His *Elements of Universal Jurisprudence* (1661) was a standard text for a century. A caustic tract on German princes proposed the secularization of principalities, a confederation, and a general army supported by the people. Despite a period of imprisonment, he attained a professorship at Heidelberg, and, in the words of the title page of his major work, was "Counsellor of State to his late Swedish Majesty and to the present King of Prussia."

In 1672 he published his *Jus Naturae et Gentium* ("*Of the Law of Nature and Nations*"), which appeared in French early in the eighteenth century, and in English in 1710 from the French text, translated by Basil Kennett, with the Preface and notes of the French Barbeyrac. Excerpts below are from this English text (London, 1749, 5th ed.).

Following closely the argument of Grotius, Pufendorf reasoned as follows: Beginning with definitions of "moral entities," conscience, and the nature of moral action, he argues that "It is not agreeable to the nature of man that he should live without law." This nature of man and of man in nature is imposed on us at birth by God himself, and cannot be altered by us. Man's rights and duties arise therefrom, and his later inventions of states and laws have their authority only as they do not conflict with the anterior laws of nature. Pufendorf often takes issue with Hobbes in this book, and disagrees with the latter's limitation on men as equal only in strength and fear. Some British influence is shown, too, in his quotations from Selden. It is interesting, too, to observe Pufendorf's use of Lucretius on the origin of man and the state in nature.* In saying that "The will of the state is but the sum of the individual wills that constitute it," Pufendorf would appear to have anticipated Rousseau.

Subsequent chapters of this book discuss reparations for injuries, the natural equality of man, the nature of promises and compacts, and of oaths, partnerships, and matrimony, the origin of property and its transfer, how compacts are entered into and dissolved (an obligation ceases upon the perfidy of either party), the origin, establishment, and structure of civil societies ("to guard themselves against those injuries which one man was in danger of sustaining from another"), the powers, duties, and limitations of sovereigns, and the rights of war.

It will be seen below, page 226, how the American John Wise made use of Pufendorf in his *Vindication* (1717), even to the point of almost verbatim quotation from the English text, and yet how Wise also adapted his text to his own purposes. ৡৢ

The Law of Nature

[Bk. II, Ch. III]. Since then it appears inconsistent with the nature and the condition of man that he should live entirely loose from all law, and perform his actions by a wild and wandering impulse, without regard to any standard or measure, it follows that we make enquiry into that most general and universal rule of human actions, to which every man is obliged to conform, as he is a reasonable creature. To this rule custom hath given the name of Natural Law, and we may call it likewise the Law Universal and Perpetual; the former, in regard that it binds the whole body of the human race, the latter, because it is not subject to change. . . .

Therefore when we acknowledge the Law of Nature to be the Dictate of Right Reason, our sense and meaning is this, that the understanding of man is endued with such a power as to be able, from the con-

* The English text uses Creech's translation of Lucretius in the footnotes. See Creech above, page 66.

templation of human condition, to discover a necessity of living agreeably to this Law; as likewise to find out some principle by which the precepts of it may be clearly and solidly demonstrated. Nor is it any rub or prejudice to this doctrine that the artificial method of demonstrating these natural precepts is not known or apprehended by all men; and that most persons both learn and observe the Law of Nature by custom, and by the common course and tenor of living. For we see every day the common mechanics and artificers performing many things, either by imitation, or by the compendious direction of instruments, the proof of which they do not in the least understand; and yet this doth not hinder such operations from being truly mathematical, or from being founded on solid principles of Reason . . . The dictates of Right Reason are true principles, which agree with the Nature of things well observed and examined; and which are deduced from other true and first principles, by the rules of good consequence [i.e., logic]. On the contrary, those are dictates of depraved reason in which a man either lays down false principles, or by a wrong method deduces false conclusions. For at the same time as we affirm the Law of Nature to be imprinted on us by the nature of things, we imply that it is most true and infallible; since Nature presents us with nothing but what really exists, and produces no effect that can be charged with falsehood: all falsity arising from the mistakes of men, whilst they either divide such notions as naturally cleave together, or join such together as Nature hath separated and placed at a distance. And this course of judging being duly followed, we need not fear that anyone shall be able to foist upon us for Natural Law either the frantic notions of his ill purged brain, or the irregular desires of his misguided mind. For 'tis in vain for that man to make his appeal to Reason who cannot demonstrate his assertions from principles of unquestioned truth, and such as agree with the nature of things.

Sociableness, and the Dignity and Equality of Man

[Bk. II, Ch. III. After arguing that self-love and self-preservation are fundamental:]

This then will appear a fundamental Law of Nature, *Every man ought as far as in him lies, to promote and preserve a peaceful sociableness with others, agreeable to the main end and disposition of the human race in general.* . . . By this term of sociableness we would imply such a disposition of one man toward all others as shall suppose him united to them by benevolence, by peace, by charity, and so as it were by a silent and a secret obligation. . . .

[Bk. III, Ch. II]. The word MAN is thought to carry somewhat of *dignity* in its sound; and we commonly make use of this as the last and most prevailing argument against a rude insulter, *I am not a Beast, a Dog, but I am a Man as well as yourself.* Since then human nature agrees equally to all persons, and since no one can live a sociable life with another who does not own and respect him as a Man; it follows as a command of the Law of Nature *that every man esteem and treat another as one who is naturally his equal, and who is a Man as well as he.* . . .

For as in well-ordered commonwealths, one subject may exceed another in riches or in honor, but all are equal sharers in the common Liberty, so under this regulation of Nature, how much soever a man may surpass his neighbors as to bodily or intellectual endowments, he is still obliged to pay all natural duties as readily and as fully as he expects to receive them; nor do those advantages give him the least power or privilege to oppress his fellows. Nor, on the other side, does the bare unkindness of nature or of fortune set a man in a worse condition than others as to the enjoyment of common rights. But whatever one man requires or expects from others, the same may others (all circumstances being alike) demand from him; and the same judgment one decrees against another, he is obliged in the like case to submit to himself. On this account, we can by no means admit of Cicero's rule which he lays down in his third book of Offices: *Lex ipsa naturae*, etc. "The Law of Nature itself, which preserves and holds together the common profit of mankind, does decree that things necessary for life and sustenance may be transferred from an idle and useless person to a man of wisdom, goodness and valor who, should he be suffered to perish, would exceedingly prejudice the public by his death. . . ."

This Equality being admitted, there flow from it several precepts, the observation of which bears a very great force in the maintaining of peace and friendship amongst men. And this in the first place is most manifest, that he who would use the assistance of others in promoting his own advantage, ought as freely to be at their service, when they want his help on the like occasions. One good turn requires another, is the common proverb. For he must certainly esteem others unequal to himself who constantly demands their aid, and as constantly denies his own. And whoever is of this insolent temper cannot but highly displease and provoke those about him, and soon give occasion to a breach of the common peace. It was a manly and a gallant reproof which Caractacus gave the Romans, *Num si* [etc.] . . . "Because you desire to be masters of all men, does it follow that all men must desire to be your slaves?" . . . Hence it is a command of Nature's Law that *no man who has not obtained a particular and especial right shall arrogate to himself a larger share than his fellows; but shall admit others to an enjoyment of equal privileges with himself.*

Montesquieu
1689–1755

"The oracle who is always consulted and cited on the subject [i.e., the separation of powers], is the celebrated Montesquieu. If he be not the author of this invaluable precept in the science of politics, he has the merit of at least displaying and recommending it most effectively to to the attention of mankind." James Madison, *Federalist Papers*, No. 47

⋦ Montesquieu's admirers have credited him with directing America toward its theory of checks and balances, the separation of powers, and even a federal constitution; and his weight in these directions is undeniable. Yet Jefferson, who quoted Montesquieu liberally in his earlier notebooks, came to caution others about him, as about Blackstone, because of their leanings toward monarchy, British style. Washington read him, Hamilton strongly felt his influence, and few French authors are more generally quoted at that period on forms of political institutions.

Yet Charles Louis de Secondat, Baron de Montesquieu, was no radical. Born to estate and title, he felt strongly that French liberties were all but lost under a decadent absolutism. From his travels in other lands, especially in England around 1730, he drew his plan of examination of political forms and so, perhaps, inaugurated comparative politics. Important, too, is his emphasis upon the influence of climate, and of social customs, upon government. For he desired to write empirically, from observations, and did so within limits (he also drew heavily on the analogies of Roman history). The only check on power, he thought, was power; hence the desirability of divided governmental powers, each acting as a check on the others. Laws of nature and government he assumed, and that a conformity to them was necessary for success in government. Human laws he saw as natural phenomena, varying like plants with the milieu. Man, being man, he said, must seek justice, even if there be no sure grounds for belief in its existence. His use of a modern term, "relative to," is notable.

Montesquieu's great work, *The Spirit of Laws* (*Esprit des Lois*, 1748), discussed governments and laws, customs and climate, religion, taxes, and ancient history in a style eminently readable. The whole was written in thirty books, with many brief chapters, and often with short, almost aphoristic sentences, and a clarity which tempts the reader to credit the author with more depth than he has.

As France moved toward revolution, Montesquieu's influence declined. He was too conservative for the Encyclopedists, too secular for the Jesuits, too Anglophile for the patriots, too abstract for the economists. Yet his book remains readable, temperate, even wise, full of suggestion, a landmark.

His major work was translated almost at once into English (1750) by Thomas Nugent, whose work is still standard. It went through many editions in various languages. Selections below are from the Worcester, Massachusetts, edition (1802) from the London fifth edition by Mr. Nugent (1773).[6] ठ∾

First Principles

[From the Preface]. I have first of all considered mankind; and the result of my thoughts has been that, amidst such an infinite diversity of laws and manners, they were not solely conducted by the caprice of fancy.

I have laid down the first principles, and have found that the particular cases apply naturally to them; that the histories of all nations are only consequences of them; and that every particular law is connected with another law, or depends on some other of a more general extent.

[Bk. I, Ch. 3]. Law in general is human reason, inasmuch as it governs all the inhabitants of the earth; the political and civil laws of each nation ought to be only the particular cases in which this human reason is applied.

They should be adapted in such a manner to the people for whom they are made as to render it very unlikely for those of one nation to be proper for another.

They should be relative to the nature and principle of the actual or intended government; whether they form it, as in the case of political laws, or whether they support it, as may be said of civil institutions.

They should be relative to the climate of each country, to the quality of the soil, to its situation and extent, to the manner of living of the natives, whether husbandmen, huntsmen or shepherds; they should have a relation to the degree of liberty which the constitution will bear; to the religion of the inhabitants, to their inclinations, riches, number, commerce, manners and customs. . . . These relations I shall examine, since all these together form what I call the SPIRIT OF LAWS.

Fundamental Laws

[Bk. II, Ch. 4]. The intermediate, subordinate, and dependant powers constitute the nature of monarchical government, I mean of that in which a single person governs by fundamental laws . . . In monarchies the prince is the source of all power political and civil. These fundamental laws necessarily suppose the intermediate channels through which the power flows: for if there be only the momentary and capricious will of a single person to govern the state, nothing can be fixed, and of course there can be no fundamental law.

The most natural, intermediate and subordinate power is that of the nobility. This in some measure seems to be essential to a monarchy, whose fundamental maxim is, no monarch, no nobility; no nobility, no monarch; but there may be a despotic prince.

There are men who have endeavored in some countries in Europe to abolish all the jurisdiction of the nobility; not perceiving that they were driving at the very thing that was done by the parliament of England. Abolish the privileges of the lords, of the clergy, and of the cities in a monarchy, and you will soon have a popular state, or else a despotic government. . . .

Though the ecclesiastic power is so dangerous in a republic, yet it is extremely proper in a monarchy, especially of the absolute kind. . . .

The English, to favor their liberty, have abolished all the intermediate powers of which their monarchy was composed. They have a great deal of reason to be jealous of this liberty; were they ever so unhappy as to lose it, they would be one of the most servile nations upon earth. . . .

It is not enough to have intermediate powers in a monarchy; there must be also a depository of the laws. This depository can be only the political bodies who promulgate the new laws and revive the obsolete. The natural ignorance of the nobility, their indolence, and contempt of civil government, require there should be a body invested with a power of reviving the laws which would be otherwise buried in oblivion. The prince's council are not a proper depository. They are naturally the depository of the momentary will of the prince, and not of the fundamental law. Besides, the prince's council is continually changing; it is neither permanent nor numerous; neither has it a sufficient share of the confidence of the people; consequently it is incapable to set them right in difficult conjunctures, or to reduce them to proper obedience.

Despotic governments, where there are no fundamental laws, have no such kind of depository. Hence it is that religion has generally so much influence in those countries because it forms a kind of permanent depository; and if this cannot be said of religion, it may of the customs that are respected instead of laws.

On Democracy

[Bk. III, Ch. 3]. There is no great share of probity necessary to support a monarchical or despotic government. The force of laws in one, and the prince's arm in the other, are sufficient to direct and maintain the whole. But in a popular state, one spring more is necessary, namely, Virtue.

What I have advanced here is confirmed by the unanimous testimony of historians, and is extremely agreeable to the nature of things. For it is clear that in a monarchy, where he who commands the execution of the laws generally thinks himself above them, there is less need of virtue than in a popular government, where the person intrusted with the execution of the laws is sensible of being subject himself to their direction.

Clear it is also that a monarch who through bad advice or indolence ceases to enforce the execution of the laws may easily repair the evil; he has only to follow other advice, or to shake off his indolence. But when in a popular government there is a suspension of the laws, as this can proceed only from the corruption of the republic, the state is certainly undone.

A very curious spectacle it was in the last century to behold the impotent efforts the English made for the establishment of a democracy. As those who had a share in the direction of public affairs were void of all virtue, as their ambition was inflamed by the success of the most daring of their members [i.e., Cromwell], as the spirit of faction was suppressed only by that of a succeeding faction, the government was continually changing; the people, amazed at so many revolutions, sought everywhere for a democracy without being able to find it. At length, after a series of tumultuary motions and violent shocks, they were obliged to have a recourse to the government which they had so odiously proscribed. . . .

The Nature of Monarchies

[Bk. III, Chs. 5, 9]. Let us compare what the historians of all ages have said concerning the courts of monarchs; let us recollect the conversations and sentiments of people of all countries, in respect to the wretched character of courtiers; and we shall find that these are not mere airy speculations, but things confirmed by a sad and melancholy experience.

Ambition joined to idleness, and baseness to pride; a desire of obtaining riches without labor, and an aversion to truth; flattery, treason, perfidy, violation of engagements, contempt of civil duties, fear of the prince's virtue are, I think, the characteristics by which most courtiers in all ages and countries have been constantly distinguished. Now it is exceeding difficult for the leading men of a nation to be knaves, and for the inferior sort of people to be honest; for the former to be cheats, and for the latter to rest satisfied to be only dupes. . . .

As virtue is necessary in a republic, and in a monarchy honor, so fear is necessary in a despotic government; with regard to virtue, there is no occasion for it, and honor would be extremely dangerous.

Here the immense power of the prince is devolved entirely upon those to whom he is pleased to intrust it. Persons capable of setting a value upon themselves would be likely to create revolutions. Fear must therefore depress their spirits and extinguish even the least sense of ambition.

A moderate government may, whenever it pleases, and without any danger, relax its springs; it supports itself by its laws and by its own force. But when a despotic prince ceases one single moment to lift up his arm, when he cannot instantly demolish those whom he has intrusted with the first post and employments, all is over; for as fear, the spring of this government, no longer subsists, the people are left without a protector.

Equality

[Bk. VIII, Ch. 3]. As distant as heaven is from earth, so is the true spirit of equality from that of extreme equality. The former does not consist in managing so that every one should command, or that no one should command, or that no one should be commanded; but in obeying and commanding our equals. It endeavors not to be without a master, but that its masters should be none but its equals.

In the state of nature, indeed, all men are born equal; but they cannot continue long in this equality. Society makes them lose it, and they recover it only by means of the laws.

Such is the difference between a well regulated democracy and one that is not so; so that in the former men are equal only as citizens, but in the latter they are also equal as magistrates, as senators, as judges, as husbands or as masters.

The natural place of virtue is near to liberty; but it is not nearer to extreme liberty than to servitude.

No Large Republic

[Bk. VIII, Ch. 16. This is a chapter to which Jefferson objected, especially the first sentence. Montesquieu had not understood the nature of *representative* government.]

It is natural to a republic to have only a small territory; otherwise it cannot long subsist. In a large republic there are men of large fortunes, and consequently of less moderation; there are trusts too great to be placed in any single subject; he has interests of his own; he soon begins to think that he may be happy, great and glorious, by oppressing his fellow citizens; and that he may raise himself to grandeur on the ruins of his country.

In a large republic, the public good is sacrificed to a thousand views; it is subordinate to exceptions and depends on accidents. In a small one, the interest of the public is easier perceived, better understood and more within the reach of every citizen; abuses have a less extent, and of course are less protected.

The Word Liberty

[Bk. XI, Chs. 2, 3, 4]. There is no word that has admitted of more various significations, and has made more different impressions on human minds, than that of *liberty*. Some have taken it for a facility of deposing a person on whom they had conferred a tyrannical authority; others for the powers of choosing a person whom they are obliged to obey; others for the right of bearing arms, and of being thereby enabled to use violence; others for the privilege of being governed by a native of their own country, or by their own laws. A certain nation for a long time thought that liberty consisted in the privilege of wearing a long beard [i.e., Russia]. Some have annexed this name to one form of government in exclusion of others; those who had a republican taste applied it to this government; those who liked a monarchical state, gave it to monarchies. Thus they have all applied the name of liberty to the government most conformable to their own customs and inclinations; and as in a republic people have not so constant and so present a view of the instruments of the evils they complain of, and likewise as the laws seem there to speak more, and the executors of the laws less, it is generally attributed to republics and denied to monarchies. In fine, as in democracies the people seem to do very nearly whatever they please, liberty has been placed in this sort of government, and the power of the people has been confounded with their liberty.

It is true that in democracies the people seem to do what they please; but political liberty does not consist in an unrestrained freedom. In governments, that is, in societies directed by laws, liberty can consist only in the power of doing what we ought to will, and in not being constrained to do what we ought not to will.

We must continually present to our minds the difference between independence and liberty. Liberty is a right of doing whatever the laws permit; and if a citizen could do what they forbid, he would no longer be possessed of liberty, because all his fellow citizens would have the same power.

Democratic and aristocratic states are not necessarily free. Political liberty is to be met with only in moderate governments; yet even in these it is not always met with. It is there only when there is no abuse of power; but constant experience shows us that every man invested with power is apt to abuse it; he pushes on till he comes to something that limits him. Is it not strange though true to say that virtue itself has need of limits?

To prevent the abuse of power, it is necessary that by the very disposition of things power should be a check to power. A government may be so constituted as no man shall be compelled to do things which the law does not oblige him, nor forced to abstain from things which the law permits.

Division of Powers

[Bk. XI, Ch. 6]. In every government there are three sorts of power: the legislative; the executive, in respect to things dependent on the law of nations; and the executive, in regard to things that depend on the civil law.

By virtue of the first, the prince or magistrate enacts temporary or perpetual laws, and amends or abrogates those that have been already enacted. By the second, he makes peace or war, sends or receives embassies; establishes the public security, and provides against invasions. By the third, he punishes criminals, or determines the disputes that arise between individuals. The latter we shall call the judiciary power, and the other simply the executive power of the state.

The political liberty of the subject is a tranquillity of mind, arising from the opinion each person has of his safety. In order to have this liberty, it is requisite the government be so constituted as one man need not be afraid of another.

When the legislative and executive powers are united in the same person, or in the same body of magistrates, there can be no liberty; because apprehensions may arise lest the same monarch or senate should enact tyrannical laws, to execute them in a tyrannical manner.

Again, there is no liberty if the power of judging be not separated from the legislative and executive powers. Were it joined with the legislative, the life and liberty of the subject would be exposed to arbitrary control; for the judge would then be the legislator. Were it joined to the executive power, the judge might behave with all the violence of an oppressor.

There would be an end of everything were the same man, or the same body, whether of the nobles or of the people to exercise those three powers, that of enacting laws, that of executing the public resolutions, and that of judging the crimes or differences of individuals.

Most kingdoms in Europe enjoy a moderate government because the prince, who is invested with the two first powers, leaves the third to his subjects. In Turkey, where these three powers are united in the sultan's person, the subjects groan under the weight of a most frightful oppression. . . .

Hence it is that many of the princes of Europe, whose aim has been levelled at arbitrary power, have constantly set out with uniting in their own persons all the branches of magistracy, and all the great offices of state. . . .

The judiciary power ought not to be given to a standing senate; it should be exercised by persons taken from the body of the people, at certain times of the year, and pursuant to a form and manner prescribed by law, in order to erect a tribunal that should last only as long as necessity requires.

By this means the power of judging, a power so terrible to mankind, not being annexed to any particular state or profession, becomes, as it were, invisible. People have not then the judges continually present to their view; they fear the office, but not the magistrate. . . .

But though the tribunals ought not to be fixed, yet the judgments ought, and to such a degree as to be always conformable to the exact letter of the law. Were they to be the private opinion of the judge, people would then live in society without knowing exactly the obligations it lays them under.

The judges ought likewise to be in the same station as the accused, or in other words, his peers, to the end that he may not imagine he is fallen into the hands of persons inclined to treat him with rigor. . . .

As in a free state, every man who is supposed a free agent, ought to be his own governor; so the legislative power should reside in the whole body of the people. But since this is impossible in large states, and in small ones is subject to many inconveniences, it is fit the people should act by their representatives what they cannot act by themselves.

[Montesquieu here argues that the nobility should handle the legislative, and should be hereditary, and so would separate privileges from popular envy; and that the executive should be in the monarch. Thus Montesquieu is not republican.]

English Liberty

[Bk. XI, Ch. 6]. Whoever shall read the admirable treatise of Tacitus on the manners of the Germans will find that it is from them the English have borrowed the idea of their political government. This beautiful system was invented first in the woods.

As all human things have an end, the state we are speaking of will lose its liberty, it will perish. Have not Rome, Sparta and Carthage perished? It will perish when the legislative power shall be more corrupted than the executive.

It is not my business to examine whether the English actually enjoy this liberty or not. It is sufficient for my purpose to observe that it is established by their laws; and I inquire no further.

Neither do I pretend by this to undervalue other governments, nor to say that this extreme political liberty ought to give uneasiness to those who have only a moderate share of it. How should I have any such design, I who think that even the excess of reason is not always desirable, and that mankind generally find their account better in mediums than in extremes?

Harrington in his *Oceana* has also inquired into the highest point of liberty to which a constitution of a state may be carried. But of him indeed it may be said that for want of knowing the nature of real liberty, he busied himself in pursuit of an imaginary one.

Religion in Monarchy and Republic

[Bk. XXIV, Ch. 5]. When a religion is introduced and fixed in a state, it is commonly such as is most suitable to the plan of government there established: for those who receive it, and those who are the cause of its being received, have scarcely any other idea of policy than that of the state in which they were born.

When the Christian religion, two centuries ago, became unhappily divided into Catholic and Protestant,* the people of the north embraced the Protestant, and those of the south adhered still to the Catholic.

The reason is plain: the people of the north have, and will forever have, a spirit of liberty and independence, which the people of the south have not; and therefore a religion which has no visible head is more agreeable to the independency of the climate than that which has one.

In the countries themselves where the Protestant religion became established, the revolutions were made pursuant to the several plans of political government. Luther, having great princes on his side, would never have been able to make them relish an ecclesiastic authority that had no exterior preeminence; while Calvin, having to do with people who lived under republic governments, or with obscure citizens and monarchies, might very well avoid establishing dignities and preeminence.

Each of these two religions was believed to be the most perfect; the

* Montesquieu was a Roman Catholic.

Calvinist judging his most conformable to what Christ had said, and
the Lutherans to what the apostles had practiced.

Jean Jacques Burlamaqui

1694–1748

✒ Burlamaqui, professor of natural and civil law at Geneva and son
of a former counselor and secretary of state of Geneva, shares with
Montesquieu a considerable influence on American political theory. His
major work, *The Principles of Natural and Politic Law* (1747), was a
text at Cambridge, Oxford, and Dublin, and was the basis of Witherspoon's lectures at Princeton from 1768 to the Revolution. Indeed, according to the one book on the subject in this country, R. F. Harvey's
Burlamaqui, to which this brief sketch is indebted, Burlamaqui was
more printed in America than Locke's *Treatises* or Montesquieu. Strange,
then, that his name is so little remembered.

Burlamaqui's *Principes du Droit Naturel* was put into English in
1748 by the same Mr. Nugent who did Montesquieu two years later.
In various languages, the book went through fifty-eight editions by
1875, six in America after 1792. The title appears in this country in the
1750s, in New England sermons and James Otis' speeches in the 1760s;
the book was owned by Adams by 1763, and is quoted by all the revolutionary leaders. The influence of Burlamaqui on the English Blackstone is unquestioned, and Jefferson knew him both at first hand and
through James Wilson, student of Burlamaqui and first lecturer on law
in the new country. Burlamaqui's work was a text at William and Mary
from 1779 down to 1840, and the Reverend John Clarke, urging a chair
of politics at Harvard, argued that Burlamaqui "would lay a foundation
for that political knowledge which is of infinite importance to a free
country."[7]

According to Harvey, Burlamaqui may be a source for Jefferson's
emphasis in the Declaration of Independence on "happiness" instead of
the Lockean "property." For the Swiss jurist saw the state as a natural
expression of man's experience, and its function as that of collective
happiness by way of individual happiness through social justice. For
Burlamaqui sees no conflict between man and state, neither Hobbes'
fear nor Locke's elaborate need to provide some mode of contract. On
the contrary, men, being men, will evolve naturally modes of living
together, and these ways will be tested by time and utility. Thus the
state is no longer negative, a restraint on man, but positive, a human
creation for its own needs and uses, open to evolution and improvement
by experiment.

Hence, Burlamaqui can proceed to an examination of practical methods, such as separation of powers, checks and balances, and judicial review, as well as the pretenses of unchallenged power. "It does not follow," he says (reminding one of Thoreau), "that because I am incapable to resist a person, he has therefore a right to command me." Burlamaqui recommends a fundamental law or constitution, which shall be both a source of governmental powers and a check upon them, a basis for civil laws yet superior to them, but in no sense mysterious of origin nor sacred. This is, indeed, what the American Constitution became, a human, practical document. Perhaps here is also a source of John Adams' vigorous statement, quoted above (p. 13), that the revolutionary committees made no pretenses of "interviews with the gods," but proceeded as a wise architect would.

Quotations below are from the fourth edition of Burlamaqui's *Principles of Natural and Politic Law*, Boston, 1792. ࣸ

General Principles

[Pt. I, Ch. I]. My design is to inquire into these rules which nature alone prescribes to man, in order to conduct him safely to the end which every one has, and indeed ought to have, in view, namely, true and solid happiness. The system or assemblage of these rules, considered as so many laws imposed by God on man, is generally distinguished by the name of *Natural Law*. This science includes the most important principles of morality, jurisprudence and politics; that is, whatever is most interesting in respect as well to man as to society. There can be nothing more deserving of application of a rational being, of a being that has its perfection and felicity seriously at heart. A just knowledge of the maxims which we ought to follow in the course of life, is the principle object of wisdom; and virtue consists in putting them constantly in practice, without being ever diverted from so noble a pursuit.

The idea of *Right*, and much more that of *Natural Right*, is undoubtedly relative to the nature of man. It is from this nature therefore, from the constitution and state of man, that we are to deduce the principles of this science. . . .

We must therefore set out with acknowledging as a fixed and incontestable principle, that the human understanding is naturally right, and has within itself a strength sufficient to arrive at the knowledge of truth, and to distinguish it from error; especially in things wherein our respective duties are concerned, and which are requisite to form man for a virtuous, honorable, and quiet life; provided, however, he employs all the care and attention that lies in his power.

Sense and experience concur to convince us of the truth of this principle; which is the hinge, as it were, whereon the whole system of humanity turns. It cannot be called in question without sapping the foundation, and entirely subverting the whole structure of society; because this would be annulling all manner of distinction between truth and error, and between good and evil; and by a natural consequence of this subversion, we should find ourselves reduced to the necessity of doubting everything; which is the highest pitch of human extravagance.

Those who pretend that reason and its faculties are depraved in such a manner as to be no longer capable of serving as a sure and faithful guide to man, either in respect to his duties, or particularly with regard to religion, do not reflect that they have adopted for the basis of their system a principle destructive of all truth, and consequently of religion.

Original State of Society

[Pt. I, Ch. IV]. Another primitive and original state is that wherein men find themselves in respect to one another. They are all inhabitants of the same globe, placed in a kind of vicinity to each other; have all one common nature, the same faculties, same inclinations, wants and desires. They cannot do without one another; and it is only by mutual assistance they are capable of attaining to a state of ease and tranquillity. Hence we observe a natural inclination in mankind that draws them towards each other, and establishes a commerce of services and benevolences between them, from whence results the common good of the whole, and the particular advantage of individuals. The natural state therefore of men among themselves is a state of union and society; society being nothing more than the union of several persons for their common advantage. Besides, it is evident that this must be a primitive state, because it is not the work of man but established by divine institution. Natural society is a state of equality and liberty; a state in which all men enjoy the same prerogatives, and an entire independence on any other power but God. For every man is naturally master of himself and equally [equal?] to his fellow creatures, so long as he does not subject himself to another person's authority by a particular convention. . . .

But among all the states established by the act of man, there is none more considerable than the civil state, or that of civil society and government. The essential character of this society which distinguishes it from the fore-mentioned society of *nature*, is the subordination to a supreme authority, exclusive of equality and independence. Mankind were originally divided into families only, and not into nations. Those families lived under the paternal government of the person who was their chief, as their father or grandfather. But when they came afterwards to increase and unite for their common defence, they composed a national body, governed by the will of him or those on whom they had conferred the authority. This is the origin of what we call civil government, and of the distinction of sovereign and subjects. . . .

As these different modifications of the primitive state of man are the effects of his natural liberty, the new relations of different states thence arising may be very well considered as so many natural states; provided however that the use which men make of their liberty, in this respect, has nothing in it unconformable to their natural constitution, that is, to reason and the state of society.

It is therefore proper to observe, in relation to this subject, that when we speak of the natural state of man, we are to understand not only that natural and primitive state in which he is placed, as it were, by the hands of nature herself; but moreover all these into which man enters by his own act and agreement, and that are conformable in the main to his nature, and contain nothing but what is agreeable to his constitution and the end for which he was formed.

Of the Law of Nature

[Pt. II, Chs. I, V]. By natural law we understand a law that God imposes on all men, and which they are able to discover and know by the sole light of reason, and by attentively considering their state and nature.

Natural law is likewise taken for the system, assemblage, or body of the laws of nature.

Natural jurisprudence is the art of attaining to the knowledge of the laws of nature, of explaining and applying them to human actions. . . .

[Pt. II, Ch. IV]. Let us afterwards observe that the first principles of natural laws ought to be not only true, but likewise simple, clear, sufficient, and proper for these laws.

They ought to be true; that is, they should be taken from the very nature and state of the thing. False or hypocritic principles must produce consequences of the same nature; for a solid edifice can never be raised on a rotten foundation. They ought to be simple and clear of their own nature, or at least easy to apprehend and unfold. For the laws of nature being obligatory for all mankind, their first principles should be within every body's reach, so that whosoever has common sense may be easily acquainted with them.[8] . . .

[Vol. II, Pt. I, Ch. iii]. To give an adequate definition of civil liberty, we must say that it is natural liberty itself, divested of that part which constituted the independence of individuals, by the authority which it confers on sovereigns, and attended with a right of insisting on his making a good use of his authority, and with a moral security that this right will have its effect. . . . All this is performed by means of covenants. . . .

[Vol. II, Pt. I, Ch. vi]. But if the sovereign should push things to the last extremity, so that his tyranny becomes insupportable, and it appears evident that he has formed a design to destroy the liberties of his subjects, then they have a right to rise against him, and even to deprive him of the supreme power.

Salus Populi Summa Lex

[Vol. II, Pt. II, Ch. vii]. *Let the safety of the people be the supreme law.* This ought to be the chief end of all his [i.e., the sovereign's] actions. The supreme authority has been conferred upon him with this view; and the fulfilling of it is the foundation of his right and power. The prince is properly the servant of the public. He ought, as it were, to forget himself, in order to think only on the advantage and good of those whom he governs. He ought not to look on any thing as useful to himself which is not so to the state. This was the idea of the heathen philosophers. They defined a good prince [as] one who endeavors to render his subjects happy; and a tyrant, on the contrary, one who aims only at his own private advantage.

The very interest of the sovereign demands that he should direct all his actions to the public good. By such a conduct he wins the hearts of his subjects, and lays the foundation of solid happiness and true glory.

Where the government is most despotic, these sovereigns are least powerful. They ruin everything, and are the sole possessors of the whole country; but then the state languishes, because it is exhausted of men and money; and that first loss is the greatest and most irreparable.

His subjects seem to adore him and to tremble at his very looks: But see what will be the consequence of the least revolution; then we find that this monstrous power, pushed to excess, cannot long endure, because it has no resource in the hearts of the people. On the first blow, the idol tumbles down and is trampled underfoot. The king who in his prosperity found not a man who durst tell him the truth, shall not find one, in his adversity, that will vouchsafe either to excuse or defend him against his enemies. It is therefore equally essential to the happiness of the people and of sovereigns that the latter should follow no other rule in the manner of governing than that of the public welfare.

Civil Laws May Change Natural Laws

[Vol. II, Pt. III, Ch. 1]. But we must be careful not to confound two things entirely distinct, I mean the State of Nature and the Laws of Nature. . . . The civil laws may produce a few changes in the natural state, and consequently make some regulations unknown to the law of nature, without containing anything contrary to that law, which supposes the state of liberty in its full extent, but nevertheless permits mankind to limit and restrain that state, in the manner which appears most to their advantage.

We are, however, far from being of the opinions of those writers [i.e., Hobbes] who pretend that it is impossible the civil laws should be repugnant to that of nature, because, say they, there is nothing either just or unjust antecedently to the establishment of those laws [i.e., the civil]. What we have above advanced, and the principles we have established in the whole course of this work, sufficiently evince the absurdity of that opinion.

It is as ridiculous to assert that before the establishment of civil laws and society there was no rule of justice to which mankind were subject, as to pretend that truth and rectitude depend on the will of man, and not on the nature of things. . . .

If the abuse of the legislative power proceeds to excess, and to the subversion of the fundamental principles of the laws of nature, and of the duties which it enjoins, it is certain that under such circumstances, the subjects are by the laws of God not only authorized, but even obliged to refuse obedience to all laws of this kind.

But this is not sufficient. That the laws may be able to impose a real obligation and reckoned just and equitable, it is necessary the subjects should have a perfect knowledge of them. . . . Since the first quality of laws is that they be known, sovereigns ought to publish them in the clearest manner. In particular, it is absolutely necessary that the laws be written in the language of the country.

[As to religion, Burlamaqui declares that the state takes precedence in a conflicting order, e.g., to report for army duty and to go to church, but that a sovereign cannot forbid preaching nor establish a new worship.]

[Vol. III, Pt. III, Ch. iii]. The sovereign cannot lawfully assume to himself an empire over consciences. . . . It is therefore no less absurd than impious to endeavor to constrain consciences, and to propagate religion by force of arms.

Jean Jacques Rousseau
1712–1778

&⸱ Into the sober debates of classical and seventeenth- and eighteenth-century authors Jean Jacques Rousseau injected a different note, one destined to revolutionary implications. His influence is impossible to evaluate with clarity. His personal imbalance (he was an orphaned son of refugee parents, a mixture of egoism and self-doubt), his inconsistencies, his mingled logic and mysticism, leave us as he left his own day, unsure of his motives and at times of his integrity.

Acquainted with the writings of Hobbes, Locke, and Montesquieu, and the classics, even if superficially, he made use of the familiar appeal to "nature," but with a difference. For Rousseau conceived of "man in nature" as a kind of primitive garden of innocence, a life of simplicity and virtue, "peasants directing affairs of state under an oak," now long since corrupted by society. Most familiar of Rousseau's ideas is that of man's loss of freedom because of this social corruption. Free man moved, or should move, from the free state to a state which was the expression of the general will. Instead of Hobbes' absolute sovereign or Locke's compact between people and sovereign, Rousseau has the state expressive of and subservient to the general will.

According to Rousseau, the rights of the people are inalienable and cannot be taken away by any state. Laws are the expression of the public will, and even the church exists but to teach public and civil morality, its dogmas being no concern of the state as such. If the people agree merely to obey a state, the contract is already broken, since people cannot sign away their freedom, the community being but an expression of themselves. For the people only are the depository of government. One might say that Rousseau was thus feeling toward a conception of the individual as willingly yielding to majority opinion for the general good, suppressing self-desire and obeying even distasteful laws when they are an expression of the general welfare, yet never surrendering participation in the state.

Nevertheless, critics have been quick to point out the paradox of a dominant general will forcing the individual to be free. If, on the one hand, Rousseau may be linked with the simple and natural man of Wordsworth, or the later tide of romanticism with its emphasis on individual intuition, on the other he may foreshadow a doctrine of arbitrary majority will, a Fascist state pretending to be the voice of the *Volk* and riding ruthlessly over the individual or the dissident minority. How the general will, unchallenged and unchallengeable, can be trusted to represent always the voice of freedom is not at all clear. Though a power for popular revolt against arbitrary governments, Rousseau could also be a voice for an irrational and mystical kind of anarchy and demogoguery.

It may be questioned whether Rousseau had much direct influence upon American political documents. Nevertheless, his *Discourse on the Origin and Foundations of Inequality among Men* appeared in 1753, his famous *Social Contract* in 1762. Both were published in London in English in the early 1760s, and later in America. Possibly our "We, the people" owes something to his emphasis on the popular will. The first American edition of the *Social Contract*, Albany, 1797, said in the Preface: "His political works especially . . . are repeatedly referred to by eminent writers on government, and the framers of numerous constitutions . . . appear to have eyed them with deference, copied them in some particulars and made improvements in others."

Quotations below are made from the anonymous translation published in London in 1764 and soon circulated in America. Its title read: *A Treatise on the Social Compact or the Principles of Politic Law*, and it is the text followed by the Albany publication of 1797. A later translation, also anonymous, London, 1791, changed the title to *Contract*. This latter is the text used for some present editions, for example, the Hafner Library of Classics, New York, 1947.[9]

The Social Compact: Man Born Free; The First Society

[I, 1]. Man is born free, and yet is universally enslaved. At the same time, an individual frequently conceives himself to be the lord and master over others, though only more eminently deprived of liberty. Whence can this change arise? Are there any means by which it may be rendered lawful? The former question I cannot answer, though I imagine myself capable of resolving the latter.

If I took into consideration only the existence and effect of power,

I should say, So long as a people are compelled to obey, they do well to be obedient; but, as soon as they are in a capacity to resist, they do better to throw off the yoke of restraint: For, in recovering their liberty on the same plea by which they lost it, either they have a just right to reassume it, or those could have none who deprived them of it. But it is an inviolable right founded on the very nature of society, which serves as the basis of all others. Man doth not derive this right, however, immediately from nature; it is founded on mutual convention. We must proceed, then, to inquire of what kind such convention must have been. But, before we come to argue this point, I should establish what I have already advanced.

[I, 2]. The most ancient of all societies, and the only natural one, is that of a family. And even in this, children are no longer connected with their father than while they stand in need of his assistance. When this becomes needless, the natural tie is of course dissolved, the children are exempted from the obedience they owe their father, and the father is equally so from the solicitude due from him to his children; both assume a state of independence respecting each other. They may continue, indeed, to live together afterwards; but their connection, in such a case, is no longer natural, but voluntary; and even the family union is then maintained by mutual convention.

This liberty, which is common to all mankind, is the necessary consequence of our very nature; whose first law being that of self-preservation, our principal concerns are those which relate to ourselves; no sooner, therefore, doth man arrive at years of discretion than he becomes the only proper judge of the means of that preservation, and of course his own master.

In a family, then, we may see the first model of political societies: their chief is represented by the father, and the people by his children, while all of them being free and equal by birth, they cannot alienate their liberty, but by their common interest. All the difference between a father and a state lies in this, that, in the former, the love which a father naturally bears to his children is a compensation for his sollicitude concerning them; and, in the latter, it is the pleasure of command that supplies the place of this love, which a chief doth not entertain for his people. . . .

It is then doubtful, according to Grotius, whether the whole race of mankind, except about an hundred individuals, belong to those individuals, or whether the latter belong to the whole race of mankind; and he appears, throughout his whole work, to lean to the former opinion. This is also the opinion of Hobbes. Thus they divide the human species into herds of cattle, each of which hath a keeper who protects it from others only that he may make a property of it himself. . . .

Aristotle had said, indeed, before either of them, that men were not naturally equal; but that some of them were born to slavery, and others to dominion.

Aristotle was right as to the fact, but mistook the effect for the cause. Nothing is more certain than that every man born in slavery is born to be a slave. In such a state, men lose even the desire of freedom, and prefer subjection . . . If there are any slaves, therefore, by nature, it is because they are slaves contrary to nature. Power first made slaves, and cowardice hath perpetuated them.

Force and Slavery

[I, 3, 4]. The strongest is not strong enough to continue always master, unless he transforms his power into a right to command, and obedience into a duty. Hence is deduced the right of the strongest; a right taken ironically in appearance, and laid down as an established principle in reality. But will this term never be rightly explained? Force, in the simplest sense, is a physical power; nor can I see what morality can result from its effects. To yield to superior force is an act of necessity, not of the will; at most it is but an act of prudence. And in what sense can this be called a duty?

Let us suppose, however, for a moment, this pretended right established, and we shall see it attended with inexplicable absurdities; for, if it be admitted that power constitutes right, the effect changes with the cause, and every succeeding power, if greater than the former, succeeds also to the right; so that men may lawfully disobey, as soon as they can do it, with impunity; and, as right is always on the strongest side, they have nothing more to do than to acquire superior force. Now what kind of right can that be, which vanishes with the power of enforcing it? If obedience be only exacted by compulsion, there is no need to make such obedience a duty, as when we are no longer compelled to obey, we are no longer obliged to it. It appears, therefore that the word *right* adds nothing in this case to that of force, and, in fact, is a term of no signification.

THE CONTINENTAL STREAM

Be obedient to the higher powers. If by this precept is meant, *subject to a superior force*, the advice is good, though superfluous; I will answer for it, such a rule will never be broken. All power, I own, is derived from God; but every corporeal malady is derived also from the same source. But are we therefore forbid to call in the physician? If a robber should stop me on the highway, am I not only obliged, on compulsion, to give him my purse, but am I also obliged to it in point of conscience, though I might possibly conceal it from him? This will hardly be averred; and yet the pistol he holds to my breast is, in effect, a superior force.

On the whole, we must conclude, then, that mere power doth not constitute right, and that men are obliged only to pay obedience to lawful authority. Thus we are constantly recurring to my first question.

As no man hath any natural authority over the rest of his species, and as power doth not confer right, the basis of all lawful authority is laid in mutual convention. . . .

It may be said, a monarch maintains among his subjects the public tranquillity. Be it so; I would be glad to know of what they are gainers, if the wars in which his ambition engages them, if his insatiable avarice, or the oppressions of his ministers, are more destructive than civil dissensions? Of what are they the gainers, if even this tranquillity be one cause of their misery? A prisoner may live tranquil enough in his dungeon; but will this be sufficient to make him contented there? . . .

To renounce one's natural liberty is to renounce one's very being as a man; it is to renounce not only the rights, but even the duties of humanity. And what possible indemnification can be made for a man who thus gives up his all? Such a renunciation is incompatible with our very nature; for to deprive us of the liberty of the will is to take away all morality from our actions. In a word, a convention which stipulates on the one part absolute authority, and on the other implicit obedience, is, in itself, futile and contradictory. Is it not evident that we can lie under no reciprocal obligation whatever to a person of whom we have a right to demand everything; and doth not this circumstance, against which he has no equivalent, necessarily infer such act of convention to be void? For what claim can my slave have upon me, when he himself and all that belongs to him are mine? His claims are of course my own, and to say those can be set up against me is to talk absurdly. . . .

Thus, in whatever light we consider this affair, the right of making men slaves is null and void, not only because it is unjust, but because it is absurd and insignificant. The terms *slavery* and *justice* are contradictory and reciprocally exclusive of each other. Hence the following proposal would be equally ridiculous, whether made by one individual to another, or by a private man to a whole people: "I enter into an agreement with you, altogether at your own charge, and solely for my profit, which I will observe as long as I please, and which you are to observe also, as long as I think proper."

The Social Compact

[I, 6, 8]. I suppose mankind arrived at that term when the obstacles to their preservation in a state of nature prevail over the endeavors of individuals to maintain themselves in such a state. At such a crisis this primitive state therefore could no longer subsist, and the human race must have perished, if they had not changed their manner of living.

Now as men cannot create new powers, but only compound and direct those which really exist, they have no other means of preservation than that of forming, by their union, an accumulation of forces, sufficient to oppose the obstacles to their security, and of putting these in action by a first mover, capable of making them act in concert with each other.

This general accumulation of power cannot arise but from the concurrence of many particular forces; but the force and liberty of each individual being the principal instruments of his own preservation, how is he to engage them in the common interest without hurting his own and neglecting the obligation he lies under to himself? This difficulty, being applied to my present subject, may be expressed in the following terms:

"To find that form of association which shall protect and defend, with the whole force of the community, the person and property of each individual, and in which each person, by uniting himself to the rest, shall nevertheless be obedient only to himself and remain as fully at liberty as before." Such is the fundamental problem, of which the social compact gives the solution.

The clauses of this compact are so precisely determined by the nature of the act that the least restriction or modification renders them void and of no effect; in so much that, although they may perhaps never have been formally promulgated, they are yet universally the same, and are everywhere tacitly acknowledged and received. When the social pact, however, is violated, individuals recover their natural liberty, and are re-invested with their original rights, by losing that conventional liberty for the sake of which they had renounced them. . . .

If, therefore, we take from the social compact everything that is not essential to it, we shall find it reduced to the following terms: "We, the contracting parties, do jointly and severally submit our persons and abilities to the supreme direction of the general will of all, and, in a collective body, receive each member into that body, as an indivisible part of the whole."

This act of association accordingly converts the several individual contracting parties into one moral collective body, composed of as many members as there are votes in the assembly, which receives also from this same act its unity and existence. This public personage, which is thus formed by the union of all its members, used formerly to be denominated a *City*, and at present takes the name of a *republic* or *body politic*. . . . With regard to the associates themselves, they take collectively the name of the *people*, and are separately called *citizens*, as partaking of the sovereign authority, and *subjects*, as subjected to the laws of the state.

On Sovereignty

[II, 1, 3]. The first and the most important consequence to be drawn from the principles already established, is that the general *will* only can direct the forces of the state agreeable to the end of its original institution, which is the common good; for, though the opposition of private interests might make the establishment of societies necessary, it must have been through the coalition of those interests that such establishment became possible. The bonds of society must have been formed out of something common to those several interests, for, if there had been no point to which they could have been reconciled, no society could possibly have subsisted. Now it is only on these points that the government of society should be founded.

I say, therefore, that the sovereignty, being only the exertion of the general will, cannot be alienated, and that the sovereign, which is only a collective being, cannot be represented but by itself: the power of a people may be transmitted or delegated, but not their will. . . .

It follows, from what has been said, that the general Will is always in the right, and constantly tends to the public good; it does not follow, however, that the deliberations of the people will always be attended with the same rectitude. We are ever desirous of our own good, but we do not always distinguish in what it consists. A whole people never can be corrupted, but they may be often mistaken, and it is in such a case only that they appear to seek their own disadvantage.

The Dissolution of the State

[III, 10]. The dissolution of the state indeed may happen two ways. First, when the prince does not govern according to law; but arrogates the sovereign power to himself: in which case he effects a remarkable change, whereby not the government but the state itself is contracted. What I mean to say is that the great state is thence dissolved, and that he forms another within it, composed only of the members of the government, who are only the masters and tyrants over the rest of the people. So that when the government usurps the sovereignty, at that instant the social compact is broken, and the individuals who were citizens before are restored to the rights of natural liberty, and are compelled, not legally obliged, to obedience.

It is the same thing when the members of government assume separately the power they are entitled to exercise only collectively; which is no less an infringement of the laws, and is productive of still worse consequences. For, in this case, there may be said to be as many princes as magistrates; while the state, no less divided than the government, is totally dissolved or changes its form.

French Ideologists: Raynal, Volney

§ The whole intellectual climate of the French ideologists, so-called, is of interest; but it lies somewhat outside of this book, apart from the limitations on space, for two reasons: its influence was mostly after the American revolution, and its figures possessed a somewhat limited appeal in this country.

French literature, as was indicated above, circulated increasingly in America after the Treaty of Paris, 1763, and French thinkers were far from unknown; nor was the American experience without admirers in France. For example, a work appeared in France in "the third year of Liberty" (1795), entitled (to translate) *Declaration of the Rights of Man and the Citizen, Compared with the Declarations of the United*

States of America. "After centuries of ignorance," it proclaimed, "the science of politics has emerged from the shadows," and France was "destined to serve as a model." The constitutions of Pennsylvania and of Massachusetts were compared with the French declarations, and the opening paragraph of our Declaration of Independence was copied with great admiration.

Nevertheless, John Adams, writing to Jefferson in later life, thought the Encyclopedists might have been of service had they not been so devoid, he said, of common sense, so sure of their own rightness, and so atheistic. Jefferson, less perturbed by their irregularities, replied that Baron Grimm had been the pleasantest of men and Helvetius one of the best on earth. Noah Webster, in his *Miscellaneous Papers* (1794), remarked: "The philosophical researches of Voltaire, Rousseau, and the Abbe Raynal had long unchained the minds of that part of the French nation who reads; a respectable class of men. These men understood the errors of their government and the nature of liberty."

The whole effect of these French thinkers was that of critical analysis, in a tradition dating back to Francis Bacon and Descartes, and looking ahead to French positivism. Their examination of the flimsy grounds for aristocratic pretensions, of the abuses of taxation and tithes and of land holding, became common property and had far-reaching effects. History became a tool for examination, with overtones of evolution in the emphasis on progress.

The ideologists found in self-interest, enlightened by tolerance and mutual aid, the key to man's history. They replaced Descartes' *Cogito, ergo sum* by *Sentio, ergo sum*, "I feel, therefore I exist"; for their psychology was based on sensation, not intuition. Their center was the "law of nature," and they interpreted it with optimism and a hope of man's perfectibility through a proper education. Such optimism found a ready ear in the new world, and unquestionably entered into American plans for public education.

Much of their literature, however, appeared subsequent to the American Revolution, such as the writings of Mably or Raynal on American institutions, or the commentaries of Destutt de Tracy on Montesquieu, which led Jefferson to write their author that he had once seen much merit in Montesquieu but had since come to find a mixture of truth and error. Jefferson translated and published de Tracy in Philadelphia in 1811. Du Pont de Nemours' *Physiocratie*, published in 1768, charmed many Americans, and is linked with Crevecoeur's idyllic picture of life in Orange County, New York. Condillac and Condorcet were well known in the 1790s, the latter going through many editions. His *Sketch of a Historical View of the Progress of the Human Mind* (1795) contains an interesting statement about the new nation: "One sees for the first time a great people delivered from all its chains, giving itself peacefully the constitution and the laws which it thinks most fitting for happiness."[10] Thus America appeared to justify the long argument for the right of peoples to dissolve old governments and form new to their own taste; and Americans came thus to see themselves reflected in French eyes as makers of history and leaders in the march to a better world. ᠈᠊

Guillaume-Thomas François Raynal (1711–1796)

᠈᠊ The Abbé Raynal's *Philosophical History* was once in every hand and his name in every mouth, said the old *Biographie Universelle* (Paris, 1824). Educated as a Jesuit priest, he turned *philosophe*, and wrote with vigor if not always with judgment. He represents the more inflammatory literature of the period. His *Philosophical History* went through many editions, and appeared in Philadelphia in four volumes in 1770. A later edition was burned in 1780 in France. Americans read with interest his *Revolution of the American Colonies*, published in French in 1781, and in English in Philadelphia the following year. The excerpt is from this latter edition. The tone is that of Tom Paine, and the overtone that of an enemy of the French monarchy. ᠈᠊

THE AMERICAN COLONIES

The pretentions of the colonists rested on the nature of their charters, and on the still more solid basis of the rights of every English subject, not to be taxed without the consent expressed by himself or his representatives. This right, which ought to be that of every people, since it is founded on the eternal law of reason, originated so far back as in the reign of the first Edward. From this epoch the Englishman has never lost sight of it. In peace, in war, under weak or wicked Kings, in slavish or tumultuous times, it has been his unremitted claim . . . It was in the defense of it that he has shed rivers of blood, that he has punished or dethroned his Kings. In short, at the Revolution of 1688, that right was solemnly acknowledged by the celebrated act in which liberty was seen to trace, with the same hand with which it had driven out the royal despot, the conditions of a contract between a nation and the sovereign it had newly chosen. This prerogative of a people, much more sacred without all question than so many imaginary rights which superstition would sanctify in tyrants, was, with regard to England, at once both the instrument and the rampart of her liberty. . . . The Englishman, in founding his colony, had carried with him these principles beyond the seas; and the same ideas had been transmitted to his progeny. . . .

The knowledge, and the discoveries of the mother country were turned against herself, and she was told that . . .

Society originates in the wants of men, government in their vices. Society tends always to good; government ought always to tend to the repressing of evil. Society is the first, it is in its origin independent and free; government was instituted for it, and is but its instrument. It is for one to command; it is for the other to obey. Society created the public power; government, which has received it from society, ought to consecrate it entirely to its use. . . .

There is no form of government which has the prerogative to be immutable. No political authority, which is created yesterday or a thousand years ago, may not be abrogated in ten year's time or tomorrow. No power, however respectable, however sacred, that is authorized to regard the state as its property.

Whoever thinks otherwise is a slave. It is to be an idolater of the work of his own hands . . .

All authority in the world has begun either by the consent of the subjects or by the power of the master. In both one and the other case, it may justly end. There is no prescription in favor of tyranny against liberty.

The truth of these principles is so much the more essential, because that all power by its very nature tends to despotism, even in the most jealous nations, even in yours, ye Englishmen, yes, even yours.

Constantin Volney (1757–1820)

◄§ Volney has a peculiar interest to Americans because of his residence in this country, and because his book, *The Ruins* (called *The Ruins of Empire* in the American translations), held a fascination for a later American, Abraham Lincoln. An Oriental traveler and linguist, Volney had some political experience in France and Corsica before he published in 1791 his *The Ruins* and two years later his *Treatise on the Law of Nature*. Following imprisonment and then a series of lectures on history, he migrated in search of freedom. His *The Ruins of Empire* had been published in London in 1797, but with a rendering too cautious for Volney's taste. A "new translation" appeared in Philadelphia in 1799, the text of which is followed below; and a very similar translation appeared in Paris in 1802, aided in part by Joel Barlow. Jefferson, too, had a hand in further revision of the work for less wordiness, and editions appeared in Albany (1822), Boston (1833), etc.

Volney's *Ruins* opened with the melancholy reflections of the traveler upon the ruins of Palmyra. An apparition expounded to the solitary traveler a better future for mankind, on the principles of the laws of nature. After reviewing man's history and his follies, the book ended with a kind of catechism on the law of nature (not in earlier issues), which is quoted in part below from the edition of 1802. One might compare its tenets with the letters of Franklin and Jefferson on Deism, or Freneau's poem on "The Religion of Nature." ❧

THE RUINS OF EMPIRE

[Ch. 15, entitled "The New Age"]. And the civil governors said: The people are mild and tractable, and naturally servile; we must speak to them in the name of the king and the law, and they will shortly return to their duty. People! It is the royal will and pleasure of our sovereign lord the King, he commands and graciously ordains.

PEOPLE. The king has no will or pleasure of his own, in his political capacity, independent of the safety and welfare of the people; he can neither command nor ordain but according to the sovereign voice of the law, under which, like ourselves, he is a subject.

CIVIL GOVERNORS. The law calls upon you for submission.

PEOPLE. The law is the *general* will; and a reformation of abuses is our will.

CIVIL GOVERNORS. Ye are in that case, a rebellious people.

PEOPLE. Nations never revolt; tyrants only are rebels.

CIVIL GOVERNORS. The king is on our side, and he enjoins you to submit.

PEOPLE. Kings cannot be separated from their respective nations, of which they form a constituent part or member. The king of ours cannot, of course, be on your side; ye can, therefore, have nothing but his bare shadow to substantiate your pretensions.

Then the military governors advanced and said: "The people are timid; let us threaten them; there is no way of bringing them to obedience but by force. Soldiers, chastise this insolent rabble!"

PEOPLE. Soldiers, are we not all of one kindred and children of the same national family? Will you strike your own brethren? If the people be destroyed, who will support the army?

And the soldiers, grounding their arms, said to their chiefs: "We too are a part of the people; show us the enemy."

Then the ecclesiastical governors said: There is now but one resource left. The people are superstitious; we must awe and intimidate them with the names of God and of religion.

Our dearly beloved brethren! our faithful children! God has specially commissioned us to govern you.

PEOPLE. Produce the patent of his commission.

PRIESTS. You must have faith; reason bewilders and leads men astray.

PEOPLE. And would you govern without recourse to reason?

PRIESTS. God is the God of peace! Religion enjoins you to obey.

PEOPLE. Peace naturally supposes justice; and obedience implies the observance of an acknowledged and pre-existent law.

PRIESTS. Men are only sent into this world for trial and suffering.

PEOPLE. Show us then the example by suffering yourselves.

PRIESTS. Would you live without Gods or kings?

PEOPLE. We wish to live without tyrants.

PRIESTS. Ye cannot do without mediators to intercede and act in your behalf.

PEOPLE. Ye mediators with God and with kings! Ye courtiers and priests! your services are too expensive; henceforth we mean to take the management of our affairs into our own hands.

Then the small group exclaimed: We are lost, it is all over with us; the people is enlightened.

And the people replied: No, no, by being lost ye are saved; for, since we are enlightened, our power shall not be abused: our desires extend not beyond our just rights. Resentment it were impossible not to feel, but we shall now bury it in the grave of oblivion. We were slaves, we can now command; but our will is only to be free, and by willing it, we are so.

THE LAW OF NATURE

Q. What is the law of nature?

A. It is the constant and regular order of facts, by which God governs the universe; an order which his wisdom presents to the senses and to the reason of men, as an equal and common rule for their actions, to guide them, without distinction of country or of sect, towards perfection and happiness.

Q. Give a clear definition of the word law.

A. The word law, taken literally, signifies lecture, because, originally, ordinances and regulations were lectures, preferably to all others, made to the people, in order that they might observe them, and not incur the penalties attached to the infraction of them: whence it follows that the original custom explaining the true idea. [*Sic*; *it* and *that* were later omitted.]

The definition of law is, "An order or prohibition to act, with the express clause of a penalty attached to the infraction, or of a recompense attached to the observance of that order."

Q. Do such orders exist in nature?

A. Yes.

Q. What does the word nature signify?

A. The word nature bears three different senses:

1. It signifies the universe, the material world: in this first sense we say the beauties of nature, the richness of nature, that is to say, the objects in the heavens and on the earth exposed to our sight;

2. It signifies the power that animates, that moves the universe, considering it as a distinct being, such as the soul is to the body: in this second sense we say, "The intentions of nature, the incomprehensible secrets of nature."

3. It signifies the partial operations of that power on each being, or on each class of beings; and in this third sense we say, "The nature of man is an enigma; every being acts according to his nature."

Wherefore, as the actions of each being or of each species of beings are subjected to constant and general rules, which cannot be infringed without interrupting and troubling the general or particular order, those rules of action and of motion are called natural laws, or laws of nature.

Q. Give me examples of those laws.

A. It is a law of nature that the sun illuminates successively the surface of the terrestial globe;—that its presence causes both light and heat; —that heat acting upon water, produces vapors;—that those vapors rising in clouds into the regions of the air, dissolve into rain or snow, and renew incessantly the waters of fountains and of rivers. . . .

Wherefore, as all those and similar facts are immutable, constant and regular, so many real *orders* result from them for man to conform himself to, with the express clause of punishment attending the infraction of them, or of welfare attending their observance. . . . And as the only and common end of all those laws, considered relatively to mankind, is to preserve and render them happy, it has been agreed upon to reduce the idea to one simple expression, and to call them collectively, the *law of nature*. . . .

[Volney then defines ten attributes of the law of nature: it is primitive (i.e., anterior to all others), immediate, universal, invariable, evident, reasonable, just, pacific, beneficent, and alone sufficient. He denies the charge of atheism. He then takes up in detail individual and social morality.]

Q. What do you conclude from all this?

A. I conclude from it that all the social virtues are only the habitude of actions useful to society and to the individual who practices them; that they all refer to the physical object of man's preservation; that nature having implanted in us the want of that preservation, has made a law to us of all its consequences, and a crime of everything that deviates from it; that we carry in us the seed of every virtue, and of every perfection; that it only requires to be developed; that we are only happy inasmuch as we observe the rules established by nature for the end of our preservation; and that all wisdom, all perfection, all law, all virtue, all philosophy, consist in the practice of these axioms founded on our own organization:

> Preserve thyself; Instruct thyself; Moderate thyself;
> Live for thy fellow-citizens, that they may live for thee.

Tom Paine (1737–1809)

๛ We may summon Tom Paine's gift of clarity here for a final definition of "natural rights." The passage will be found in *The Writings of Tom Paine* (G. P. Putnam's Sons, 1899). "The Rights of Man," 1792. Vol. II, p. 306.

DEFINITION OF NATURAL RIGHTS

Man did not enter into society to become *worse* than he was before, nor to have fewer rights than he had before, but to have those rights better secured. His natural rights are the foundation of all his civil rights. . . .

Natural rights are those which appertain to man in right of his existence. Of this kind are all the intellectual rights, or rights of the mind, and also all those rights of acting as an individual for his own comfort and happiness, which are not injurious to the natural rights of others.

Civil rights are those which appertain to man in right of his being a member of society. Every civil right has for its foundation some natural right pre-existing in the individual, but to the enjoyment of which his individual power is not, in all cases, sufficiently competent. Of this kind are all those which relate to security and protection. . . . Society *grants* him nothing. Every man is a proprietor in society, and draws on the capital as a matter of right. . . .

A Declaration of Rights is, by reciprocity, a Declaration of Duties also. Whatever is my right as a man is also the right of another; and it becomes my duty to guarantee, as well as to possess.

PART IV · THE EMERGING
PATTERN: 1700–1790

"QUERY: What used to be the pride of the Americans?
ANSWER: To indulge in the fashions and manufactures of Great Britain.
QUERY: What is now their pride?
ANSWER: To wear their old clothes over again, 'till they can make new ones."
Benjamin Franklin, examination before the British House of Commons, February 3, 1766

"The body politic is formed by a voluntary association of individuals. It is a social compact, by which the whole people covenants with each citizen, and each citizen with the whole people, that all shall be governed by certain laws for the common good." State Constitution of Massachusetts, 1780

"The truth is that in our governments, the supreme, absolute and uncontrollable power remains in the people. As our constitutions are superior to our legislatures, so the people are superior to our constitutions. . . . These important truths, sir, are far from being merely speculative: we, at this moment, speak and deliberate under their immediate and benign influence." James Wilson, speech before the Pennsylvania Convention, November 26, 1787

"After centuries of ignorance, the science of politics has emerged from the shadows." *Declaration of the Rights of Men and of the Citizen*, French National Assembly, 1795.

THE EMERGING PATTERN: 1700–1790

Тне century of struggle in England was followed by a general desire for peace and harmony. This desire expressed itself in a philosophy of common sense, reasonableness, moderation, and *pas de zèle* (no zeal, no excessive enthusiasm), and in the middle-class virtues of thrift, utilitarianism, and practicality—in short, in Whiggism in politics and society. It was an age of conservative liberalism, and its temper lingered longer in the colonies than in the home land.

Yet it was not wholly a period of calm. War with France early in the century united parliamentarians and merchants behind the Whig leaders, especially as victories accumulated. At the accession of George I in 1714, a powerful House of Commons strengthened that leadership for decades to come, despite less successful wars, until a growing corruption and complacency hastened the crisis at home and within the colonies.

For it had been, too, an age of colonial expansion. By the treaty of 1713, England had acquired the vast Hudson Bay country, Nova Scotia, and Newfoundland. Colonial population expanded rapidly, from a bare 250,000 in 1700 to ten times that figure by the time of the American Revolution. The American seacoast was no longer the "wilderness," but the scene of a growing industry and prosperity, and was therefore involved in every decision made in the home country for an expanding empire.

The colonies felt the impact of renewed war with France. New Englanders captured the strong Fort Louisburg in 1745; and Virginians took part in the western campaigns of the next decade. The colonists rejoiced as at a common victory when Quebec fell (1759) and the western forts came into British hands. It was during this decade (1754) that Franklin proposed a confederation of the colonies for mutual protection and mutual benefits. The plan failed of achievement, but the seed had been sown. Americans, despite protestations of loyalty and intervals of hope of redress, became increasingly critical of a colonial policy which taxed and regulated them in the name of home interests, and forbad them representation in legislative councils. They had contributed much to the prosperity of England; and they thought they should share as equals in the benefits. More Whig than the Whigs of England, they circulated the old language of "rights" in a manner already somewhat dated in the mother country. But not wholly so; for Whig opinion in England tended often to favor the American cause. Understandably, the writers of such opinion were popular in the colonies.

It is possible to see the American revolutionary period in three stages: (1) that of the original reliance on the language of "British rights," of parliamentarian government under the Whig tradition and in the language of Locke and his disciples; (2) that of uneasy protest and, as British law failed them, the increasing use of the larger claims of the metaphysical heritage of "human rights," and the "law of nature and of nations"; and (3) that of independence and the sobering realization that a new and sound government must be formed. Here the Americans once again reviewed history, being determined to retain much of the British precedent but not to be bound within it if they might profit by the lessons of history and of political philosophers. This third phase falls somewhat outside of the latter limits of this study, and is but suggested in the conclusion.

In England, the language of American patriots encountered a new temper. Skeptics like Hume had cut under the myth of primitive man and his supposed compact government within the beneficent laws of nature. A critical spirit had replaced the old abstract historical generalizations. As Americans became more Whig, England moved steadily toward Tory preferences. What might have been the result of a more lenient policy toward the colonies is, of course, only a subject for speculation. In actuality, aided by the rise of newspapers and magazines in both countries, the dissemination of political argument flourished, and the divergences mounted.

Below are samplings of some of the British writers most popular in the colonies. On the ground that the colonials were still, up to 1775, British in spirit and in fact, and, however recalcitrant, still far from advocating separation, these British writers have been paralleled with a few American expressions of opinion, especially before 1766, the date of the repeal of the Stamp Act. It is unfortunate that space and our major purpose will not permit mention of equally popular literary figures from Dryden and Pope to Gray and Goldsmith, or sermonizers like Tillotson and Bishop Butler. Instead, we shall glance at Shaftesbury and Addison, Bolingbroke, Blackstone and Burke, Price and Priestley, as more strictly in the political tradition, and also at a few representative American pamphleteers. These will suggest some of the contemporary currents, and the heritage closest in time to the actual revolution.

Anthony Ashley Cooper, Third Earl of Shaftesbury

1671-1713

◄§ Shaftesbury, whose education had been directed by John Locke, was a delicate, studious man, yet a sturdy advocate of an independent Parliament and people. His Whig convictions he applied to literature and the arts, arguing that the free artists flourished best in free countries. His *Characteristicks (sic) of Men, Manners, Opinions, Times*, 3 volumes, London, 1711, was widely popular, perhaps because its style was easy and readable, though somewhat mannered. In this book he spoke for humor and gentle satire as the best weapons against fanaticism, and for moderation as preferable to persecution. His views were fashionable in his day, and found a more enduring expression in Pope's *Essay on Man*.

Shaftesbury may be recognized in America in the young Franklin, and for example, in William Parks' "Plain Dealer" essays in the *Maryland Gazette* as early as 1728. Excerpts here are from the sixth edition of 1737. §►

The Freedom of Wit and Humour

[I, Treatise II]. According to the notion I have of Reason, neither the written treatises of the learned nor the set discourses of the eloquent are able of themselves to teach the use of it. 'Tis the habit alone of reasoning that can make a Reasoner. And men can never be better invited to the habit than when they find pleasure in it. A freedom of raillery, a liberty in decent language to question everything, and an allowance of unravelling or refuting any argument, without offence to the arguer, are the only terms which can render such speculative conversations any way agreeable. . . .

Nor is it a wonder that men are generally such faint reasoners, and care so little to argue strictly on any trivial subject in company, when they dare so little exert their reason in greater matters, and are forced to argue lamely where they have need of the greatest activity and strength. The same thing therefore happens here as in strong and healthy bodies which are debarred their natural exercise and confined in a narrow space. They are forced to use odd gestures and contortions. They have a sort of action, and move still, though with the worst grace imaginable. . . .

If men are forbid to speak their minds seriously on certain subjects, they will do it ironically. If they are forbid to speak at all upon such subjects, or if they find it really dangerous for 'em to do so, they will then redouble their disguise, involve themselves in mysteriousness, and talk so as hardly to be understood, or at least not plainly interpreted, by those who are disposed to do 'em a mischief. And thus Raillery is brought more in fashion, and runs into extreme. 'Tis the persecuting spirit has raised the bantering one; and want of liberty may account for want of a true politeness, and for the corruption or wrong use of pleasantry and humor.

Liberty and Literature

[I, Treatise III]. And now that I am fallen unawares into such profound reflections on the periods of government, and the flourishing and decay of Liberty and Letters . . . I must wonder still more when I consider how after the extinction of the Caesarian and Claudian family, and a short interval of princes raised and destroyed with much disorder and public ruin, the Romans should regain their perishing dominion and retrieve their sinking state, by an after-race of wise and able princes successively adopted, and taken from a private state to rule the Empire of the World . . . They did what was in their power to restore Liberty, and raise again the perishing Arts and decayed virtue of Mankind. But the season was now past! The fatal form of government was become too natural; and the world, which had bent under it, and was become slavish and dependent, had neither power nor will to help itself. The only deliverance it could expect was from the merciless hands of the Barbarians . . . Even Barbarity and Gothicism were already entered into Arts e'er the savages had made any impression on the Empire. . . . Not a statue, not a medal, not a tolerable piece of architecture, could shew itself afterwards. Philosophy, Wit and Learning, in which some of those good princes had themselves been so renowned, fell with them, and ignorance and darkness overspread the world, and fitted it for the chaos and ruin which ensued.

We are now in an age when Liberty is once again in the ascendant. And we are ourselves the happy nation who not only enjoy it at home, but by our greatness and power give life and vigour to it abroad; and are the head and chief of the European League founded on this common cause. Nor is it to be feared that we should lose this noble ardour or faint under the glorious toil; though, like ancient Greece, we should for succeeding ages be contending with a foreign power, and endeavoring to reduce the exorbitancy of a Grand Monarch. 'Tis with us at present as with the Roman People in those early days, when they wanted only repose from arms to apply themselves to the improvement of arts and studies. We should in this case need no ambitious Monarch to be allured, by hope of fame or secret views of power, to give pensions abroad as well as at home, and purchase flattery from every profession and science. We should find a better fund within ourselves, and should, without such assistance, be able to excel by our own virtue and emulation.

A Discussion of Deism

[II, Treatise V, Sec. 3. Shaftesbury here defends Deists against the charge of atheism, arguing that writers are caught between those alarmed at free discussion and those respecting "natural religion." "We are too lazy and effeminate," says Shaftesbury, "and withal a little too cowardly, to dare doubt. . . . Thus we will needs *know* everything and be at pains of examining nothing." Franklin, Jefferson, Ethan Allen, Tom Paine, and other Americans followed such argument with interest.]

Where Force is necessary, Reason has nothing to do. But on the other hand, if Reason be needful, Force in the meanwhile must be laid aside: for there is no enforcement of Reason but by Reason, and therefore if Atheists are to be reasoned with at all, they are to be reasoned with like other men; since there's no other way in nature to convince 'em. . . .

What was never *questioned* was never *proved* . . . whatever subject had not, at some time or other, been examined with perfect indifference [i.e. disinterestedness], was never rightly examined, nor could rightly be believed. . . .

For whilst you are laboring to unhinge Nature; whilst you are searching Heaven and Earth for prodigies, and studying how to miraculize everything, you bring confusion into the world, you break its uniformity, and destroy that admirable simplicity of Order, from whence the One infinite and perfect Principle is known. Perpetual strifes, convulsions, violences, breach of laws, variation and unsteadiness of order, shew either no control, or several uncontrolled and unsubordinate powers in Nature. We have before our eyes either the Chaos and Atoms of the atheists,* or the magic and daemons of the Polytheists. Yet is this tumultuous system of the universe asserted with the highest zeal by some who would maintain a Deity. This is that face of things, and these the features by which they represent Divinity. Hither the eyes of our more inquisitive and ingenuous youth are turned with care, lest they see anything otherwise than in this perplexed and amazing view. As if Atheism were the most natural inference which could be drawn from a regular and orderly state of things! But after all this mangling and disfigurement of Nature, if it happens that the amazed disciple coming to himself, and searching leisurely into Nature's ways, finds more of Order, Uniformity, and Constancy in things than he suspected, he is of course driven into Atheism: and this merely by the impressions he received from that preposterous system, which taught him to seek for Deity in Confusion and to discover Providence in an *irregular disjointed world.* . . .

Compare our own Machines with the great One; and see whether by their Order, Management and Motions, they betoken either so perfect a Life, or so consummate an Intelligence. The one is regular, steady, permanent; the others are irregular, variable, inconstant. In one there are the marks of wisdom and determination; in the other, of whimsy and conceit. In one there appears judgment; in the other fancy only. In one Will; in the other, Caprice. In one, Truth, Certainty, Knowledge; in the other, Error, Folly and Madness. But to be convinced there is something above, which thinks and acts, we want, it seems, the *latter* of these signs; as supposing there can be no Thought or Intelligence but what is like our own. We sicken and grow weary with

* A reference to Lucretius?

the order and regular course of things. Periods, and stated Laws, and Revolutions just and proportionable, work not upon us, nor win our admiration. We must have riddles, prodigies, matter for surprise and horror. By Harmony, Order and Concord we are made Atheists; by Irregularity and Discord, we are convinced of Deity! The world is mere accident, if it proceed in course; but an effect of wisdom, if it runs mad!

Joseph Addison
1672–1719

⁌ It is difficult for the modern reader to understand the one-time popularity of Addison's play, *Cato*. Yet it ran through eight editions in its first year (1713), and was hailed as "nobler" and "loftier" than anything since Shakespeare. Part of this extravagant praise is explained by its supposed political implications as a protest against a possible Stuart restoration in the event of Queen Anne's death. Between its lines, too, one must read the persistence of Plutarch's *Lives* and the old admiration for the Stoic virtues. The plot is that of Cato's resistance to Caesar, and his demand that the usurper yield to the people and the Senate. When Caesar stands at the gates, Cato, after fortifying himself with Plato on immortality, falls on his sword and thus deprives Caesar of victory over the last of the old Romans.

Cato was played in America from Boston to Charleston, and printed in Boston in 1750. George Washington longed to play Juba opposite Sally Fairfax as Marcia, and went to see the play performed at every opportunity. At Valley Forge he drew strength from Cato's "The virtue of adversity is fortitude." Nothing better proves the appeal of the Stoic virtues than the success of this sententious play. The text followed below is found in the *Works* of Joseph Addison, edited by Mr. Tickell, London, 1746, Volume II. ⁌

Prologue by Alexander Pope

He bids your breasts with ancient ardor rise,
And calls forth Roman drops from British eyes.
Virtue confessed in human shape he draws,
What Plato thought, and God-like Cato was . . .
A brave man struggling in the storms of fate,
And greatly falling with a falling state!
While Cato gives his little Senate laws,
What bosom beats not in his country's cause? . . .

Her last good man dejected Rome adored,
And honored Caesar's less than Cato's sword.

Character of Cato

[Juba, prince of Numidia, speaks. (I, iv):]

A Roman soul is bent on higher views:
To civilize the rude unpolished world,
And lay it under the restraint of laws;
To make man mild and sociable to man;
To cultivate the wild, licentious savage
With wisdom, discipline, and liberal arts—
Th' embellishments of life: Virtues like these,
Make human nature shine, reform the soul,
And break our fierce barbarians into men. . . .
To strike thee dumb, turn up thy eyes to Cato!
There may'st thou see to what a godlike height
The Roman virtues lift up mortal man.
While good, and just, and anxious for his friends,
He's still severely bent against himself;
Renouncing sleep, and rest, and food, and ease,
He strives with thirst and hunger, toil and heat;
And when his fortune sets before him all
The pomps and pleasures that his soul can wish,
His rigid virtue will accept of none. . . .
Where shall we find the man that bears affliction
Great and majestic in his griefs, like Cato?
Heavens, with what strength, what steadiness of mind,
He triumphs in the midst of all his sufferings!
How does he rise against a load of woes,
And thank the gods that throw the weight upon him!

Cato Refuses Compromise

[Dialogue between Cato and Caesar's ambassador (II, ii)].

CATO. My life is grafted on the fate of Rome:
Would he save Cato? bid him spare his country.
Tell your dictator this, and tell him, Cato
Disdains a life which he has power to offer. . . .

  Bid him disband his legions,
  Restore the commonwealth to liberty,
  Submit his actions to the public censure,
  And stand the judgment of a Roman Senate.
  Bid him do this, and Cato is his friend.

DECIUS. Cato, the world talks loudly of your wisdom—

CATO. Nay, more, tho' Cato's voice was ne'er employed
  To clear the guilty, and to varnish crimes,
  Myself will mount the rostrum in his favor.
  And strive to gain his pardon from the people.

DECIUS. A style like this becomes a conqueror.

CATO. Decius, a style like this becomes a Roman.

DECIUS. What is a Roman that is Caesar's foe?

CATO. Greater than Caesar: he's a friend to virtue.

DECIUS. Consider, Cato, you're in Utica,
  And at the head of your own little Senate;
  You don't now thunder in the Capitol,
  With all the mouths of Rome to second you.

CATO. Let him consider that who drives us thither:
  'Tis Caesar's sword has made Rome's Senate little,
  And thinned its ranks. Alas, thy dazzled eye
  Beholds this man in a false glaring light,
  Which conquest and success have thrown upon him;
  Didst thou but view him right, thou'dst see him black
  With murder, treason, sacrilege, and crimes
  That strike the soul with horror but to name 'em.
  I know thou look'st on me as on a wretch
  Beset with ills, and covered with misfortunes;
  But, by the gods I swear, millions of worlds
  Should never buy me to be like that Caesar.

DECIUS. Does Cato send this answer back to Caesar,
  For all his generous cares and preferred friendship?

CATO. His cares for me are insolent and vain:
  Presumptuous man! The gods take care of Cato.
  Would Caesar show the greatness of his soul?
  Bid him employ his care for these my friends,
  And make good use of his ill-gotten power,
  By sheltering men much better than himself.

DECIUS. Your high, unconquered heart makes you forget
You are a man. You rush on your destruction.

Stoic Virtue

[Cato to Juba (II, iv)].

But know, young prince, that value soars above
What the world calls misfortune and affliction.
These are not ills; else would they never fall
On Heaven's first favourites, and the best of men.
The Gods, in bounty, work up storms about us,
That give mankind occasion to exert
Their hidden strength, and throw out into practice
Virtues, which shun the day, and lie concealed
In the smooth seasons and the calms of life. . . .
The hand of fate is over us, and Heaven
Exacts severity from all our thoughts:
It is not now a time to talk of aught
But chains or conquest; liberty, or death.

Cato's Death

[IV, iv: Cato reads from Plato's book on the Immortality of the Soul, saying that Plato reasons well, but that he wonders when or where "this world was made for Caesar." Before killing himself, he lies down to sleep, "Indifferent in his choice to sleep or die." Lucius makes the final speech:]

LUCIUS. From hence, let fierce contending nations know
What dire effects from civil discord flow.
'Tis this that shakes our country with alarms,
And gives up Rome a prey to Roman arms,
Produces fraud, and cruelty, and strife,
And robs the guilty world of Cato's life.

Cato's Letters: John Trenchard

1662-1723

In the early seventeen twenties John Trenchard wrote in the *London Journal* and the *British Journal* a series of letters signed merely "Cato." Though they seem today a rather unoriginal restatement of Whig philosophy, they were immensely popular, perhaps especially so in the colonies.[2] The excerpt below on "Freedom of Speech" was quoted by the boy Franklin as early as 1721, in his "Dogood Papers" in the *Boston Courant*. John Adams rated the papers highly. In 1724 Thomas Gordon (translator of Tacitus) collected the papers, and they were re-issued in four volumes in 1733, 1748, and thereafter. Provoked originally by the South Sea scandal, they diverged soon to political topics in general, always from the Whig predilections. The brief excerpts below are from the original London edition of 1724, Volume I. ⚜

Freedom of Speech

Without freedom of thought, there can be no such thing as Wisdom; and no such thing as Liberty without freedom of speech; which is the right of every man, as far as by it he does not hurt or control the right of another; and this is the only check it ought to suffer, and the only bounds it ought to know.

This sacred privilege is so essential to free governments, that the security of property and the freedom of speech always go together; and in those wretched countries where a man cannot call his tongue his own, he can scarce call anything else his own. Whoever would overthrow the liberty of a nation must begin by subduing the freeness of speech.

Praise of Sidney

[Trenchard quoted often from the classics, translating a lengthy letter of Brutus to Cicero in which Brutus scorns to receive mercy from Octavius Caesar, and regrets Cicero's submissiveness. Here he praises Sidney, in a preface to a long quotation from him.]

I send you, for the entertainment of your readers this week, two or three passages out of the great Algernon Sydney: an author who can never be too much valued or read; an author that does honor to the English nobility, and to the English name; an author who writ better upon Government than any Englishman, and as well as any foreigner; and an author who was a martyr for that liberty which he has so amiably described and so nobly defended. He fell a sacrifice to the vile and corrupt Court of our pious Charles the Second. He had asserted the rights of mankind, and shewed the odiousness of tyranny; he had exposed the absurdity and vileness of the sacred and fashionable doctrine of those days, passive obedience and hereditary right; doctrines which give the lie to common sense, and would destroy all common happiness and security amongst men! Doctrines which were never practiced by those that preached them! and doctrines which are big with nonsense, contradiction, impossibility, misery, wickedness and desolation! These were his crimes, and these his glory.

The book is every way excellent; he has read and digested all history; and this performance of his takes in the whole business of Government: It makes some amends for the loss of Cicero's Books *De Republica*. Col. Sydney (*sic*) had all the clear and comprehensive knowledge, and all the dignity of expression of that great master of eloquence and politics; his love of liberty was as warm, his honesty as great, and his courage greater.

Henry St. John, Lord Bolingbroke

1678–1751

◄§ Bolingbroke's reputation was at one time that of a stylist and orator. His influence on Pope is well known, and even his enemies paid him the tribute of attack. He was accused of writing for royal favor; and he early went into exile and retirement. Though a Tory and a high churchman, he returned to the seventeenth-century argument against the divine rights of kings and in favor of a balanced government. He also followed Locke in the latter's insistence that the "unerring mark" of the love of truth was "the not entertaining any proposition with greater assurance than the proofs it is built upon will warrant." [3]

His *On the Study and Use of History* (written in 1735, published in 1752) taught Jefferson, so he said, to respect original documents over commentators; and his *Idea of a Patriot King* (written in 1738, also published in 1752) was held in esteem by John Adams. The first selection below is from *Letters on the Spirit of Patriotism: On the Idea of a Patriot King* (London, 1752). The first essay complains of the loss of the ancient British spirit of liberty, and urges remembrance of the British constitution. The second selection below treats of the "uses of history." ◄►

On Divine Rights

The notions concerning the divine institution and right of kings, as well as the absolute power belonging to their office, have no foundation in fact or reason, but have risen from an old alliance between ecclesiastical and civil policy. The characters of king and priest have been sometimes blended together: and when they have been divided, as kings have found the great effects wrought in government by the empire which priests obtain over the consciences of mankind, so priests have been taught by experience that the best method to preserve their own rank, dignity, wealth and power, all raised upon a supposed divine right, is to communicate the same pretension to kings, and, by a fallacy common to both, impose their usurpations on a silly world. This they have done: and in the state, as in the church, these pretensions to a divine right have been carried highest by those who have had the least pretension to the divine favor. . . .

A divine right to govern ill is an absurdity: to assert it is blasphemy. . . . God has made us to desire happiness; he has made our happiness dependent on society; and the happiness of society dependent on good or bad government. His intention, therefore, was that government should be good. . . .

I will not say that the essential form of monarchy should be preserved though the preservation of it were to cause the loss of liberty. *Salus reipublicae suprema lex esto* is a fundamental law: and sure I am the safety of a commonwealth is ill provided for if the liberty be given up. But this I presume to say, and can demonstrate, that all the limitations necessary to preserve liberty, as long as the spirit of it subsists, and longer than that no limitations of monarchy nor any other form of government can preserve it, are compatible with monarchy. I think on these subjects neither as the Tories nor as the Whigs have thought: at least I endeavor to avoid the excesses of both. . . . My aim is to fix this principle; that limitations on a crown ought to be carried as far as it is necessary to secure the liberties of a people; and that all such limitations may subsist, without weakening or endangering monarchy.

Uses of History

[The text is Bolingbroke, *Works*, Volume II, London, 1777, p. 345. History is "for our improvement in wisdom and virtue."]

Man is the subject of every history; and to know him well, we must see him and consider him as history alone can present him to us, in every age, in every country, in every state, in life and in death. History, therefore, of all kinds, of civilized and uncivilized, of ancient and modern nations, in short, all history that descends to a sufficient detail of human actions and characters, is useful to bring us acquainted with our species, nay, with ourselves. To teach and inculcate the general principles of virtue, and the general rules of wisdom and good policy, which result from such details of actions and characters, comes for the most part, and always should come, expressly and directly into the design of those who are capable of giving such details: and therefore, whilst they narrate as historians, they hint often as philosophers; they put into our hands, as it were, on every proper occasion, the end of a clue that serves to remind us of searching, and to guide us in the search of that truth which the example before us either establishes or illustrates. . . .

We are not only passengers or sojourners in this world, but we are absolute strangers at the first step we make in it. Our guides are often ignorant, often unfaithful. By this map of the country which history spreads before us, we may learn, if we please, to guide ourselves. In our journey through it, we are beset on every side. We are besieged, sometimes even in our strongest holds. Terror and temptation, conducted by the passions of other men, assault us; and our passions, that correspond with these, betray us. History is a collection of the journals of those who have travelled through the same country, and been exposed to the same accidents; and their good and their ill success are equally instructive. In this pursuit of knowledge an immense field is opened to us: general history, sacred and profane; and histories of particular countries, particular events, particular orders, particular men; memorials, anecdotes, travels. . . .

In free governments . . . it is incumbent on every man to instruct himself, as well as the means and opportunities he has permit, concerning the nature and interests of the government, and those rights and duties that belong to him, or to his superiors, or to his inferiors. This in general, but in particular it is certain that the obligations under which we lie to serve our country increase, in proportion to the ranks we hold, and other circumstances of birth, fortune, and situation that call us to their service; and above all, to the talents which God has given us to perform it.

[Later letters give a long review of history from the fifteenth century on, and call on the King to restore England.]

Two New England Clergymen

John Wise (1652–1725)

◄§ The part played by the Puritan clergy was mentioned briefly above, and the early Thomas Hooker appears elsewhere.* John Wise, born the son of an indentured servant in the time of Cromwell, is noteworthy in the early eighteenth century on two counts: (1) He foreshadowed the democratic spirit of the colonies, and (2) he gave evidence of colonial knowledge of the literature of liberty, notably Pufendorf.[4] A graduate of Harvard and a clergyman, he tangled with Governor Andros by refusing to accept a tax levy without the general consent, and suffered arrest and a heavy fine. Later, resenting the Mather oligarchy in the New England churches, he wrote *The Churches' Quarrel Espoused* (1711), and then in 1717, *Vindication of the Government of the New England Churches*. So widely did he range in his argument beyond the local quarrel that his essay was reprinted in 1772 as appropriate to the political issues of the day.

His argument is a familiar one: the law of nature is written on men's hearts; man is inherently good and reasonable and by nature free-born; and mixed government, after the British manner, is best. In the church-y part of his text he had quoted Tertullian and Cyprian to show that congregationalism was historically sound and that the primitive churches "were distinct political bodies," for the early church had elected officials and encouraged lay participation in "mixed administration," in "perfect and complete societies incorporate." From this he led into the text given below, quoting Plato, Aristotle, Plutarch, Cicero, Coke, and Hooker, and especially Pufendorf. He could not have written so boldly had he not been able to count on a receptive audience, already aware of the arguments for self-determination. The text here is that of the Boston edition of the *Vindication*, 1717 (microfilm), somewhat modernized in spelling and form. 𝄢

THE VINDICATION

The constitution of New England churches, as settled by their platform, may be fairly justified from antiquity, the light of Nature, Holy Scripture, and from the noble and excellent nature of the constitution itself, and lastly from the Providence of God dignifying of it. . .

To me it seems most apparent that under Christ the reason of the constitution of these and the primitive churches is really and truly owing to the Original State and Liberty of Mankind, and founded peculiarly in the light of nature. . . . It seems to me as though wise and provident Nature by the dictates of Right Reason excited by the moving suggestions of humanity, and armed with the just demands of Natural Liberty, Equity, Equality and Principles of Self-Preservation,

* Wise makes no mention of Locke. Note that he precedes Montesquieu and Burlamaqui.

originally drew up the scheme, and then obtained the royal approbation. . . . This is granted by the London ministers . . . "That that which is evident by and consonant to the true Light of Nature, or Natural Reason, is to be accounted *jure divino* in matters of religion. . . ."

[Pt. II, Ch. II]. I shall disclose several principles of Natural Knowledge; plainly discovering the Law of Nature, or the true sentiments of Natural Reason, with respect to man's being and government. And in this essay I shall peculiarly confine the discourse to two heads, viz.

1. Of the Natural (in distinction to the Civil) and then
2. Of the Civil being of man. And I shall principally take Baron Puffendorff [*sic*] for my chief guide and spokesman.

1. I shall consider man in a state of Natural Being, as a free-born subject under the crown of Heaven, and owing homage to none but God himself. It is certain Civil Government in general is a very admirable result of Providence, and an incomparable benefit to mankind, yet must needs be acknowledged to be the effect of human Free-Compacts and not of Divine institution; it is the produce of man's Reason, of human and rational combinations, and not from any direct orders of Infinite Wisdom, in any positive Law wherein is drawn up this or that scheme of Civil Government. . . .

The prime immunity in man's state is that he is most properly the subject of the law of Nature. He is the favorite animal on earth, in that this part of God's image, viz. Reason is congenate with his nature, wherein by a law immutable, instampt upon his frame, God has provided a rule for men in all their actions, obliging each one to the performance of that which is right, not only as to justice, but likewise as to moral virtues, the which is nothing but the Dictate of Right Reason founded in the soul of man . . . That which is to be drawn from man's Reason, flowing from the true current of that faculty, when unperverted, may be said to be the Law of Nature; on which account the Holy Scriptures declare it written on men's hearts. . . . The way to discover the Law of Nature in our own state is by a narrow watch, and accurate contemplation of our natural condition and propensions. Others say this is the way to find out the Law of Nature. . . . But more particularly in pursuing our condition for the discovery of the Law of Nature, this is very obvious to view, viz.

1. A principle of Self-Love, and Self-Preservation, is very predominant in every man's being.
2. A Sociable Disposition.
3. An Affection or Love to mankind in general. . . .

2. The second great immunity of man is an Original Liberty instampt upon his rational nature. He that intrudes upon this Liberty violates the Law of Nature. . . . This liberty does not consist in a loose and ungovernable freedom, or in an unbounded license of acting. Such license is disagreeing with the condition and dignity of man, and would make man of a lower and meaner constitution than brute creatures; who in all their liberties are kept under a better and more rational government by their instincts. Therefore as Plutarch says, "Those persons only who live in obedience to Reason are worthy to be accounted free: they alone live as they will who have learnt what they ought to will." . . .

Man's external personal, Natural Liberty, antecedent to all human parts or alliances must also be considered. And so every man must be conceived to be perfectly in his own power and disposal, and not to be controled by the authority of any other. And thus every man must be acknowledged equal to every man, since all subjection and all command are equally banished on both sides; and considering all men thus at liberty, every man has a prerogative to judge for himself, viz. what shall be most for his behoof, happiness, and well-being.

3. The third capital immunity belonging to man's nature is an equality amongst men; which is not to be denied by the Law of Nature, till man has resigned himself with all his Rights for the sake of a Civil State; and then his personal liberty and equality is to be cherished and preserved to the highest degree, as will consist with all just distinctions amongst men of honor, and shall be agreeable with the public good. . . . The word Man, says my author, is thought to carry somewhat of dignity in its sound; and we commonly make use of this as the most proper and prevailing argument against a rude insulter, viz. "I am not a beast or a dog, but am a Man as well as your self." Since then human nature agrees equally with all persons; and since no one can live a sociable life with another that does not own or respect him as a man; it follows as a command of the Law of Nature, that every man esteem and treat another as one who is naturally his equal, or who is a man as well as he. . . .

Every man considered in a natural state must be allowed to be free, and at his own disposal; yet to suit man's inclinations to society, and in a peculiar manner to gratify the necessity he is on of public rule and order, he is impelled to enter into a Civil Community; and divests himself of his natural freedom, and puts himself under government. . . . So that,

The first human subject and original of Civil Power is the People. For as they have a power every man over himself in a natural state, so upon a combination they can and do bequeath this power unto others; and settle it according as their united discretion shall determine. For that this is very plain, that when the subject of sovereign power is quite extinct, that power returns to the People again. And when they are free, they may set up what species of government they please; or if they rather incline to it, they may subside into a state of natural being, if it be plainly for the best. . . .

The formal reason of government is the will of a community, yielded up and surrendered to some other subject, either of one particular person, or more, conveyed in the following manner.

Let us conceive in our mind a multitude of men, all naturally free and equal; going about voluntarily to erect themselves into a new Commonwealth. Now their condition being such, to bring themselves into a politic body, they must needs enter into divers covenants.

1. They must interchangeably each man covenant to join in one lasting society, that they may be capable to concert the measures of their safety, by a public vote.

2. A vote or decree must then nextly pass to set up some particular species of government over them. And if they are joined in their first compact upon absolute terms to stand to the decision of the first vote concerning the species of government: then all are bound by the Majority to acquiesce in that particular form thereby settled, though their own private opinion incline them to some other model.

3. After a decree has specified the particular form of government, then there will be need of a new Covenant, whereby those on whom sovereignty is conferred engage to take care of the common peace and welfare. In which Covenant is included that submission and union of wills, by which a state may be conceived to be but one person. So that the most proper definition of a Civil State is this, viz. A Civil State is a compound moral person, whose will (united by those covenants be-

fore passed) is the will of all; to the end it may use and apply the strength and riches of private persons toward maintaining the common peace, security, and well-being of all. . . .

The chief end of civil communities is that men thus conjoined may be secured against the injuries they are liable to from their own kind. For if every man could secure himself singly, it would be great folly for him to renounce his natural liberty, in which every man is his own king and protector.

[Wise concludes by defining three kinds of state, giving most attention to democracy, but finding mixed governments best: "that which has a regular monarchy (in distinction to what is despotic) settled upon a noble democracy as its basis." This he finds best exemplified in England; but he defends democracy in church government, on the grounds that a Christian people may settle what species of government they prefer.]

Jonathan Mayhew (1720–1766)

◄§ Jonathan Mayhew stepped into the limelight with a sermon in 1749 protesting the anniversary effort to make a saintly martyr of Charles I. Always fearful of an English episcopate in New England, he preached in 1765 a sermon on lawful resistance against both episcopacy and the Stamp Act, and in 1766 a sermon of rejoicing at the repeal of the Stamp Act, called "The Snare Broken." A student of Cicero, Harrington, Sidney, Locke, and *Cato's Letters*, he argued submission to governors so long as they were proper trustees of power. Review of those in responsible power, and even resistance, became thus religious and political duties; for the end of government was usefulness and happiness, tested by consent to being governed. John Adams and James Otis testified to Mayhew's influence by quoting him in political contexts.

Three excerpts will show his quality: the first two are from sermons of 1749, the third is from the sermon of thanksgiving at the repeal of the Stamp Act. The text is Alden Bradford's *Memoir of the Life and Writings of the Reverend Jonathan Mayhew* (Boston, 1838). ➢

The Duty of Private Judgment

Reason is no enemy to free inquiry and private judgment in religious matters. The cause of error and superstition may suffer by a critical examination. Its security is to lurk in the dark. But true religion flourishes the more, the more people exercise their rights of private judgment. . . .

Are Christians bound in conscience to believe and conform to that religion, whatever it may be, which is established by law, in the countries where they respectively live? This is a plain question: and they either are, or are not so obliged. There is no medium. If they are not so obliged, but only when they apprehend the established religion is agreeable to the word of God, this implies a right of private judgment, and gives up the point in question. But if they are bound in conscience to conform in the manner before expressed, it follows that he who lives in Scotland is bound in conscience to be a Presbyterian; he who lives in England to be an Episcopalian; he who lives in France, Italy or Spain to be a Roman Catholic; he who lives in Turkey to be a Mahometan; and he who lives in a heathan, idolatrous country, to be a pagan and a worshipper of idols; and thus one must be a polytheist and idolator, in order to obey the *gospel* concerning submission to the powers that be. And in order to know the true religion, we must examine the law-books of the country where we reside or travel through. . . .

Let us endeavor to find the truth, and after we are settled in our judgment as to any religious doctrine, to adhere to it with constancy of mind, till convinced of our error in a rational way . . . No man whatever, whether of a civil or sacred character, has any authority to control us, except by the gentle methods of argument and persuasion . . . Did I say, we have a *right* to judge and act for ourselves? It is our solemn *duty* to do it. We cannot relinquish the right, nor neglect the use of it, without being highly culpable. . . .

While we assert our own liberty and our Christian rights, let us be consistent and uniform, and not attempt to encroach on the rights of others. They have the same right to judge, and to chose their own religion, with ourselves. For nothing is more incongruous than for an advocate of liberty to tyrannize over his neighbors.

DISOBEDIENCE A DUTY

[Mayhew's sermon on Charles I was entitled in full: "Discourse Concerning Unlimited Submission and Non-resistance to the Higher Powers: With Some Reflections on the Resistance to King Charles I, on the Anniversary of his Death: In Which the Mysterious Doctrine of that Prince's Saintship and Martyrdom is Unriddled." This sermon, printed in Boston in 1750, commented ironically on "divine rights," and the worship of the beheaded monarch. It found circulation also in England, and was reprinted in Boston in 1818.]

We may safely assert these two things, in general, without undermining civil government: One is that no civil rulers are to be obeyed when they enjoin things inconsistent with the word and commands of God. All disobedience, in such case, is lawful and *glorious*; particularly if people refuse to comply with any legal establishment of religion, because it is a gross perversion and corruption of a pure and divine religion, brought from God to man by the Son of God himself, the only head of the Christian church. All commands running counter to the revealed will of God are null and void; and disobedience to them is not a crime, but a duty.

Another thing may be asserted, with equal truth and safety; which is that no government is to be submitted to, at the expense of that which is the great and sole end of government, the common good and welfare of society.

AMERICAN RIGHTS

[Mayhew was asked to preach the sermon of thanksgiving for the repeal of the Stamp Act, in 1766. Published in Boston in 1766, the sermon was entitled "The Snare Broken." Quotation is from the original printing, microfilm. Mayhew said he had no wish to go into political considerations, but would "briefly premise a few things."]

We have a natural right to our own, till we have freely consented to part with it either in person, or by those whom WE have appointed to represent and to act for us.

It should be taken for granted that this natural right is declared, affirmed, and secured to us, as we are British subjects, by Magna Charta; all acts contrary to which are said to be *ipso facto* null and void. . . .

It is taken for granted also that the right of trial by juries is a constitutional one with respect to all British subjects in general, particularly to the colonists. . . .

[Mayhew lists other rights, e.g., right to petition Parliament, etc. He sees the growth of the colonies as "chiefly owing, under God, to the liberty enjoyed here." He condemns rioting and expresses thankfulness for the restoration of order. At the conclusion, he extends a welcome to the oppressed of other lands and pleas for peace and harmony.]

Let none suspect that, because I thus urge the duty of cultivating a close harmony with our mother country, and a dutiful submission to the King and Parliament, our chief grievances being redressed, I mean to dissuade people from having a just concern for their own rights, or legal, constitutional privileges. History, one may presume to say, affords no example of any nation, country or people long free, who did not take some care of themselves; and endeavor to guard and secure their own liberties. . . .

Having been initiated in youth in the doctrines of civil liberty, as they were taught by such men as Plato, Demosthenes, Cicero and other renowned persons among the ancients; and such as Sidney and Milton, Locke and Hoadley, among the moderns, I liked them; they seemed rational. Having earlier still learnt from the holy scriptures that the wise, brave and vertuous were always friends of liberty; that God gave the Israelites a king (or absolute monarch) in his anger, because they had not sense and vertue enough to like a free commonwealth, and to have himself for their King; that the son of God came down from heaven to make us "free indeed," and that "where the spirit of the Lord is, there is liberty," this made me conclude that freedom was a great blessing.

Sir William Blackstone

1723–1780

⪙ In the very year of the American outbursts over the Stamp Act, there appeared in England a book destined to have a powerful effect on both sides of the Atlantic—Blackstone's *Commentaries on the Laws of England*. Published in London in 1765, and in Philadelphia in 1771, it was based on lectures given at Oxford from 1753 onward. Fully 2500 copies are said to have circulated in the colonies before the Revolution.

The book clarified for Americans the status of British subjects; for, using Fortescue, Coke, Grotius, Pufendorf, Montesquieu, and Burlamaqui (Blackstone owed not a little to the last), the author reviewed the history of British common law. "A competent knowledge of the laws of that society in which we live," he wrote, "is a proper accomplishment of every gentleman and scholar." James Wilson, first American lecturer on law, made one significant change—"should be the study," he said, "of every free citizen, and of every free man."

From Blackstone, Americans learned of the rights of Englishmen: personal life, liberty, habitation, property, movement, right of petition, right to bear arms in self-defense, rights by which "the meanest individual is protected from the insults and oppression of the greatest."

Yet Blackstone was no radical. His purpose was a summation of English practice. For Americans his common-sense view of law was of great importance; for he saw law as a natural growth, by trial and error, by experience and testing. Here was no appeal to divine vengeance against changes, no nebulous Rousseauistic "general will." There might be a hint of Hobbes in the finality of his Parliamentarian control; and, indeed, Jefferson complained that Blackstone made Tories of all England. Americans, however, might make additions to his summary, adding a written constitution and providing for judicial review of legislative acts, as a limit on unchallenged powers.

No longer an authority, Blackstone still gives us an excellent and readable view of his age and of the British tradition, without which the American story is inconceivable. Extracts are from the Philadelphia edition of 1771. ❧

On the Nature of Law in General

[Intro., Sec. 2]. This law of nature, being co-eval with mankind and dictated by God himself, is of course superior in obligation to any other.* It is binding over all the globe, and all countries, and at all times: no human laws are of any validity if contrary to this; and such of them as are valid derive all their force, and all their authority, mediately or immediately from this original.

But in order to apply this to the particular exigencies of each individual, it is still necessary to have recourse to reason; whose office it is to discover, as was before observed, what the law of nature directs in every circumstance of life; by considering what method will tend most effectually to our own substantial happiness. . . .

In a state of nature we are all equal, without any superior but Him who is the author of our being. But man was formed for society; and, as is demonstrated by the writers on this subject, is neither capable of living alone, nor indeed has the courage to do it. . . . Hence arises a third kind of law to regulate this mutual intercourse, called "the law of nations:" which, as none of these states will acknowledge a superiority in the other, cannot be dictated by either, but depends entirely upon the rules of natural law, or upon mutual compacts, treaties, leagues, and agreements between these several communities: in the construction also of which compacts we have no other rule to resort to but the law of nature; being the only one to which both communities are equally subject. . . .

The only true and natural foundations of society are the wants and fears of individuals. Not that we can believe with some theoretical

---

* Blackstone here, it is true, repeats the familiar "law of nature." It was left for Bentham to study government as utilitarian only, thus avoiding these metaphysical enigmas. Hamilton quotes this passage in *The Farmer Refuted*, 1775.

writers that there ever was a time when there was no such thing as society; and that, from the impulse of reason, and through a sense of their wants and weaknesses, individuals met together in a large plain, entered into an original contract, and chose the tallest man present to be their governor. . . . But though society had not its formal beginning from any convention of individuals, actuated by their wants and fears, yet it is the *sense* of their weakness and imperfection that *keeps* mankind together: that demonstrates the necessity of this union; and that therefore is the solid and natural foundation, as well as the cement, of society. And this is what we mean by the original contract of society; which, though perhaps in no instance it has ever been formally expressed at the first institution of a state, yet in nature and reason must always be understood and implied, in the very act of associating together; namely, that the whole should protect all its parts, and that every part should pay obedience to the will of the whole; or, in other words, that the community should guard the rights of each individual member, and that (in return for this protection) each individual should submit to the laws of the community; without which submission of all it was impossible that protection could be certainly extended to any.

Of the Laws of England

[Intro., Sec. 3]. Our ancient lawyers, and particularly Fortescue, insist with abundance of warmth, that these customs are as old as the primitive Britons, and continued down, through the several mutations of government and inhabitants, to the present time, unchanged and unadulterated. This may be the case as to some; but in general, as Mr. Selden in his notes observes, this assertion must be understood with many grains of allowance; and ought only to signify, as the truth seems to be, that there never was any formal exchange of one system of laws for another: though doubtless by the intermixture of adventitious nations, the Romans, the Picts, the Saxons, the Danes, and the Normans, they must have insensibly introduced and incorporated many of their own customs with those that were before established; thereby in all probability improving the texture and wisdom of the whole, by the accumulated wisdom of divers particular countries.

On the Rights of Persons

[From Bk. I, Ch. I]. For the principal aim of society is to protect individuals in the enjoyment of those absolute rights which were vested in them by the immutable laws of nature; but which could not be preserved in peace without that mutual assistance and intercourse which is gained by the institution of friendly and social communities. Hence it follows that the first and primary end of human laws is to maintain and regulate those *absolute* rights of individuals. Such rights as are social and *relative* result from, and are posterior to, the formation of states and societies: so that to maintain and regulate these is clearly a subsequent consideration. And therefore the principal view of human law is, or ought always to be, to explain, protect, and enforce such rights as are absolute, which in themselves are few and simple, and then, such rights as are relative, which arising from a variety of connections, will be far more numerous and more complicated. . . .

The absolute rights of man . . . are usually summed up in one general appellation, and denominated the natural liberty of mankind. This natural liberty consists properly in a power of acting as one thinks fit, without any restraint or control, unless by the law of nature; being a right inherent in us by birth, and one of the gifts of God to man at his creation, when he endued him with the faculty of free-will. But every man, when he enters into society, gives up a part of his natural liberty, as the price of so valuable a purchase; and, in consideration of receiving the advantages of mutual commerce, obliges himself to conform to these laws which the community has thought proper to establish. . . .

The idea and practice of this political or civil liberty flourish in their highest vigor in these kingdoms, where it falls little short of perfection, and can only be lost or destroyed by the folly or demerits of its owner; the legislature, and of course the laws of England, being peculiarly adapted to the preservation of this inestimable blessing even in the meanest subjects. Very different from the modern constitutions of other states, on the continent of Europe, and from the genius of the imperial law; which in general are calculated to vest an arbitrary and despotic power, of controlling the actions of the subject, in the prince or in a few grandees. And this spirit of liberty is so deeply implanted in our constitution, and rooted even in our very soil, that a slave or a negro, the moment he lands in England, falls under the protection of the laws, and so far becomes a freeman; though the master's right to his service may possibly still continue. . . .

The rights themselves, thus defined by these several statutes, consist in a number of private immunities; which will appear, from what has been premised, to be indeed no other than either that *residuum* of natural liberty which is not required by the laws of society to be sacrificed to public convenience, or else those civil privileges which society hath engaged to provide, in lieu of the natural liberty so given up by individuals. . . . And these may be reduced to three principal or primary articles: the right of personal security, the right of personal liberty, and the right of private property.

Colonies

[Of special interest to Blackstone's American audience was his review of countries subject to or colonies of England. The latter are of three sorts, he says: provincial, having crown commissions; proprietary, being crown grants; and charter, being civil corporations with power to make their own laws. None is, of course, independent of the laws of England, whatever local adaptations may have been demanded by circumstances. All colonies and plantations, by a ruling under George III, are subordinate and dependent upon the imperial crown and the Parliament of Britain.]

Appeal to British Tradition

THE STAMP ACT ERA, 1764–1766

◄§ James Otis' "Rights of the British Colonies Asserted and Proved" appeared in Boston in 1764. Its sentiments, said John Adams, were "as familiar to me as my alphabet." He was, said Adams, "a great master of the law of nature and of nations. He had read Pufendorf, Grotius, Barbeyrac, Burlamaqui, Vattel." Adams himself in his twenties had embarked upon a severe program of studies, "to examine the systems of all the legislators, ancient and modern . . . and the result of this long examination is a settled opinion that the liberty, the inalienable, indefeasible rights of man, the honor and dignity of human nature, the grandeur and glory of the public, and the universal happiness of individuals, were never so skillfully and successfully consulted as in that most excellent monument of human art, the common law of England." [5]

Thus the era of the Stamp Act aroused in the American colonies a flood of political documents aimed one and all at an assertion of American rights as British citizens. Not yet was the period of gropings toward independence, for none was yet so bold as to contemplate this step. Even Patrick Henry's vigorous protest in the Virginia House of Burgesses (1765) was framed on British rights; and the so-called Stamp Act Congress, representatives of nine colonies meeting in New York, drew up its "Declaration of the Rights and Grievances of the Colonists in America" as an expression of its "duty" to assert "the most essential rights and liberties of the colonists," as "inherent rights and privileges of his [Majesty's] natural born subjects within the kingdom of Great Britain." Among these rights were no taxation without consent, and representation from persons chosen by themselves. Daniel Dulany's "Considerations on . . . Imposing Taxes in the British Colonies" (Annapolis, 1765), calling on Magna Charta, Hampden, and the Bill of Rights, or Stephen Hopkins' "The Rights of Colonies Examined" (Providence, 1765, and London, 1765) showed the same concern. Perhaps only Samuel Adams, firebrand of Massachusetts, in the resolves of the Massachusetts Assembly extended his language to "certain essential rights of the British Constitution of government, which are founded in the law of God and nature, and are the common rights of mankind;" and "no law of society can . . . divest them of those rights." But he, too, reaffirmed full loyalty to the Crown.

In England, Benjamin Franklin, there to present a Pennsylvania petition and to protest the Stamp Act, repeated his old argument that the American colonies would one day be the cornerstone of the Empire. He was summoned to appear before the House of Commons and there questioned. His clear answers made him a hero at home and a figure to reckon with abroad. In his replies, printed in London and Boston in 1766, he made a clean distinction between mob action and public assembly, between unlawful rebellion and lawful protest as British citizens. In the *London Chronicle* in February 1766, he wrote an open letter outlining what the American people "will be apt to think and say." They will suppose, for example, that it is "an undoubted right of Englishmen not to be taxed but by their own consent, given through their representatives. . . . That compelling the colonies to pay money without their consent would be rather like raising contributions in an enemy's country, than taxing Englishmen for their own public benefit. That it would be treating them as a conquered people, and not as true British subjects." [6]

Let us examine, then, the language of a few of these documents which assert the traditional rights of Englishmen. ह

James Otis (1725–1783)

James Otis was eighteen when Samuel Adams in 1743 submitted for graduation at Harvard his thesis entitled "The Doctrine of the Lawfulness of Resistance to the Supreme Magistrate if the Commonwealth Cannot Otherwise be Preserved." Jefferson was born that year and Washington was but eleven.

Advocate general under the Crown, Otis resigned his office in 1761 in protest against the Writs of Assistance, which authorized officers to enter any house without warrant to search for smuggled goods. He grounded his case on British and "natural" rights, and argued that any act of Parliament against these was automatically null and void. Man, he said, was an independent sovereign, subject to laws written by nature within himself, whose rights were inherent, inalienable, and indefeasible by any laws, pacts, contracts, covenants, or stipulations. American independence, said John Adams later, "was then and there born."

Otis' "Rights of the British Colonists Asserted and Proved" appeared in Boston in 1764, from which document (microfilm) the extracts below are taken. In 1772 he drew up with Samuel Adams the "Rights of the Colonists" (see below, Appendix A, pp. 267–268). A member of the colonial assembly and of the Continental Congress, Otis was active until physical and mental health failed him. ৯৯

FOUNDATIONS OF GOVERNMENT

I think it has an everlasting foundation in the unchangeable will of God, the author of nature, whose laws never vary. . . . Government is therefore most evidently founded on the *necessities of our nature.* It is by no means an arbitrary thing, depending merely on compact or human will for its existence. . . .

This supreme absolute power is *originally* and *ultimately* in the people; and they never did in fact *freely*, nor can they *rightfully*, make an absolute, unlimited renunciation of this divine right. It is ever in the nature of the thing given in *trust*, and on a condition, the performance of which no mortal can dispense with; namely, that the person or persons on whom the sovereignty is conferred by the people, shall *incessantly* consult *their* good. . . .

It is evidently contrary to the first principles of reason that supreme unlimited power should be in the hands of *one* man. It is the greatest "idolatry, begotten by flattery, on the body of pride," that could induce one to think that a *single mortal* should be able to hold so great a power, if ever so well inclined. . . .

The end of government being the good of mankind, points out its great duties: It is above all things to provide for the security, the quiet, and happy enjoyment of life, liberty, and property. There is no one act which a government can have a *right* to make that does not tend to the advancement of the security, tranquility and prosperity of the people. If life, liberty and property could be enjoyed in as great perfection in solitude as in society, there would be no need of government. But the experience of ages has proved that such is the nature of man, a weak, imperfect being, that the valuable ends of life cannot be obtained without the union and assistance of many. . . .

The form of government is by *nature* and by right so far left to the individuals of each society that they may alter it from a simple democracy, or government of all over all, to any other form they please. Such alteration may and ought to be made by express compact. But how seldom this right has been asserted, history will abundantly show. . . . But if every prince since Nimrod had been a tyrant, it would not prove a *right* to tyrannize. There can be no prescription old enough to supersede the law of nature, and the grant of God almighty, who has given to all men a natural right to be *free*, and they have it ordinarily in their power to make themselves so, if they please.

[Otis continues by discussing how civil powers "remain in the whole body of the people," and by rehearsing the story of the abdication of James II, and the Bill of Rights, quotes them in detail so that all may know them.]

NATURAL RIGHTS OF THE COLONIES

[The colonists have the same rights, as "the noble discoverers and settlers of a new world."]

In return for which those colonies have received from the several states of Europe, except from Great Britain only since the revolution, nothing but ill usage, slavery and chains, as fast as the riches of their own earnings could furnish the means of forging them.

A plantation or colony is a settlement of subjects in a territory disjoined or remote from the mother country, and may be made by private adventurers or the public; but in both cases the colonists are entitled to as ample rights, liberties and privileges as the subjects of the mother country are, and in some respects to more. . . . [Otis here quotes Grotius, Pufendorf, and Thucydides on colonies.]

The colonists are by the law of nature free born, as indeed all men are, white or black. . . . [Here, quoting Montesquieu and Locke, Otis attacks the slave trade.]

The colonists, being men, have a right to be considered as equally entitled to all the rights of nature with the Europeans, and they are not to be restrained in the exercise of any of these rights, but for the evident good of the whole community.

By being and becoming members of society, they have not renounced their natural liberty in any greater degree than other good citizens, and if 'tis taken from them without their consent, they are so far enslaved.

[After briefly tracing liberty from the Norman times to William and Mary, and asserting that the colonies proved their loyalty in the last war, 1748, Otis continues:]

He that would palm the doctrine of unlimited passive obedience and non-resistance upon mankind, and thereby or by any other means serve the cause of the Pretender, is not only a fool and a knave, but a rebel against common sense, as well as the laws of God, of Nature, and his country. . . .

I am aware some will think it is time for me to retreat, after having expressed the power of the British parliament in quite so strong terms. But 'tis from and under this very power and its acts, and from the common law, that the political and civil rights of the colonists are derived. And upon those grand pillars of liberty shall my defense be rested. . . .

I have waited years in hopes to see some one friend of the colonies pleading in public for them. I have waited in vain. One privilege is taken away after another and where we shall be landed, God knows, and I trust will protect and provide for us even should we be driven and persecuted into a more western wilderness, on the score of liberty, civil and religious, as many of our ancestors were, to these once inhospitable shores of America.

Stephen Hopkins (1717–1785)

⋈§ Stephen Hopkins' *The Rights of Colonies Examined* was printed in Providence and London in 1765. Governor of Rhode Island and member of the Providence committee to draft instructions on the Stamp Act, Hopkins was a member of the Board of Commissioners in Albany in 1754, and later a delegate to the General Congress in Philadelphia and a signer of the Declaration of Independence. The text is that of the Providence printing of twenty-four pages (microfilm). ह∾

ON LIBERTY

Liberty is the greatest blessing that men enjoy, and slavery the heaviest curse that human nature is capable of. This being so, makes it a matter of utmost importance to men which of the two shall be their portion. Absolute Liberty is, perhaps, incompatible with any kind of government. The safety resulting from society and the advantage of

just and equal laws, hath caused men to forego some parts of their natural liberty, and submit to government. This appears to be the most
rational account of its beginning. . . .

This glorious constitution [the British], the best that ever existed
among men, will be confessed by all to be founded by compact and
established by consent of the people. By this most beneficent compact,
British subjects are to be governed only agreeable to laws to which
themselves have some way consented, and are not compelled to part
with their property, but as it is called for by the authority of such
laws. . . .

"For liberty solely consists in an independency upon the will of another; and by the name of slave, we understand a man who can neither
dispose of his person or goods, but enjoys all at the will of his master,"
says Sidney on government. . . .

New England was first planted by adventurers who left England,
their native country, by permission of King Charles the first, and, at
their own expense, transported themselves to America . . . Before their
departure, the terms of their freedom and the relation they should
stand in to the mother country, in their emigrant state, were fully settled; they were to remain subject to the King, and dependent on the
kingdom of Great Britain. In return, they were to receive protection,
and enjoy all the rights and privileges of free-born Englishmen. . . .

To illustrate this [freedom of colonies], permit us to examine what
hath generally been the condition of colonies with respect to their
freedom; we will begin with those who went out from the ancient
common-wealths of Greece, which are the first, perhaps, we have any
good account of. Thucidides [sic], that grave and judicious historian,
says of one of them, "They were not sent out to be slaves, but to be
the equals of those who remain behind"; and again, the Corinthians
gave public notice, "that a new colony was going to Epidamnus, into
which all that would enter, should have equal and like privileges with
those who staid at home." This was uniformly the condition of all the
Grecian colonies. . . .

If we pass from the Grecian to the Roman colonies we shall find
them not less free: But this difference may be observed between them,
that the Roman colonies did not, like the Grecian, become separate
states, governed by different laws, but always remained a part of the
mother state; and all that were free of the colonies, were also free of

Rome, and had right to an equal suffrage in making all laws, and appointing all officers for the government of the whole common-wealth. For the truth of this, we have the testimony of St. Paul, who though born at Tarsus, yet assures us he was born free of Rome. And Grotius gives us the opinion of a Roman king, concerning the freedom of the colonies: King Tullius says: "for our part, we look upon it to be neither truth nor justice, that mother cities ought of necessity, and by the law of nature, to rule over their colonies."

[Hopkins examines royal and Parliamentarian rulings on the American colonies, commerce, the distance from England which precludes knowledge of American conditions, unjust taxes, and the attention given to "informers"; the latter, he says, will remind the reader of "Tacitus's account of the miserable condition of the Romans, in the reign of Tiberius."]

John Adams (1735–1826)

❧ A proper examination of the mighty figures of Franklin, Adams, and Jefferson must be left to other texts. From Adams, however, we may quote a passage from this same year of 1765, a product of the course of studies mentioned above (p. 238).

For Adams the loose phrases of popular rebellion could not suffice. This man, whose sense of duty led him to defend the British soldiers who participated in the Boston massacre (he opened his defense with Beccaria and closed with Sidney), desired not revolution, but the orderly processes of law. Indeed, he was all but suspected at times of monarchical leanings. Yet the American cause had few sturdier defenders.

In order to set a historical background for the day, he produced from his studies *A Dissertation on the Canon and the Feudal Law*, printed in the *Boston Gazette* in 1765, and later in pamphlet and book form. Despite its youthful extremism in spots, it forecast the prevailing opinions of Adams' life. Quotations are from *The Works of John Adams*, ed. Charles F. Adams (Boston, 1850–1856), Vol. III. ❧

THE PURITAN SPIRIT OF 1765

It was this great struggle [the British struggle culminating in 1688] that peopled America. It was not religion alone, as is commonly supposed; but it was a love of universal liberty, and a hatred, a dread, a horror, of the infernal confederacy before described, that projected, conducted, and accomplished the settlement of America. . . .

After their arrival here, they began their settlement, and formed their plan, both of ecclesiastical and civil government, in direct opposition to the canon and the feudal system. The leading men among them, both of the clergy and the laity, were men of sense and learning. To many of them the historians, orators, poets, and philosophers of Greece and Rome were quite familiar; and some of them have left libraries that are still in being, consisting chiefly of volumes in which the wisdom of the most enlightened ages and nations is deposited. . . .

They knew that government was a plain, simple, intelligible thing, founded in nature and reason, and quite comprehensible by common sense. . . .

They were convinced by their knowledge of human nature, derived from history and their own experience, that nothing could preserve their posterity from the encroachments of the two systems of tyranny . . . but knowledge diffused generally through the whole body of the people. . . . For this purpose they laid very early the foundations of colleges, and invested them with ample privileges and emoluments. . . .

They [the people] have a right, an indisputable, unalienable, indefeasible, divine right to that most dreaded and envied kind of knowledge, I mean, of the characters and conduct of their rulers. Rulers are no more than attorneys, agents, and trustees, for the people: and if the cause, the interest and trust, is insidiously betrayed, or wantonly trifled away, the people have a right to revoke the authority that they themselves have deputed, and to constitute abler and better agents, attorneys, and trustees. And the preservation of the means of knowledge among the lowest ranks is of more importance to the public than all the property of all the rich men of the country. It is even of more consequence to the rich themselves, and to their posterity. . . .

Let us take it for granted that the same great spirit which once gave Caesar so warm a reception, which denounced hostilities against John till Magna Carta was signed, which severed the head of Charles the First from his body, and drove James the Second from his kingdom; the same great spirit . . . which first seated the great grandfather of his present most gracious majesty on the throne of Britain,—is still alive and active and warm in England; and that the same spirit in America, instead of provoking the inhabitants of that country, will endear us to them forever, and secure their good-will.

This spirit, however, without knowledge, would be little better than a brutal rage. Let us tenderly and kindly cherish, therefore, the means of knowledge. Let us dare to read, think, speak, write. . . . Let us study the law of nature; search into the spirit of the British constitution; read the histories of ancient ages; contemplate the great examples of Greece and Rome; set before us the conduct of our own British ancestors, who have defended for us the inherent rights of mankind against foreign and domestic tyrants and usurpers, against arbitrary kings and cruel priests, in short, against the gates of earth and hell. Let us read and recollect and impress upon our souls the views and ends of our own more immediate forefathers in exchanging their native country for a dreary, inhospitable wilderness. Let us examine into the nature of that power, and the cruelty of that oppression which drove them from their homes. . . .

Let the pulpit resound with the doctrines and sentiments of religious liberty. Let us hear the danger of thraldom to our consciences from ignorance, extreme poverty and dependence, in short, from civil and political slavery. . . .

Let the bar proclaim "the laws, the rights, the generous plan of power" delivered down from remote antiquity . . . Let it be known that British liberties are not the grants of princes or parliaments, but original rights, conditions of original contracts, coequal with prerogative, and coeval with government; that many of our rights are inherent and essential, agreed on as maxims, and established as preliminaries, even before a parliament existed. Let them search for the foundations of British laws and government in the frame of human nature, in the constitution of the intellectual and moral world . . .

In a word, let every sluice of knowledge be opened and set a-flowing.

Edmund Burke

1729–1797

⊷§ Of British statesmen during the critical period preceding the American Revolution, Edmund Burke and the elder Pitt particularly endeared themselves to the colonists by their consideration of the colonial cause. William Pitt, first earl of Chatham, concerned over the ineptitude of British ministers in foreign affairs, repeatedly urged a more considerate treatment of the colonists, including the recall of troops, the repeal of assessments, bills for the relief of dissenters, and the cessation of hostilities. "When your Lordships consider their decency, firmness and wisdom," he said in the House of Lords, "you cannot but respect their cause and wish to make it your own. For myself, I must avow that in all my reading—and I have read Thucydides, and have studied and admired the master states of the world—for solidity of reasoning, force and sagacity and wisdom of conclusion under a complication of difficult circumstances, no body of men can stand in preference to the general Congress at Philadelphia. The histories of Greece and Rome give us nothing equal to it, and all attempts to impose servitude upon such a mighty continental nation must be in vain." His words found enthusiastic quotation on the American side of the water.

Burke's fame in America rested heavily on his famous *Speech on Conciliation with the Colonies*, made on March 22, 1775, and immediately reprinted in New York. Guided like Pitt by a desire to save England from its blunders, he was nevertheless sincere in his argument that the colonists were not subdued peoples but Englishmen, with a more than common love of British freedoms. To prove that they must be held in bondage, said Burke, Englishmen must attack their own liberties. Well into the twentieth century, this speech was required study in American high schools; for Burke taught Americans to think well of themselves. Excerpts below are from the New York 1775 edition, collated with the London second edition of the same year, for reasons that appear below. ❧

Character of the Americans

In this character of the Americans, a love of freedom is the predominating feature, which marks and distinguishes the whole: and as an ardent is always a jealous affection, your colonies become suspicious, restive and untractable, whenever they see the least attempt to wrest from them by force, or shuffle from them by chicane, what they think the only advantage worth living for. This fierce spirit of liberty is stronger in the English colonies probably than in any other people of the earth; and this from a great variety of powerful causes; which, to understand the true temper of their minds, and the direction which this spirit takes, it will not be amiss to lay open somewhat more largely.

First, the people of the colonies are descendents of Englishmen. England, Sir, is a nation which still I hope respects, and formerly adored her freedom. The colonists emigrated from you, when this part of your character was most predominant; and they took this bias and direction the moment they parted from your hands. They are therefore not only devoted to liberty, but liberty according to English ideas, and on English principles. Abstract liberty, like other mere abstractions, is not to be found. Liberty inheres in some sensible object; and every nation has formed to itself some favorite point which by way of eminence becomes the criterion of their happiness. It happened, you know, Sir, that the great contests for freedom in this country were from the earliest times chiefly upon the question of taxing. Most of the contests in the ancient commonwealths turned primarily on the right of election of Magistrates; or on the balance among the several orders of the state. The question of money was not with them so immediate. But in England it was otherwise; on this point of taxes the ablest pens and most eloquent tongues, have been exercised; the greatest spirits have acted and suffered. In order to give the fullest satisfaction concerning the importance of this point, it was not only necessary for those who in argument defended the excellence of the English constitution, to insist on this privilege of granting money as a dry point of fact, and to prove that the right had been acknowledged in ancient parchments to [and ?] blind usages, to reside in a certain body called a House of Commons. They went much farther; they attempted to prove, and they succeeded, that in theory it ought to be so, from the particular nature of a House of Commons as an immediate representative of the people; whether the old records had delivered this oracle or not. They took infinite pains to inculcate as a fundamental principle, that in all monarchies the people must in effect themselves mediately or immediately possess the power of granting their own money, or no shadow of liberty could subsist. The colonies draw from you, as with their life-blood, these ideas and principles. Their love of liberty, as with you, fixed and attached on this specific point of taxing. Liberty might be safe, or might be endangered in twenty other particulars, without their being much pleased or alarmed. Here they felt its pulse; and as they found that beat, they thought themselves sick or sound. . . . And your mode of governing them, whether through lenity or indolence, through wisdom or mistake, confirmed them in the imagination that they, as well as you, had an interest in the common principles.

They were farther confirmed in this pleasing error by the form of their provincial legislative assemblies. Their governments are popular in an high degree; some are merely popular; in all, the popular representative is the most weighty; and this share of the people in their ordinary government never fails to inspire them with lofty sentiments, and with a strong aversion from whatever tends to deprive them of their chief importance.

Religions of America

The people are Protestants; and of that kind which is the most adverse to all implicit submission of mind and opinion. This is a persuasion not only favorable to liberty, but built upon it. I do not think, Sir, that the reason of this averseness in the dissenting churches from all that looks like absolute government is so much to be sought in their religious tenets, as in their history. . . . The dissenting interests have sprung up in direct opposition to all the ordinary powers of the world; and could justify that opposition only on a strong claim to natural liberty. Their very existence depended on the powerful and unremitted assertion of that claim. All Protestantism, even the most cold and passive, is a sort of dissent. But the religion most prevalent in our northern [colonies is a refinement on the principle of resistance; it is the dissidence of dissent, and the Protestantism of the Protestant religion. This religion, under a variety of denominations agreeing in nothing but the communion of the spirit of liberty, is predominant in most of the northern] * provinces; where the Church of England, notwithstanding its legal rights, is in reality no more than a sort of private sect, not composing most probably the tenth of the people. The colonists left England when this spirit was high; and in the emigrants was the highest of all, and even that strain of foreigners, which has been constantly flowing into these colonies, has, for the greatest part, been composed of dissenters from the establishments of their several countries; and have brought with them a temper and character far from alien to that of the people with whom they mixed.

Education of the Colonies

In no country, perhaps, in the world, is the law so general a study. The profession itself is numerous and powerful, and in most provinces it takes the lead. The greater number of the deputies sent to the Congress were lawyers. But all who read, and most do read, endeavor to obtain some smattering in that science. I have been told, by an eminent bookseller, that in no branch of his business, after tracts of popular devotion, were so many books as those on the law exported to the plantations. The colonists have now fallen into the way of printing them for their own use. I hear that they have sold nearly as many of Blackstone's

* This passage in brackets appears to have slipped out of the American text, probably by skipping to the repetition of the word "northern," and is here supplied from the second London edition of 1775.

Commentaries in America as in England. . . . This study renders men acute, inquisitive, dextrous, prompt in attack, ready in defence, full of resources. In other countries, the people more simple, and of a less martial ["mercurial," (London, 1775)] cast, judge of an ill principle in government only by an actual grievance; here they anticipate the evil, and judge of the pressure of the grievance by the badness of the principle. They augur misgovernment at a distance, and snuff the approach of tyranny in every tainted breeze.

New Things in America

I do not mean to commend either the spirit in this excess, or the moral causes that produced it. Perhaps a more smooth and accomodating spirit of freedom in them would be more acceptable to us. Perhaps ideas of liberty might be desired more reconcilable with an arbitrary and boundless authority. Perhaps we might wish the colonists to be persuaded that their liberty is more secure when held in trust for them by us . . . The question is, not whether their spirit deserves praise or blame. What, in the name of God, shall we do with it? . . . We thought, Sir, that the utmost which the discontented colonists could do, was to disturb authority; we never dreamt they could of themselves supply it; knowing in general what an operose business it is to establish a government absolutely new. But having, for our purposes in this contention, resolved that none but an obedient assembly should sit, the humors of the people there, finding all passage through the legal channel stopped, with great violence broke out another way.

Some provinces have tried their experiment, as we have tried ours; and theirs has succeeded. They have formed a government sufficient for its purposes, without the bustle of a revolution, or the troublesome formality of an election. Evident necessity, and tacit consent, have done the business in an instant. So well they have done it . . . that the new institution is infinitely better obeyed than the ancient government ever was in its most fortunate periods. . . . This new government has originated directly from the people; and was not transmitted through any of the ordinary artificial media of a positive constitution. It was not a manufacture ready formed, and transmitted to them in that condition from England.

The evil arising from hence, is this; that the colonists having once found the possibility of enjoying the advantages of order, in the midst of a struggle for liberty, such struggles will not henceforward seem so terrible to the settled and sober part of mankind, as they had appeared before the trial.

Pursuing the same plan of punishing, by the denial of the exercise of government to still greater lengths, we wholly abrogated the ancient government of Massachusetts. We were confident that the first feeling, if not the very prospect of anarchy, would instantly enforce a complete submission. The experiment was tried. A new, strange, unexpected face of things appeared. Anarchy is found tolerable. A vast province has now subsisted, and subsisted in a considerable degree of health and vigor for near twelve months, without Governor, without public council, without judges, without executive magistrates. . . . Our late experience has taught us that many of those fundamental principles, formerly believed infallible, are either not of the importance they were imagined to be; or that we have not at all adverted to some other far more important and far more powerful principles, which entirely overrule those we had considered as omnipotent. . . . In order to prove that the Americans have no right to their liberties, we are every day endeavoring to subvert the maxims which preserve the whole spirit of our own. To prove that the Americans ought not to be free, we are obliged to depreciate the value of freedom itself; and we never seem to gain a paltry advantage over them in debate without attacking some of those principles, or deriding some of those feelings for which our ancestors have shed their blood.

Joseph Priestley

1733–1804

๛ Two names reverberated around the period of the American revolution, those of Joseph Priestley and Richard Price.[1] Priestley, clergyman and man of science, famous for his work with oxygen and his ill-fated phlogiston theory, friend of Franklin and Jefferson, removed to America late in life (1793) and died here. His papers, books, and laboratory equipment had been burned by mobs in England because of his support of the French Revolution. In America he was best known for his *Essay on the First Principles of Government and on the Nature of Political, Civil and Religious Liberty*, published in 1768, and again in 1771. Quotation here is from the second edition of 1771. A large part of the book is given to an argument for religious freedom and toleration. Priestley advocated more, not fewer, sects, as a guarantee of liberty for all of them. Note his emphasis on *progress*. ঔ

Definitions

The great instrument in the hand of divine providence of this progress of the species towards perfection is *society*, and consequently *government*. . . . Government being the great instrument of this progress of the human species towards this glorious state, that form of government will have a just claim to our approbation which favors this progress, and that must be condemned in which it is retarded. . . .

In all states, great or small, the sentiments of that body of men in whose hands the supreme power of the society is lodged, must be understood to be the sentiments of the whole body, if there be no other method in which the sentiments of the whole body can be expressed. . . .

Political liberty, I would say, consists in the power which the members of the state reserve to themselves, of arriving at the public offices, or at least of having votes in the nomination of those who fill them; and I would chose to call civil liberty that power over their own actions which the members of the state reserve to themselves, and which their officers must not infringe. [This last paragraph of definition is in italics.]

On Political Liberty

[Sect. II]. In countries where every member of the society enjoys an equal power of arriving at the supreme offices, and consequently of directing the strength and the sentiments of the whole community, there is a state of the most perfect political liberty. On the other hand, in others where a man is, by birth or fortune, excluded from these offices, or from a power of voting for proper persons to fill them, that man, whatever be the form of the government, or whatever civil liberty or power over his own actions he may have, has no power over those of another; he has no share in the government, and therefore has no political liberty at all. Nay, his own conduct, as far as the society does interfere, is in all cases directed by others.

It may be said that no society on earth was ever formed in the manner represented above. I answer, it is true; because all governments whatever have been, in some measure, compulsory, tyrannical and oppressive in their origin; but the method I have described must be allowed to be the only equitable and fair method of forming a society. And since every man retains, and can never be deprived of his natural right (founded on a regard to the general good) of relieving himself from all oppression, that is, from everything that has been imposed upon him without his own consent; this must be the only true and proper foundation of all the governments subsisting in the world, and that to which the people who compose them have an unalienable right to bring them back.

It must necessarily be understood, therefore, whether it be expressed or not, that all people live in society for their mutual advantage; so that the good and happiness of the members of any state is the great standard by which everything relating to that state must finally be determined. . . .

I own it is rather matter of surprise to me that this great object of all government should have been so little insisted on by our great writers who have treated of this subject, and that more use hath not been made of it. . . .

But if there be any truth in the principles above laid down, it must be a fundamental maxim in all governments that if any man hold what is called a high rank, or enjoy privileges and prerogatives in a state, it is because the good of the state requires that he should hold that rank, or enjoy those privileges; and such persons, whether they be called kings, senators, or nobles, or by whatever names or titles they be distinguished, are, to all intents and purposes, the *servants of the public*, and accountable to the people for the discharge of their respective offices.

If such magistrates abuse their trust, in the people, therefore, lies the right of *deposing*, and consequently of *punishing* them. . . .

To say that these forms of government have been long established, and that these oppressions have been long suffered, without any complaint, is to supply the strongest arguments for their abolition.

[Without further quotation, we may point out that Priestley discusses education in the free state as individuals acting independently yet collectively toward truth, without legislative interference. Suppose, he says, that Alfred had been able to fix Oxford's education; and remember how Oxford at one time tried to forbid the study of Newton and Locke. Much subsequent argument is for religious liberty. He advocates abandonment of the traditional restrictions on Roman Catholics, and objects to confusion of ecclesiastical and civil offices. An established church he considers of doubtful value, as the early churches existed without civil aid, even with persecution; and to lean on civil aid is an admission of weakness. Yet he advocates reform rather than change, such as fewer articles of belief, more equal livings, greater toleration, and exclusion of clergy from civil duties.]

Richard Price
1723–1791

◄§ Richard Price's *Observations on the Nature of Civil Liberty* became, along with Tom Paine's *Common Sense*, a bible of the American Revolution. Published just before the Declaration of Independence in the spring of 1776, it went through thirteen editions in London alone in the same year, plus reprintings in Edinburgh, Boston, New York, and Philadelphia, and translation into the French. It is said that 60,000 copies were sold in the one year; and one John Stevenson complained that it was "replete with destruction to almost every state under heaven."

Price's book was, however, a restatement of familiar argument, not without its debt to Priestley, and couched in a language for popular comprehension. "We are not maintaining but violating our own constitution in America," was his contention; and he argued that discussion presupposed an understanding of liberty, divided by him into physical, moral, religious, and civil, the last subsuming the others, since "self-direction or self-government" is the one idea that runs through them all. Excerpts are from the Philadelphia edition, 1776 (microfilm). ⅋◦

Government of the People

It is obvious that all civil government, as far as it can be denominated *free*, is the creature of the people. It originates with them. It is conducted under their direction; and has in view nothing but their happiness. All its different forms are no more than so many different modes in which they choose to direct their affairs, and to secure the quiet enjoyment of their rights. In every free state every man is his own Legislator. All *taxes* are free-gifts for public service. All *laws* are particular provisions or regulations established by COMMON CONSENT for gaining protection and safety. And all *Magistrates* are Trustees or Deputies for carrying these regulations into execution.

Liberty, therefore, is too imperfectly defined when it is said to be "a Government by Laws, and not by Men." If the laws are made by one man, or a junto of men in a state, and not by COMMON CONSENT, a government by them does not differ from slavery. In this case, it would be a contradiction in terms to say that the state governs itself. . . .

Though all the members of a State should not be capable of giving their suffrages on public measures, individually and personally, they may do this by the appointment of Substitutes or Representatives. They may entrust the powers of Legislation, subject to such restrictions as they shall think necessary, with any number of *Delegates*; and whatever can be done by such delegates within the limits of their trust, may be considered as done by the united voice and counsel of the community. In this method a free government may be established in the largest state; and it is conceivable that by regulations of this kind, any number of states might be subjected to a scheme of government that would exclude the desolations of war, and produce universal peace and order. . . .

Government, as has been before observed, is in the very nature of it a Trust; and all its powers a Delegation for gaining particular ends. This trust may be misapplied and abused. It may be employed to defeat the very ends for which it was instituted; and to subvert the very rights which it ought to protect. . . . Nothing, then, can be more absurd than a doctrine which some have taught, with respect to the omnipotence of parliaments. They possess no power beyond the limits of the trust for the execution of which they were formed. If they contradict this trust, they betray their constituents, and dissolve themselves. All delegated power must be subordinate and limited. If omnipotence can, with any sense, be ascribed to a legislature, it must be lodged where all legislative authority originates; that is, in the PEOPLE. For *their* sakes government is instituted; and theirs is the only real omnipotence.

The Colonies

We have been so used to speak of the colonies as *our* Colonies, and to think of them as in a state of subordination to us, and as holding their existence in America only for our use, that it is no wonder the prejudices of many are alarmed, when they find a different doctrine maintained. The meanest person among us is disposed to look upon himself as having a body of subjects in America; and to be offended at the denial of his right to make laws for them, though perhaps he does not know what color they are of, or what language they talk. . . .

I have chosen to try this question by the general principles of Civil

Liberty; and not by the practice of former times; or by the Charters granted the colonies . . . The question with all liberal enquiries ought to be, not what jurisdiction over them Precedents, Statutes and Charters give, but what reason and equity and the rights of humanity give. This is, in truth, a question which no Kingdom has ever before had occasion to agitate. The case of a free country branching itself out in the manner Britain has done, and sending to a distant world colonies which have there, from small beginnings and free legislatures of their own, increased and formed a body of powerful states, likely soon to become superior to the parent state—this is a case which is new in the history of mankind; and it is extremely improper to judge of it by the rules of any narrow and partial policy; or to consider it on any other ground than the general one of reason and justice. . . .

The enquiry whether the war with the Colonies is a just war will be best determined by stating the power over them, which it is the end of the war to maintain: and this cannot be better done than in the words of an act of parliament made on purpose to define it. That act, it is well known, declares, "That this Kingdom has power, and of right ought to have power to make laws and statutes to bind the Colonies, and the people of America, in all cases whatever." Dreadful power indeed! I defy anyone to express slavery in stronger language. It is the same with declaring "that we have a right to do with them what we please! . . ."

If it means anything, it means that the property, and the legislations of the Colonies, are subject to the absolute discretion of Great Britain, and ought of right to be so. The nature of the thing admits of no limitation. The Colonies can never be admitted to be judges, how far the authority over them in these cases shall extend. This would be to destroy it entirely. If *any* part of their property is subject to *our* discretion, the *whole* must be so. If we have a right to interfere at all in their internal legislation, we have a right to interfere as far as we think proper. It is self-evident that this leaves them nothing they can call their own.

CONCLUSION

"The American are the first people whom Heaven has favoured with an opportunity of deliberating upon, and choosing the forms of government under which they should live. All other constitutions have derived their existence from violence or from accidental circumstances, and are therefore probably more distant from their perfection, which, though beyond our reach, may nevertheless be approached under the guidance of reason and experience." John Jay, in Charge to Ulster County, N. Y., Grand Jury, 1777.

"Whereas recognition of the inherent dignity and of the equal and inalienable rights of all members of the human family is the foundation of freedom, justice and peace in the world. . . ." *Universal Declaration of Human Rights*, United Nations General Assembly, Paris, Dec. 10, 1948.

CONCLUSION

THUS was the stage set for a new drama in self-government. Opportunity, a frontier habit of self-direction, distance from traditional patterns, the new science, and familiarity with a great body of literature on liberty and tyranny and the ways of government, all had blended into one of those rare moments in history when men take control of their own destinies. The shift, however gradual, had been from government by authority to government by consent and participation. "Protections" against tyranny were no less protection against hasty, ill-considered judgments on the part of one voice or many voices. Moderation more than revolution was the classical ideal of thoughtful men, preservation of ancient rights as well as independence.

Old institutions die hard, and the metaphors and assumptions on which they rest. American indifference to kingship, hereditary privilege, religious establishment, and resignation within one's social status, all hallowed by time and by loyalty, must have seemed to many a willful and reckless rebellion. Government, even today, seems to many in some mysterious way set apart from people. Yet the great contribution of the new science had been to supply new analogies and a new "authority," that of observation, reason and experience. At the same time, men, being men, had to be reassured by a new appeal to a God of rational "law" and an orderly cosmos. A revolution of another sort lies between the Puritan of early Massachusetts and the urbane Jefferson, a difference of philosophy and intellectual habit.

In 1774 the Colonial Congress embarked on elaborate debates. "The two points most labored were," wrote John Adams: "1. Whether we should recur to the law of nature, as well as the British constitution, and our American charters and grants. Mr. Galloway and Mr. Duane were for excluding the law of nature. I was very strenuous for retaining and insisting on it, as a resource to which we might be driven by Parliament, much sooner than we were aware. 2. The other question was, what authority should we concede to Parliament?"[1]

Why this concern over the "law of nature"? Because, as has been sufficiently indicated above, it had served amazingly well in providing just such sanctions, historical and broadly religious, as men deemed necessary to justify reform and rebellion. Thus the "Rights of the Colonists," 1772, advanced a clear appeal to the metaphysical argument; and the alert reader will easily detect in its language echoes of the past, not only from Aristotle, Cicero, Polybius, the Stoics, Tacitus and Lucretius, but also more clearly Coke, Harrington, Milton, Hooker, Grotius, Pufendorf, Locke, Burlamaqui and Blackstone. This document antedated the Declaration of Independence by four years. The "Declaration of Rights" of two years later opened with a literal quotation from its ancestor of 1688: "do in the first place, as Englishmen, etc. . . . Declare . . ."

Adams, put on the committee to draft the final form of this document, records that section four was opposed by Galloway who quoted "Burlamaqui, Grotius, Pufendorf, Hooker." Here, too, are plentiful echoes of Magna Carta, Coke, seventeenth century petitions, as well as Thucydides, Somers, Locke, Henry Care and Montesquieu. The word "liberty" alone in these early documents would provide material for a lengthy essay. These, too, were Declarations, not humble petitions.

In 1774 there appeared also Josiah Quincy's *Observations on . . . the Boston Port Bill*, John Adams' *History of the Dispute with America*, Jefferson's *Summary View*, product of intensive reading in the documentation of British liberties; and the "Virginia Declaration of Rights," most vigorous of them all, and thoroughly saturated with the ancient language; and finally, the Declaration of Independence," most historic, felicitous, and frugal statement of the political theory of the Revolution."[2] And in 1777 appeared in a report of a Virginia committee the "Virginia Statute of Religious Freedom," anticipated by section 16 of the Virginia Declaration of 1776, but not passed until 1785, after a spirited defense by James Madison. Its phrasing shows not a little of the

CONCLUSION

influence of Milton, Locke's *Essay on Toleration*, Shaftesbury, Voltaire, Deism, and Joseph Priestley. Finally, the Bill of Rights needed but the model of the old Declaration of 1688.

"The freedom of America," said Madison, "did not wait till usurped power had strengthened itself by exercise, and entangled the question in precedents . . . They avoided the consequences by denying the principle." "The establishment of civil and religious liberty," wrote George Washington, "was the motive which induced me to the field."[3]

Of the state constitutions which came up rapidly for revision, hardly a one failed to reaffirm the general principles of the day. "The body politic," said the Massachusetts constitution, 1780, a model for many others, "is formed by a voluntary association of individuals. It is a social compact, by which the whole people covenants with each citizen, and each citizen with the whole people, that all shall be governed by certain laws for the common good." Power is affirmed as in the people, and magistrates are seen as "substitutes and agents . . . as at all times accountable to them." Titles, exclusive privilege, government for profit or special interest, are all declared "absurd."[4]

In 1787, John Adams, then residing in England as American minister, began his *Defense of the Constitutions of Government of the United States of America*, published in three volumes in London. Once again he reviewed the long histories of Greece and Rome and the modern ideas of Montesquieu and Rousseau. In America the new Constitution was defended by the famous *Federalist Papers*, written by Hamilton, Madison, and Jay (only five papers). Numbers 18 through 20, jointly written, reviewed again the history of the Greek republics, the Germanic states, and the United Netherlands. "Experience," wrote Hamilton and Madison, "is the oracle of truth." Again, in numbers 37 through 48, Madison studied the ancient lawgivers and ancient states founded on single individuals as lessons of warning against concentrated powers. Most carefully in Number 10 Madison examined the causes and the cure for "factions," reasoning closely to his conclusion in favor of the republican principle. Here one may read the sober conclusions of men now confronted with the responsibilities of government.

James Wilson, also a signer of the Constitution, defended the new document in the same year, 1787, in his "Speech at the Convention of Pennsylvania." Vigorously he upheld the thesis that America had given birth to something new in government. "The science of government itself," he said, "seems yet to be almost in its state of infancy. Governments, in general, have been the result of force, of fraud, and of accident. After a period of six thousand years have elapsed since the creation, the United States exhibit to the world the first instance, as far as we can learn, of a nation, unattacked by external force, unconvulsed by domestic insurrections, assembling voluntarily, deliberating fully, and deciding calmly, concerning that system of government under which they would wish that they and their posterity should live. . . . One thing is very certain, that the doctrine of representation in government was altogether unknown to the ancients. Now the knowledge and practice of this doctrine is, in my opinion, essential to every system that can possess the qualities of freedom, wisdom and energy. . . . For the American states were reserved the glory and the happiness of diffusing this vital principle through all the constituent part of government."[5]

This is a significant statement. Years later, Jefferson reaffirmed it in a letter to a friend. "The full experiment of *government democratical, but representative*," he wrote, "*was and still is reserved for us*."[6] Again, as late as 1807, in response to a query, Jefferson can only answer that no perfect work on government has yet appeared—that for the present one must read Locke, Sidney, Priestley's *First Principles of Government*, and the *Federalist Papers*. These words link past and future, and permit no narrow chauvinism. The full text—the full heritage—was and is yet to be envisaged; for it must be the common inheritance wherever men concern themselves over good government. "The Cromwellian revolution was undefeated in America," said A. N. Whitehead, "so the two countries have developed along quite different lines."[7] The statement is illuminating, though far from sufficient. For the Americans had not looked to the past alone, nor remained Puritan alone, but were a part of the new times and the future. The old language of speculation had shifted to positive propositions, and history was to be launched on a new experiment.

A new world had, in fact, tried and found satisfactory a new way—a society unsaddled with aristocracy, with feudal or court assumptions of special privilege, with ecclesiastical hierarchies or military cliques. Ancient abuses had been modified, criminal laws rendered more humane, human equality and suffrage extended, free land and individual self-respect more widely distributed than ever before in history, church and state separated in mutual consideration, government by consent brought within practical range, principles of human right asserted and protected by checks and balances and frequent review, education made more generally available, and the humblest man inspired with aspirations beyond all former dreams. These were not trivial items in history.

With independence there would arise a new pride in autonomy and a new self-respect, the soberer side of the raucous boasting of a new land. Bryant and Cooper would reflect wonder in the presence of what Whitman called "the large unconscious scenery of my land with its lakes and forests." Emerson, Thoreau, Whitman would explore the resources of the democratic individual. Melville and Hawthorne would endeavor to exorcise the lingering shadows of Puritanism; and Lincoln would arise as a symbol of the native potential, patient, self-taught, simple and wise. Men abroad would study the new phenomenon: poets like Burns and Wordsworth and Goethe, students of politics like John Stuart Mill, observers like De Tocqueville and James Bryce.

In time, along with physical and industrial expansion, would come other reforms: the emancipation of slaves, the secret ballot, a more direct participation in elections, review and recall of officials, arbitration of labor disputes, a new alertness to the abuses of unchecked competition, a new homogeneity making less of origin or creed; and finally, the sobering reminder that the old forces of tyranny never rest, but arise with every opportunity to seize on history and to manipulate people in old and new cruelties.

Who shall say, even today, that there shall be no further contemplation of the conditions of human freedom? Every form of tyranny, in whatever degree, is based ultimately on a contempt for man in the large, on some creed of his static, unimprovable nature; "men led by men who do not believe in men," as Whitman warned. On what grounds are the exploiters exempt from the common lot? The answer is rarely forthcoming, for it rests finally on arrogance, seizure of power and privilege, an assumption of some mystic elevation or the compulsion of some secret ambition. The true qualifications for leadership, said Jefferson, are merit, and a value returned.

"Natural law" may have served its purpose in a bygone age. It is no longer a sacred fiction. Nevertheless, its force is felt whenever men speak of inherent rights; or when judges, finding themselves without precedents, speak in the name of what seems to them justice, equity, fair decision; for natural law is, after all, what is in the nature of things nearest to the common conception of justice, without reference to special advantages. To abandon the traditional appeal to human rights, rooted in the common nature of all men and his pragmatic presence in every state and in every form of government, would be to put trust in armed might alone.

Freedom, finally, is not an end, but a condition, a measure of the *quality* of living, a continual resistance to whatever debases mankind, a tension between the extremes of a brutish apathy and a ruthless exploitation of men, between the rights of the individual without whom there is no society, and the necessary concessions to society without which the individual is but a fragment of himself.

APPENDIXES AND INDEX

APPENDIX A

The purpose of Appendix A is to excerpt a few historic American documents for those who may wish to compare them with the main text.

The Rights of the Colonists, 1772. (For complete text, see *The Writings of Samuel Adams*, ed. H. A. Cushing, New York: G. P. Putnam's, 1904, II, 350ff.) In the following excerpts, punctuation has been modernized.

Among the natural rights of the Colonists are these: First, a right to Life; secondly, to Liberty; thirdly, to Property; together with the right to support and defend them in the best manner they can. These are evident branches of, rather than deductions from the Duty of Self Preservation, commonly called the First Law of Nature.

All men have a right to remain in a State of Nature as long as they please: and in case of intollerable oppression, civil or religious, to leave the Society they belong to, and enter into another.

When men enter into Society, it is by voluntary consent; and they have a right to demand and insist upon the performance of such conditions and previous limitations as form an equitable *original compact.*

Every natural right not expressly given up or from the nature of a Social Compact necessarily ceded remains.

All positive and civil laws should conform as far as possible to the law of natural reason and equity.

As neither reason requires, nor religion permits the contrary, every man living in or out of a state of civil society has a right peaceably and quietly to worship God according to the dictates of his conscience. . . .

In short, it is the greatest absurdity to suppose it in the power of one or any number of men at the entering into society, to renounce their essential natural rights, or the means of preserving those rights when the great end of civil government from the very nature of its institutions is for the support, protection and defence of those very rights; the principal of which as is before observed, are life, liberty and property. If men through fear, fraud or mistake, should *in terms* renounce and give up any essential natural right, the eternal law of reason and the great end of society would absolutely vacate such renunciation; the right to freedom being *the gift* of God Almighty, it is not in the power of man to alienate this gift, and voluntarily become a slave. . . .

All persons born in the British American Colonies are by the laws of God and nature, and by the Common law of England, *exclusive of all charters from the Crown*, well entitled, and by the Acts of the British Parliament are declared to

INTELLECTUAL ORIGINS

be entitled to all the natural essential, inherent and inseparable Rights, Liberties and Privileges of Subjects born in Great Britain, or within the Realm. . . .

It is utterly irreconcileable to these principles, and to many other fundamental maxims of the common law, common sense and reason, that a British house of commons, should have a right, at pleasure, to give and grant the property of the colonists.

Declaration of Rights, Continental Congress of 1774. (For text, see *Works of John Adams*, ed. C. F. Adams, Boston, 1856, II, 374ff and 535ff.)

[After the Whereas clauses of abuse of power on the part of the British]:

The good people of the several colonies . . . justly alarmed at these arbitrary proceedings of Parliament and the Administration have severally elected, constituted and appointed deputies, to meet and sit in General Congress, in the city of Philadelphia, in order to obtain such establishment as that their religion, laws, and liberties may not be subverted. Whereupon the deputies so appointed, being now assembled, in a full and free representation of these Colonies, taking into their most serious consideration the best means of attaining the ends aforesaid, do in the first place, as *Englishmen*, their ancestors, in like cases have usually done, for asserting and vindicating their rights and liberties, DECLARE—

That the inhabitants of the English Colonies in North America, by the immutable laws of nature, the principles of the English Constitution, and the several charters or compacts, have the following RIGHTS:

1. That they are entitled to life, liberty, and property, and that they have never ceded to any sovereign power whatsoever a right to dispose of either, without their consent.

2. That our ancestors, who first settled these Colonies, were, at the time of their emigration from the mother country, entitled to all the rights, liberties and immunities of free and natural born subjects, within the realm of England.

3. That by such emigration they by no means forfeited, surrendered, or lost any of those rights, but that they were, and their descendents now are, entitled to the exercise and enjoyment of all such of them, as their local and other circumstances enable them to exercise and enjoy.

4. That the foundation of English liberty, and of all free government, is a right in the people to participate in their legislative council; and as the English colonists are not represented . . . in the British Parliament, they are entitled to a free and exclusive power of legislation in their several Provincial Legislatures, where their right of representation can alone be preserved, in all cases of taxes and internal polity, subject only to the negative of their sovereign, in such a manner as has been hitherto used and accustomed. But, from the necessity of the case, and a regard to the mutual interest of both countries, we cheerfully consent to the operation of such acts of the British Parliament as are, *bona fide*, restrained to the regulation of our external commerce, for the purpose of securing the commercial advantages of the whole empire to the mother country, and the commercial benefits of its respective members; excluding every idea of taxation, internal or external, for raising a revenue on the subjects of America, without their consent.

5. That the respective Colonies are entitled to the common law of England, and more especially to the great and inestimable privilege of being tried by their peers of the vicinage, according to the course of that law.

6. That they are entitled to the benefit of such of the English statutes as existed at the time of their colonization, and which they have, by experience, respectively found to be applicable to their several local and other circumstances.

7. That these, his Majesty's Colonies, are likewise entitled to all the immunities and privileges granted and confirmed to them by royal charters, or secured by their several codes of provincial laws.

8. That they have a right peaceably to assemble, consider of their grievances, and petition the King; and that all prosecutions, prohibitory proclamations, and commitments for the same, are illegal.

9. That the keeping a standing army in these Colonies, in times of peace, without the consent of the Legislature of that Colony in which such army is kept, is against law.

10. It is indispensably necessary to good government, and rendered essential by the English Constitution, that the constituent branches of the Legislature be independent of each other; that therefore the exercise of legislative power in several Colonies, by a Council appointed during pleasure by the Crown, is unconstitutional, dangerous, and destructive to the freedom of American legislation.

All and each of which the aforesaid deputies, in behalf of themselves and their constituents, do claim, demand, and insist on, as their indubitable rights and liberties; which cannot be legally taken from them, altered or abridged, by any power whatever, without their own consent, by their representatives in their several Provincial legislatures. . . .

[The document concludes with a list of "infringements and violations of the foregoing rights" to which Americans cannot submit, but hopes that happiness and prosperity may be restored by peaceable measures.]

The Virginia Declaration of Rights. (This document was adopted almost a month before the Declaration of Independence. It was one of the most forthright of all colonial documents. The text is taken from *A Collection of all such Acts of the General Assembly of Virginia,* Richmond, 1794.)

A DECLARATION OF RIGHTS made by the Representatives of the good people of Virginia, assembled in full and free Convention, which rights do pertain to them, and their Posterity, as the basis and Foundation of Government.

1. That all men are by nature equally free and independent, and have certain inherent rights, of which, when they enter into a state of society, they cannot, by any compact, deprive or divest their posterity; namely, the enjoyment of life and liberty, with the means of acquiring and possessing property, and pursuing and obtaining happiness and safety.

2. That all power is vested in, and consequently derived from, the people; that Magistrates are their trustees and servants, and at all times amenable to them.

3. That government is, or ought to be, instituted for the common benefit, protection and security of the people, nation, or community; of all the various modes and forms of government, that is best, which is capable of producing the greatest degree of happiness and safety, and is most effectually secured against the danger of mal-administration; and that when any government shall be found inadequate or contrary to these purposes, a majority of the community hath an indubitable, unalienable, and indefeasible right to reform, alter, or abolish it, in such manner as shall be judged most conducive to the public weal.

4. That no man, or set of men, are entitled to exclusive or separate emoluments or privileges from the community, but in consideration of public services; which not being descendible, neither ought the offices of Magistrate, Legislator, or Judge, to be hereditary.

5. That the Legislative and Executive powers of the state should be separate and distinct from the Judiciary; and that the members of the two first may be restrained from oppression, by feeling and participating the burthens of the people, they should, at fixed periods, be reduced to a private station, return into that body from which they were originally taken, and the vacancies be supplied by frequent, certain, and regular elections, in which all, or any part of the former members, to be again eligible, or ineligible, as the laws shall direct.

6. That elections of members to serve as representatives of the people, in Assembly, ought to be free; and that all men having sufficient evidence of permanent

ommon interest with, and attachment to, the community, have the right of suffrage, and cannot be taxed or deprived of their property for public uses, without heir own consent, or that of their representatives so elected, nor bound by any w to which they have not, in like manner, assented, for the public good.

7. That all power of suspending laws, or the execution of laws, by any author-·y without consent of the representatives of the people, is injurious to their rights, nd ought not be exercised.

8. That in all capital or criminal prosecutions, a man hath a right to demand the cause and nature of his accusation, to be confronted with the accusers and witnesses, to call for evidence in his favor, and to a speedy trial by an impartial ·ury of his vicinage, without whose unanimous consent he cannot be found guilty, 1or can he be compelled to give evidence against himself; that no man be deprived >f his liberty except by the law of the land, or the judgment of his peers.

9. That excessive bail ought not to be required, nor excessive fines imposed, nor ·ruel and unusual punishments inflicted.

10. That general warrants, whereby an officer or messenger may be commanded to search suspected places without evidence of a fact committed, or to seize any person or persons not named, or whose offence is not particularly described and supported by evidence, are grievous and oppressive, and ought not to be granted.

11. That in controversies respecting property, and in suits between man and man, the ancient trial by jury is preferable to any other, and ought to be held sacred.

12. That the freedom of the press is one of the great bulwarks of liberty, and can never be restrained but by despotic governments.

13. That a well regulated militia, composed of the body of the people, trained to arms, is the proper, natural and safe defence of a free state; that standing armies, in time of peace, should be avoided, as dangerous to liberty; and that in all cases, the military should be under strict subordination to, and governed by, the civil power.

14. That the people have a right to uniform government; and therefore, that no government separate from, or independent of, the government of *Virginia*, ought to be erected or established within the limits thereof.

15. That no free government, or the blessing of liberty, can be preserved to any people but by a firm adherence to justice, moderation, temperance, frugality, and virtue, and by a frequent recurrence to fundamental principles.

16. That religion, or the duty which we owe to our Creator, and the manner of discharging it, can be directed only by reason and conviction, not by force or violence; and therefore all men are equally entitled to the free exercise of religion, according to the dictates of conscience; and that it is the mutual duty of all to practise Christian forbearance, love, and charity towards each other.

The Virginia Statute of Religious Freedom, 1777-1785. (Even more startling to the traditionalists must have been this statute, regarded by Jefferson with pride as one of his three major achievements. Written in 1777, it was affirmed by the Virginia legislature in 1785. Quotation is from the *Report of the Committee of Revisors Appointed by the General Assembly of Virginia, 1776*, as printed in Richmond in 1784. Italics are used to indicate phrases omitted in the form reaffirmed in 1794 and following.)

AN ACT FOR ESTABLISHING RELIGIOUS FREEDOM. *Well aware that the opinion and beliefs of men depend not on their own will, but follow involuntarily the evidence proposed to their minds; that* [Whereas] Almighty God hath created the mind free, *and manifested his supreme will that free it shall remain by making it altogether insusceptible of restraint;* that all attempts to influence it by temporal punishment, or burdens, or by civil incapacitations, tend only to beget habits of hypocrisy and meanness, and are a departure from the plan of the holy author of our religion, who being lord both of body and mind, yet chose not to propagate it by coercions on either, as was in his Almighty power to do, *but to extend it by its influence on reason alone*; that the impious presumption of legislators and rulers, civil as well as ecclesiastical, who, being themselves but fallible and unin-spired men, have assumed dominion over the faith of others, setting up their own opinions and modes of thinking as the only true and infallible, and as such, en-deavoring to impose them on others, have established and maintained false religions over the greatest part of the world, and through all time; that to compel a man to furnish contributions of money for the propagation of opinions which he dis-believes *and abhors* is sinful and tyrannical; and even the forcing him to support this or that teacher of his own religious persuasion, is depriving him of the com-fortable liberty of giving his contributions to the particular pastor whose morals he would make his pattern, and whose powers he feels most persuasive to right-eousness; and is withdrawing from the ministry those temporary rewards which proceeding from an approbation of their personal conduct, are an additional in-citement to earnest and unremitting labors for the instruction of mankind; that our civil rights have no dependence on our religious opinions, any more than our opinions in physics or geometry; that therefore the proscribing any citizen as un-worthy the public confidence by laying upon him an incapacity of being called to offices of trust and emolument, unless he profess or renounce this or that re-ligious opinion, is depriving him injuriously of those privileges and advantages to which, in common with his fellow-citizens, he has a natural right; that it tends also to corrupt the principles of that *very* religion it is meant to encourage, by bribing, with a monopoly of worldly honors and emoluments, those who will externally profess and conform to it; that though indeed these are criminal who do not with-stand such temptation, yet neither are those innocent who lay the bait in their way; *that the opinions of men are not the object of civil government, nor under its jurisdiction*; that to suffer the civil magistrate to intrude his powers into the field of opinion and to restrain the profession or propagation of principles on sup-position of their ill tendency is a dangerous fallacy, which at once destroys all religious liberty, because he being of course judge of that tendency will make his opinions the rule of judgment, and approve or condemn the sentiments of others only as they shall square with or differ from his own; that it is time enough for the rightful purposes of civil government for its officers to interfere when prin-ciples break out into overt acts against peace and good order; and finally, that truth is great and will prevail if left to herself; that she is the proper and suffi-cient antagonist to error, and has nothing to fear from the conflict unless by human interposition disarmed of her natural weapons, free argument and debate; errors ceasing to be dangerous when it is permitted freely to contradict them:

We the General Assembly of Virginia do enact [changed to: Be it enacted by the general assembly] that no man shall be compelled to frequent or support any religious worship, place, or ministry whatsoever, nor shall be enforced, restrained, molested, or burdened in his body or goods, nor shall otherwise suffer, on account of his religious opinions or belief; but that all men shall be free to profess, and by argument to maintain, their opinions in matters of religion, and that the same shall in no wise diminish, enlarge, or affect their civil capacities.

And though we well know that this Assembly, elected by the people for the ordinary purposes of legislation only, have no power to restrain the acts of suc-ceeding Assemblics, constituted with powers equal to our own, and that therefore to declare this act *to be* irrevocable would be of no effect in law; yet we are free to declare, and do declare, that the rights hereby asserted are of the natural rights of mankind, and that if any act shall be hereafter passed to repeal the present, or to narrow its operation, such Act will be an infringement of natural right.

INTELLECTUAL ORIGINS

For those who may wish to refresh their minds on the wording of the Declaration of Independence and the Constitution, they are given in part below.

Declaration of Independence. When, in the course of human events, it becomes necessary for one people to dissolve the political bands which have connected them with another, and to assume, among the powers of the earth, the separate and equal station to which the laws of nature and of nature's God entitle them, a decent respect to the opinions of mankind requires that they should declare the causes which impel them to the separation.

We hold these truths to be self-evident: that all men are created equal; that they are endowed by their Creator with certain unalienable rights; that among these are life, liberty, and the pursuit of happiness; that to secure these rights, governments are instituted among men, deriving their just powers from the consent of the governed; that whenever any form of government becomes destructive of these ends, it is the right of the people to alter or to abolish it, and to institute a new government, laying its foundations on such principles, and organizing its powers in such form, as to them shall seem most likely to effect their safety and happiness. Prudence, indeed, will dictate that governments long established should not be changed for light and transient causes; and, accordingly, all experience hath shown that mankind are more disposed to suffer, while evils are sufferable, than to right themselves by abolishing the forms to which they are accustomed. But when a long train of abuses and usurpations, pursuing invariably the same object, evinces a design to reduce them under absolute despotism, it is their right, it is their duty, to throw off such government, and to provide new guards for their future security. Such has been the patient sufferance of these colonies, and such is now the necessity which constrains them to alter their former systems of government.

[There follows the list of grievances.]

THE CONSTITUTION. *Preamble.* We, the people of the United States, in order to form a more perfect union, establish justice, insure domestic tranquility, provide for the common defense, promote the general welfare, and secure the blessings of liberty to ourselves and our posterity, do ordain and establish this Constitution for the United States of America.

THE BILL OF RIGHTS. *Amendments I–X.* Article I. Congress shall make no law respecting an establishment of religion, or prohibiting the free exercise thereof; or abridging the freedom of speech, or of the press; or the right of people peaceably to assemble, and to petition the Government for a redress of grievances.

Article II. A well-regulated militia being necessary to the security of a free State, the right of the people to keep and bear arms shall not be infringed.

Article III. No soldier shall, in time of peace, be quartered in any house without the consent of the owner, nor in time of war, but in a manner to be prescribed by law.

Article IV. The right of the people to be secure in their persons, houses, papers and effects, against unreasonable searches and seizures, shall not be violated, and no warrants shall issue but upon probable cause, supported by oath or affirmation, and particularly describing the place to be searched, and the person or things to be seized.

Article V. No person shall be held to answer for a capital or otherwise infamous crime, unless on a presentment or indictment of a grand jury, except in cases arising in the land or naval forces, or in the militia, when in actual service in time of war or public danger; nor shall any person be subject for the same offense to be twice put in jeopardy of life and limb; nor shall be compelled in any criminal case to be a witness against himself, nor be deprived of life, liberty, or property, without due process of law; nor shall private property be taken for public use without just compensation.

Article VI. In all criminal prosecutions, the accused shall enjoy a right to a speedy and public trial, by an impartial jury of the State and district wherein the crime shall have been committed, which district shall have been previously ascertained by law, and to be informed of the nature and cause of the accusation; to be confronted with the witnesses against him; to have compulsory process for obtaining witnesses in his favor, and to have the assistance of counsel for his defense.

Article VII. In suits at common law, where the value in controversy shall exceed twenty dollars, the right of trial by jury shall be preserved, and no fact tried by a jury shall be otherwise re-examined in any court of the United States than according to the rules of the common law.

Article VIII. Excessive bail shall not be required, nor excessive fines imposed, nor cruel and unusual punishments inflicted.

Article IX. The enumeration in the Constitution of certain rights shall not be construed to deny or disparage others retained by the people.

Article X. The powers not delegated to the United States by the Constitution, nor prohibited by it to the States, are reserved to the States respectively, or to the people.

APPENDIX B

Additional Reading and Notes

Some titles of general usefulness are suggested immediately below. Introductory notes and footnotes mention others for those who wish to pursue collateral readings.

For books printed in early America, see Charles Evans, *American Bibliography, 1638–1820* (Chicago, 1903–1934); also *Early American Imprints, 1639–1800* (Ed., Clifford K. Shipton, Worcester, Mass.: American Antiquarian Society, 1955-), with Readex Microprints. These, of course, do not record the vastly greater number of books imported from Europe. These must be discovered from library lists and other sources. Those interested in the education and reading of early American figures will need to delve into collected works, autobiographies, letters and papers, etc.

We need not list here the available collected works of our major colonial figures: John Adams, John Quincy Adams, Samuel Adams, John Dickinson, Benjamin Franklin, Alexander Hamilton, Thomas Jefferson (*The Papers of Thomas Jefferson*, now in progress under the direction of Julian Boyd at Princeton University, will be invaluable), James Madison, James Otis, George Washington, James Wilson, and others; as well as the *Federalist Papers*, and Max Farrand, *Records of the Federal Convention of 1787* (New Haven: Yale University Press, 1927). Jefferson alone challenges the student endlessly. See E. Millicent Sowerby's *Catalogue of the Library of Thomas Jefferson*, books by Gilbert Chinard, Karl Lehman's *Thomas Jefferson, American Humanist* (New York: Macmillan, 1947), Arthur Bestor's admirable essay on Jefferson's reading in *Three Presidents and Their Books* (Urbana: University of Illinois Press, 1955), and Trevor Colbourn's studies in the field.

There are so many studies in the area of early American history that only a few can be mentioned. The following are of interest:

Becker, Carl, *The Declaration of Independence* (New York: Harcourt, Brace, 1922).

Boorstin, Daniel, *The Americans: The Colonial Experience* (New York: Random, 1958).

Commager, Morris, *Living Ideas in America* (New York: Harper, 1951).

Corwin, Edwin S., *The 'Higher Law' Background of American Constitutional*

APPENDIX B

Law (Ithaca: Cornell Great Seal Books, 1955). A reprint of a classic statement of the concept of the "law of nature" from the Stoics on down.

Curti, Merle, *Growth of American Thought* (New York: Harper, 1943).

Hacker, Louis, *The Shaping of the American Tradition* (New York: Columbia University Press, 1947).

Koch, G. A., Republican Religion: *The American Revolution and the Cult of Reason* (New York: Holt, 1933).

Morais, Herbert, *Deism in the Eighteenth Century* (New York: Columbia University Press, 1934). The subject needs redoing.

Morgan, Edward S., *The Birth of the Republic, 1763-1789* (Chicago: University of Chicago Press, 1956).

Rossiter, Clinton, *Seedtime of the Republic* (New York: Harcourt, Brace, 1953). See footnote below.

Savelle, Max, *Seeds of Liberty* (New York: Knopf, 1948).

Shores, Louis, *Origins of the American College Library, 1638-1800* (New York: Barnes and Noble, 1935).

Wright, Benjamin F., *American Interpretations of Natural Law* (Cambridge, Mass.: Harvard University Press, 1931).

Wright, L. B., *The Cultural Life of the American Colonies* (New York: Harper, 1957).

A few general titles may be added:

Becker, Carl, *The Heavenly City of the Eighteenth Century Philosophers* (New Haven: Yale University Press, 1932).

Cassirer, Ernst, *The Philosophy of the Enlightenment* (Princeton: Princeton University Press, 1951). Also in Beacon Press paperback, 1955. See especially Chap. VI, "Law, State and Society."

Ebenstein, William, *Great Political Thinkers* (New York: Rinehart, 1941).

Edman, Irwin, *Fountainheads of Freedom* (New York: Raynal and Hitchcock, 1941).

Laski, Harold, *Political Thought in England from Locke to Bentham* (New York: Holt, 1920).

McIver, R. M., *Great Expressions of Human Rights* (New York: Harper, 1950).

Monaghan, Frank, *Heritage of Freedom* (Princeton: Princeton University Press, 1947).

Randall, J. R., *Making of the Modern Mind* (Boston: Houghton Mifflin, 1940).

Sabine, George, *A History of Political Theory* (New York: Holt, 1937). A standard work.

Notes

GENERAL INTRODUCTION

1. John Adams, "Novanglus," *Works*, ed. Ch. F. Adams (Boston, 1850-56), IV, 15. Of the "general principles" behind the Revolution, said Adams (Letter to Jefferson, June 28, 1813), "I could fill sheets of quotations from Frederic of Prussia, from Hume, Gibbon, Bolingbroke, Rousseau, and Voltaire, as well as Newton and Locke; not to mention thousands ... of inferior fame."

2. *General Laws and Liberties of the Mass. Colony* (Boston, 1672), in *Amer. Culture Ser.* (microfilm). The Mass. General Court in 1647 ordered Coke on Littleton, on Magna Carta, and Coke's Reports.

3. See Max Savelle's *Seeds of Liberty*; also Daniel Boorstin's *The Americans: The Colonial Experience*, which defends the thesis of an American contribution not dependent on bookish sources.

4. See Alice M. Baldwin, *The New England Clergy and the American Revolution* (Durham, N. Car.: Duke Univ. Press, 1928), which, perhaps, grants an undue

INTELLECTUAL ORIGINS

amount of influence to the clergy, though it was not small. Jonathan Boucher (*Reminiscences of an American Loyalist, 1738–1789*) said "Much execution was done by sermons," and accused Puritan sermons, preached and printed, of working people into a frenzy.

5. See Zoltan Haraszti, *John Adams and the Prophets of Democracy* (Cambridge, Mass.: Harvard Univ. Press, 1952), a fine study of Adams and his marginal debates with the books he read. Most of this reading, however, follows the Revolution. The quotation below ("Study governments, etc.") is from a letter to John Taylor, Nov. 16, 1814.

6. J. R. Randall, *Making of the Modern Mind*, p. 376. See especially Chapters XII-XIV, summary of the eighteenth century mind; which, says Randall (p. 309), combining the humanistic emphasis with the scientific, created a new science of human nature. Ernst Cassirer, *The Philosophy of the Enlightenment*, p. 252, says that the American States "have the distinction of being the first to convert the great ideas of the century into action."

7. John Adams (*Works*, III, 22–23): "I had read Harrington, Sidney, Hobbes, Nedham, and Locke, but with very little application to any particular views, till these debates in Congress ... turned my thoughts to these researches, which produced the 'Thoughts on Government,' the Constitution of Massachusetts, and at length the 'Defense of the Constitutions of the United States,' and the 'Discourses on Davila'"; to which writings he attributes also some of the constitutions of states and of the nation.

Clinton Rossiter's *Seedtime of the Republic* (pp. 356-361) is in substantial agreement with my general selection of sources. I should have been indebted to his study had I seen it earlier..

PART I. THE CLASSICAL HERITAGE

1. Quotation from Thomas Francklin's translation, London, 1752.

2. Of interest on the classical element in American history are:

Chinard, Gilbert, "Jefferson as a Classical Scholar," *American Scholar*, 1:132-143 (1932). Chinard makes a convincing case in his *Thomas Jefferson* (University of Michigan Paperbacks, 1957, pp. 26, 63) for the classical sources of Jefferson's politics and his personal philosophy; gathered, says Chinard, "stone by stone and maxim by maxim, from the old Greek Stoics." He "felt more kinship with Greece and Republican Rome than with the philosophers of London, Paris, or Geneva." So others; e.g., Abiel Holmes' *Life of Ezra Stiles* (Boston, 1798), in which young Stiles in the 1740's draws up his *ratio vivendi*, concluding "I consider myself a citizen of the intellectual world."

Gummere, R. M., "Socrates at the Printing Press. Franklin and the Classics," *Classical Weekly*, XXVI:17 (Dec. 5, 1932).

Holborn, Hajo, "History and Study of the Classics," *Journal of the History of Ideas*, XIV:35-50 (January 1953). A solid study.

Mullet, Charles F., "Classical Influences on the American Revolution," *Classical Journal*, 35:92-98 (November 1939).

Robanthan, Dorothy, "John Adams and the Classics," *New England Quarterly*, 19:91-98 (1946).

Smart, G. K., "Private Libraries in Colonial Virginia," *American Literature*, 10:37ff (1938-39).

Wright, L. B., "The Classical Tradition in Virginia," *Papers of the Bibliographical Society of America*, 33:85ff (1939).

————, "Jefferson and the Classics," *Proceedings of the American Philosophical Society*, 87:223-233 (1943).

APPENDIX B

See also Dumas Malone, *Jefferson and His Time* (Boston, Little Brown, 1948), Vol. I, on Jefferson's education.

3. The pervasive classical influence long antedates, of course, the American eighteenth century. For comment see Appendix C.

4. *The Cambridge History of English Literature* (1933) contains a chapter on 16 and 17th century translation. See also F. O. Mathiessen, *Translation: An Elizabethan Art* (Harvard Univ. Press, 1931). Histories of printing in Europe are available. G. H. Putnam's (1896) is still good.

5. Modern translations are Benjamin Jowett's (Oxford, 1900), and R. Crawley's (Modern Lib., 1934). Thucydides wrote on colonies (I, 34): "Every colony that is well treated honors its parent state, but becomes estranged from it by injustice. For colonies are not sent forth on the understanding that they are to be slaves... but that they are to be equals."

6. The Spens translation in Everyman's Library (1906) was replaced around 1935 by J. D. Lindslay's. Other translations are the Davies and Vaughan (1852) and Jowett's. See George Sabine's *History of Political Theory* on Plato and Aristotle.

7. The Ellis translation was from the French of Louis le Roy. Many translations of Aristotle are available. Standard are Jowett and the Smith and Ross (Oxford, 1908–1931). Errata in text: P. 43, middle line, middle parag., insert "certain" – "city is a certain number." P. 46, l. 4, insert "mutual" – "increases mutual confidence." P. 47, l. 9, Polybius, insert "its" – "into its congenial evil."

8. See Gilbert Chinard, "Polybius and the American Constitution," *Jo. of the Hist. of Ideas,* I:38–58 (Jan. 1940). Said John Adams (*Works*, IV, 440): "Polybius thinks it manifest, both from reason and experience, that the best form of government is not simple, but compounded, because of the tendency of each of the simple forms to degenerate." Polybius returned from captivity in Rome from 168 to 152 B.C. to examine how and with what institutions "almost the whole habitable world, in less than the course of fifty-three years, was reduced to the Roman yoke"; and to write the first "General History." So even was the balance, he says, that even the Romans could not be sure whether their state was an aristocracy, a democracy, or a monarchy. The mixture it seemed scarcely possible to improve upon, he thought.

9. See Virgil's *Aeneid*, Book VI, in which Anchises shows his son the long history of Rome, and apostrophizes Rome thus (freely rendered): "Forget not, O Rome, to rule the people in thy empire: these be thy arts: to impose the habits of peace; to treat subjects with forbearance, and to subdue the arrogant." (lines 851–853)

10. Cicero raises ever-practical questions: Is law merely force, or also Right? Is the only crime to be caught? Is whatever is law therefore just? What is justice, then? Could we dispense with law? Is man for the State or the State for man? Can a general law be found to which all men conform? If so, how is it known? For Cicero, the authority of government lies in established laws and public opinion. Men are equal before impartial, impersonal law. He divides law into *jus civile* (civil law, adapted to local needs), *jus gentium* (common agreement between nations), and *jus naturale* (natural law, borrowed from Stoic philosophy, the order of Nature, discoverable by reason and experience, to which all law eventually conforms. (Local laws on traffic will vary; ships on the high seas sail under international agreements; all traffic obeys laws of physical motion.)

Edwin S. Corwin (see Bibliography) says that Cicero gave to the world of law the Stoic idea of natural law; and Ch. P. Curtis (*It's Your Law*, Harvard Univ. Press, 1954, p. 33) says "The lawyer must go back of Christianity to Stoicism for the vicarious detachment which will permit him to serve his client"; for Stoicism taught craftsmanship within the possibilities, instead of the Platonic absolutes. Hiram

INTELLECTUAL ORIGINS

Haydn in *The Counter-Renaissance* (New York: Scribner's, 1950, p. 53) says: "Cicero's interpretation of the Stoic Law of Nature ... was most influential in the Renaissance movements toward a natural religion and an independent humanistic ethic." The American "Rights of the Colonists" (1772), Appendix A, echoes Cicero as does the Declaration of Independence, in "laws of nature and Nature's God."

11. Stoic thought, says Giorgio Santillana (in *Science and the Modern Mind*, ed. George Bolton, Boston: Beacon Press, 1958, p. 31) "acted as a kind of Trojan horse which established inside the consensus of public opinion the plausibility of the materialistic view." See, however, in Appendix C, Note 3, the Epicurean and Lucretian contribution.

Standard references on Stoic and Epicurean are: E. Zeller, *Stoics, Epicureans and Skeptics* (London, 1892); Cyril Bailey, *The Greek Atomists and Epicurus* (Oxford: Clarendon Press, 1929); William Oates, *The Stoic and Epicurean Philosophers* (New York: Random, 1940); and a corrective of Zeller's interpretation of the Epicureans, Norman W. DeWitt, *Epicurus and his Philosophy* (Univ. of Minnesota Press, 1954).

12. A most readable prose translation of Lucretius is R. E. Latham, in the Penguin Classics, 1951. See also George Hadzit, *Lucretius and his Influence* (New York: Longman, Green, 1935). Note 3 in Appendix C touches on the influence of Lucretius.

13. Actually, Lucretius says to live "under law and strict justice." Creech gives the passage a Whig turn by "elected." Lucretius follows this passage by an analysis of the origin of religious fears. He gives, too, an idyllic picture of primitive man, shepherd and husbandman, reclining beneath tall trees to the accompaniment of conversation, dancing and music; from which men turned to competition and wars — a source for Rousseau.

14. Seneca stressed the milder virtues, moderation, resignation to the law of the universe. "Virtue," he argued, "is open to all; as well to servants and exiles as to Princes." Montaigne was called a French Seneca, and Emerson took something from Seneca's "inner truth" and self-reliance. See R. M. Gummere, *Seneca the Philosopher* (Boston, 1922).

15. Cato was a favorite signature in colonial newspapers. Jefferson called George Wythe "the Cato of his country ... a more disinterested person never lived." (*Writings*, I, 169).

PART II. THE ENGLISH HERITAGE

1. Lyon Haștings and Herman Block, *Edward Coke, Oracle of the Law* (Boston: Houghton Mifflin, 1929, p. 49); see also Elizabeth D. Bowen, *The Lion and the Throne* (Boston: Atlantic Monthly Press, 1957). Magna Carta became a symbol of law over individual will, and of *contract* between ruler and citizen; so Fortescue interpreted it even earlier.

2. The chasm that lies between the acrimonies of the religious wars and the American late eighteenth century may be surmised from Jefferson's note to Madison, Dec. 16, 1786: "It is honorable for us to have produced the first legislature who had the courage to declare that the reason of man may be trusted with the formation of his own opinion."

Some may question the absence of St. Thomas Aquinas from American political thinking. Though he appears in some earlier libraries, he "might just as well never have written his expositions of higher law," says Clinton Rossiter (*Seedtime of the Republic*, p. 356), for all the mention of him. Whatever influence he had was indirect, via Hooker or Grotius. His political thinking was largely derivative from Aristotle, subsumed, of course, under the Church. See A. P. D'Entrères, *Saint Thomas Aquinas: Selected Political Writings* (J. G. Dawson, Ed., Oxford: Blackwell, 1949, Latin-English text). Nevertheless, the Aquinian admission of "natural law" as a part of the divine order, comprehended by reason without revelation, opened the door, it has been said, to a renewed analysis of the state on rational grounds. It appears unlikely that American political writers observed such links; for, in last analysis, Aquinas was too authoritarian and scholastic for their purpose of creating a free society of "We the people."

3. See Russell Ames, *Citizen Thomas More and his Utopia* (Princeton University Press, 1949). More's *Utopia* was scarcely democratic. More's Renaissance enthusiasm appears in his picturing the Utopians learning quickly to read Greek and setting great store by Plutarch, and others. More was to test by his death the proposition that a king could decide the religion of his subjects.

4. Sir John Fortescue, chief justice 1442–1461, wrote his *De Laudibus* in the 1460's, in exile from England. It appeared frequently in English after 1516. It presented the laws of England as materially different from those of the continent, and praised the jury system as a protection against the cruelties of torture in France. He advises the young prince to study the laws of England as the product of wise men and a protection to a sovereign.

5. Jonathan Mayhew, *Memoirs* (Boston, 1838), p. 194. Milton has been thoroughly edited in recent years. Jefferson appears to have drawn from Milton's *Reason of Church Government Urged* in his Bill for Religious Freedom, 1777. See C. R. Cragg, *Puritanism to the Age of Reason* (Cambridge Univ. Press, 1950).

6. Harrington, said Hall in his Preface, was convinced that government was not as accidental as people imagined, their being natural causes to produce natural effects. Changes were due to "changes in the balance of property." Harrington quoted Grotius, Hooker, Cicero, and others. He urged a senate to propose, people to enact through representatives, a magistracy to enforce, laws. See *The Political Writings of James Harrington* (Ed., Ch. Blitzer, New York: The Liberal Arts Press, 1955); also Theodore W. Dwight, "Harrington and his Influence upon American Political Institutions and Political Thought," *Pol. Sci. Quar.*, II (1887).

7. See Caroline Robbins, "Algernon Sidney's *Discourses*...", *William and Mary Quar.*, IV, 3 (July 1947), 267–296. The article reproduces a cartoon from the London *Political Register* of 1769, showing Americans hurling Locke, Sidney, and Calvin's Works at a departing Anglican bishop.
The temptation is very great to quote further from Sidney. Franklin proposed in 1749 that Sidney be published as a "classic"; Jefferson linked him with Locke as a prime source, and Adams called him "a great and worthy man." Franklin found useful the statement in the text (III, XXXVI) on rebellion, especially his "Men who have never been subdued cannot be said to rebel against those who wish to subdue them." Sidney argued that it was foolish to say that a good man will not abuse power; for it is power that passes on, not the man.

8. It is given to few men in history to shift a major analogy, as Locke shifted a political one from paternalism to a fiduciary trust. (Adams later finds "something fallacious in the commonplace images of mother country and children colonies.") Consider the gap between Hobbes' end of law as restraint and Jefferson's "It is to secure our rights that we resort to government."
See Merle Curti, "The Great Mr. Locke, America's Philosopher," in his *Probing our Past* (Harper, 1955). Various works study Locke's political contribution. Locke's philosophy was in line with the new atomism, and his theory of knowledge that of a Stoic and Epicurean sensory source. On Toleration, see Appendix B, Conclusion, Note 3.

9. Oxford University in 1683 condemned as "pernicious books and damnable doctrines," destructive of princes and societies, such as advocated the "contract" theory, or lawful resistance, even if the King violated the laws of God or man. Professors took oaths of complete and passive obedience. Where were they in 1685

when the King changed their religion (the Edict of Nantes was revoked also in 1685)? Where were they in 1688?

PART III. THE CONTINENTAL STREAM

1. Howard M. Jones, *America and French Culture* (University of North Carolina Press, 1927). Fenelon's *Télémaque* was widely popular.

2. Mary M. Barr, "Voltaire in America, 1744–1800," *Johns Hopkins Studies*, 39:7–150 (1941). Beccaria's *Essay on Crimes and Punishments* (London, 1767) argued that criminals were not born but made, and that punishments should be reformatory. Voltaire's *Treatise on Toleration* was translated in London, 1764, by Smollet. It mentioned Locke as a predecessor on toleration.

3. Gilbert Chinard, "Jefferson among the Philosophers," *Ethics*, 53:255–268 (July 1943). See Emile Cailliet, *La Tradition Littéraire des Idéalogues* (Philadelphia: American Philosophical Society, 1943).

4. George Sabine, *History of Political Theory*, p. 421. Hamilton Vreeland, *Hugo Grotius* (Oxford Univ. Press, 1917) is standard. See Cassirer, *Philosophy of the Enlightenment*, Chap. VI, which calls Grotius "the most important and independent thinker of the humanistic movement." Grotius' statement in the text (p. 198) about resisting sovereigns, even to putting them to death, antedated Charles I. Grotius' problem was to reconcile warring opinions, and to find sanctions for a new view without clear Biblical or ecclesiastic sanctions. Hence the use of Cicero's: The law of nature must be found in the consensus of all peoples. Grotius postulates an absolute law beyond the power of state or church to abrogate. His *Jus Naturae*, says Whewell's *Preface* (vii), "may be the mere rudiments out of which the *Jus Gentium* is to be fashioned; or it may be the lofty ideal which the *Jus Gentium* never reaches." Was the "law of nature" a Platonic original or a natural base on which the ideal was to be constructed? Grotius gropes toward an evolutionary view of law; yet he also insists that good laws cannot go against nature. If tomorrow we seek a law between nations as diverse as Christian, Moslem, Buddhist, Communist, on what, besides force, would such law rest for its sanction or validity? *The Universal Declaration of Human Rights* (United Nations General Assembly, 1948) assumes recognition of fundamental *human* rights.

5. Pufendorf defines the natural state of man as bare nativity, abstracted from all rules or institutions, of whatever source. He uses Horace and Lucretius in describing such a man, being careful to say that they did not know the Scriptures. His account (VII, V) of "factions" is of interest in the light of *Federalist Papers*, No. 10.

A word should be said of Barbeyrac, often mentioned. This French jurist who moved to Switzerland, then Germany (1674–1744) translated Pufendorf into French with a lengthy Preface of his own, showing his acquaintance with Locke, Shaftesbury, and others. The science of morality, he argued, is open to all without special revelation (quoting Cicero and the Stoics), and may be reduced to a system without worry over Pufendorf's "essences." He quotes Locke approvingly that such a science might be "by necessary consequences [i.e., logic] as incontestable as those in mathematics." He protests Genevan intolerance and the uncritical acceptance of early documents.

6. On Montesquieu see J. Dedieu, *Montesquieu* (Paris: F. Alcan, 1913) and Kingsley Martin, *French Liberal Thought in the Eighteenth Century* (Boston: Little Brown, 1929). For his influence in America, see Paul Spurlin, *Montesquieu in America* (Baton Rouge: Louisiana State Univ. Press, 1940); also Chap. V, pp. 209–216, of Cassirer, *Philosophy of the Enlightenment*.

7. Ray F. Harvey, *Burlamaqui: A Liberal Tradition in American Constitutionalism* (Univ. of No. Car. Press, 1937), p. 98. This study reveals considerable influence in America. Jefferson's "pursuit of happiness" has been attributed to Burla-

APPENDIX B

maqui's influence; and, indeed, James Wilson, in a pamphlet on legislative authority, Philadelphia, 1774, from which Jefferson took notes, asserts, giving Burlamaqui as a source, that "happiness of society is the First Law of every government." The words felicity and happiness find frequent use in Burlamaqui's work; but less as hedonism than as tests of social institutions best suited to man's needs and nature. Social institutions, for him, are rooted in "nature and nature's God," and liberty is a necessity for those who would grow in understanding.

All that man does, says Part I, V, is done with a view to man's ultimate happiness. This is "a first truth, of which we have a continual conviction from our own internal sense." This pursuit, implanted by the Creator, is as "inseparable from his [man's] nature as reason itself." Investigation of the nature of things by reason is a first need, and the origin of the term Right, which is "what reason acknowledges as a sure means of attaining happiness." Natural law is discovered only by "considering attentively the nature and constitution of man." Thus self-love is not vicious, but a source of progress; and civil society has but one origin, man's desire for his own best good. Nor are subjects obliged to "wait until the prince has rivetted their chains," but must resist when they observe that all his actions tend to oppress them. "These are truths of the last importance." John Adams quoted these ideas with approval, in *Novanglus*. Noticeable, too, is the relative absence of footnotes in Burlamaqui.

8. See Ernest Barker, *The Social Contract* (Oxford Univ. Press, 1939), a study of Locke, Hume, and Rousseau.

9. Quoted (translation mine) from Emile Cailliet, *La Tradition Littéraire des Idéalogues*, p. 200. The French *philosophes* would seem to have elaborated the concept of a Grecian Golden Age of free thought and inquiry. See Henry Guerlac, "Three Eighteenth Century Social Philosophers" in Gerald Holton, *Science and the Modern Mind* (Boston: Beacon Press, 1958).

PART IV. THE EMERGING PATTERN

1. Shaftesbury is said to have been read in America next to John Locke. His influence was marked in France. He appears to have been indebted to Seneca and other ancients. His Deistic argument (Treatise II, part III) was that those who live under a tyranny regarded as sacred are debauched in religion and morals. We Britons, thank Heaven, he says, have a better sense of government, from maxims as evident as those of mathematics. See, too, Esther Tiffany, "Shaftesbury as Stoic," PMLA, 38:642–684 (1923).

2. "Most popular, quotable, esteemed source of political ideas in the colonial period," says Clinton Rossiter, *Seedtime of the Republic*, p. 141. Letters recommended are (many reprinted in American newspapers): 38 (on capacity of people to govern); 25, 66, 73, 115 (on abuse of power); 45 (on equality); 60, 61 (on the nature of government). Papers by Gordon and Trenchard, entitled *The Independent Whig*, and often anti-establishment, were printed in Philadelphia as early as 1724. Bradford's *American Magazine*, 1741, quotes Trenchard: "That is not a free government where there is a good Prince.... but where it is so constituted that no one can be a tyrant if he would."

3. Quoted from Locke, "On Enthusiasm." John Adams said that by twenty-one he had read Bolingbroke three times.

4. Excellent chapters on Wise and Mayhew will be found in Rossiter's *Seedtime of the Republic*. On Wise, see also George A. Cook, *John Wise* (Columbia University Press, 1952). Mayhew's sermon, "The Snare Broken," was dedicated to Sir William Pitt.

5. John Adams, *Works*, III, 440. The Revolution, Adams insisted, was in the

INTELLECTUAL ORIGINS

minds and hearts of people long before hostilities, which were only the consequences of that change.

6. For the examination of Franklin and his letter to Governor Shirley, see *Writings of Franklin* (New York: Macmillan, 1905–1907). James Otis in 1762 wrote a "Vindication of the Conduct of the House," in which, with lengthy quotations from Locke, he laid down certain premises, including: That all men are naturally equal; that ideas of superiority are acquired, not innate; that Kings are for the good of the people, not the people for them; that no government has a right to make slaves of the people; that most governments are *de facto* arbitrary, but none *de jure* so; that the British constitution is the best in the world. The origin of government, he says, cannot be in brutal power, for that overturns all morality. He quotes Locke, Vattel, Harrington. For once that government has been settled by compact, he says, it has a hundred times been determined by accident or fraud or force.

American documents could be extended here. Josiah Quincy's "Observations on ... the Boston Port Bill, with Thoughts on Civil Society and Standing Armies" (Boston, Philadelphia, 1774), dedicated to freeholders and yeomanry, was vigorous. To complain of abuse of power, he says, has always been called sedition; yet the people are the sole judges of their own welfare. Mankind's motto should be *watch* and *oppose*. He quoted Montesquieu, Blackstone, Tacitus, Milton, Rapin's History, Cicero, Plutarch, the Magna Carta, Rousseau, English history, and ended with Plutarch's Brutus. From Blackstone, e.g.: "Whoever will attentively consider the English history may observe that the flagrant abuse of *any power*, by the crown or its ministers, has always been productive of a struggle, which either discovers the exercise of that power contrary to law, or (if legal) restrains it for the future." Again, Alexander Hamilton's youthful letter to the Westchester Farmer (1775), accused the bishop of holding to Hobbes' principles, and found the fundamental source of all errors in a "total ignorance of the natural rights of man." "Civil liberty is only natural liberty modified and secured by the sanctions of civil society."

7. It must not be forgotten that support for the American cause came also from England; for example, the Dunning resolution, carried in the House of Commons, 1780, "that the influence of the Crown has increased, is increasing, and ought to be diminished." The American Revolution helped strengthen popular government in England. Various studies are available; e.g., L. B. Namier, *England in the Age of the American Revolution* (London: Macmillan, 1930).

Widely read in America was James Burgh (1714–1775), *Political Disquisitions*, reprinted, Philadelphia, 1775, which book states that he had searched "a quantity of many folio volumes," among which he lists most of the major works mentioned in this text. All lawful authority, he states categorically, originates in the people. "Power in the people is like light in the sun, native, original, inherent, and unlimited by anything human." Power in governors is reflected, like light in the moon, borrowed, delegated.

Richard Price, dissenter and vigorous champion of freedom in politics and religion, was also a respected authority on public finance. He was invited to America, but declined because of poor health. Yale conferred a degree upon him. In 1785 he wrote a pamphlet urging the United States to be bold to make its revolution useful to the world, to separate religion from the state, to grant full toleration, to prohibit titles and remove slavery. Such was the rage against freedom, he wrote, that some critics lament that the ancient philosophers were not destroyed by the Goths and Vandals, along with Sidney, Locke, Montesquieu and Blackstone. "Sleep in a state," he wrote, "is always followed by slavery." See Carl B. Cone, *Torchbearer of Freedom* (University of Kentucky Press, 1952).

APPENDIX B

CONCLUSION

1. John Adams, *Works*, II, 374. Quotation on Galloway, p. 388.
2. Clinton Rossiter, *Seedtime of the Republic*, p. 353.
3. Madison, *Writings*, II, p. 185, giving his defense of the statute in the fall of 1785. For Washington's statement, *Writings*, Vol. 27, p. 249, letter of Nov. 27, 1783.
The whole story of the gradual extension of toleration deserves special study. The "Rights of the Colonists," 1772, specifically mentions Locke in connection with "mutual toleration"; and there is no doubt that Locke's essay *On Toleration*, published in Latin in Holland with his initials only, lies behind Voltaire's later essay, the essays of Priestley and Price, and the Virginia Statute of Religious Freedom. Locke's essay was reprinted in Boston in English in 1743, and in Wilmington in 1764. His third letter on toleration was expanded in 1692 to over 400 pages.

Locke's earlier argument had been that intolerance is a "principal occasion of all our miseries and confusions." The true business of religion, he argues, is not pomp, ecclesiastical dominion, nor compulsion nor orthodoxy (all are orthodox to themselves), but regulation by virtue and piety. Nor can a civil magistrate in any sense determine men's convictions, nor can confiscation or torture. A church is a free and voluntary society, not a compulsive one. No church is forced to retain unwanted members; nor can it force one to be a member. Excommunication has no right to deprive of property; nor should religion prejudice others in their civil rights. The rights of a man, as man, are not the business of religion. Locke draws, too, on his philosophical views on the limitations on human knowledge, the possibility of error, and the confusion of form for substance.

4. *Constitutions of the United States* (Lexington, Ky., 1813).
5. James Wilson, *Works*, I, 530–531. James Wilson, Scotch by birth and education, came to America in 1762, read Coke and Blackstone with John Dickinson, and in 1790 gave the first lectures on law in the new country at the College of Philadelphia, attended by George Washington and other dignitaries. Wilson shows indebtedness to Burlamaqui and Blackstone, and is rich in classical and British references. He was concerned to clarify America's unique contribution to political history.
6. *Writings*, Letter to I. H. Tiffany, Aug. 26, 1816. The 1807 letter was to John Norvell. The new principle, said Jefferson, had rendered useless almost everything before written on government.
7. *Dialogues of Alfred North Whitehead*. As Recorded by Lucien Price. (New York: Mentor Book, 1956), p. 41.

APPENDIX C

Additional Notes

1. *On Colonial Reading.* Writers such as T. G. Wright, L. B. Wright, Louis Shores or S. E. Morison have successfully challenged the picture of the colonies as a cultural vacuum. The remoteness from Europe, the lack of printing before 1735, the frontier and artisan populations, are offset by a Puritan insistence on literacy, a rising middle class, the nine colleges by 1775 (England had two), the growing libraries, bookshops, and importation of books; an intellectual leadership of men of substance, north and south; a widespread study of law; a greater cultural and economic flexibility; and the pressures of the times.

Franklin's project, the Library Company of Philadelphia, 1731, became, he said, "the mother of all the American subscription libraries, now so numerous." "They have made the common tradesmen and farmers," he added (*Autobiography*), "as intelligent as most gentlemen from other countries, and perhaps have contributed in some degree to the stand generally made throughout the colonies in defense of their privileges." This early library ordered Pufendorf, Sidney, *Cato's Letters*, and classic authors in English; to which Franklin added Woodward on geology, Voltaire's *Elements of Newton's Philosophy*, Montesquieu, Burlamaqui and Bolingbroke. Social libraries numbered into the fifties by the Revolution; and Philadelphia by 1760 had fifty bookshops, with Boston not far behind.

In 1714 Yale College received a gift of some 800 volumes, with a considerable impact on student thinking, for they included Boyle, Locke, Newton, Bacon, Milton and Shaftesbury. A still larger gift followed in 1733 from Bishop Berkeley, including also Grotius, Erasmus, Machiavelli, Gassendi, Pufendorf, Newton and Shakespeare. Princeton in 1755 received a similar donation, with classic and English titles. Already in the 1730's Isaac Greenwood was lecturing at Harvard on "the incomparable Newton"; and Thomas Hollis, English self-styled "citizen of the world," had begun a half century of Hollis-family gifts to Harvard and American friends, books Whiggish in intent, documents of British liberties.

Finally, thumb-nail sketches of Revolutionary figures left by William Pierce of Georgia (see Max Ferrand, *Records of the Federal Convention of 1787*) testify to their love of reading: of Jared Ingersol, "A man of very extensive reading"; of George Wythe, "A complete knowledge of the dead languages.... No man ... understands the history of government better"; of Charles Pickney, "Government, Law, History and Physics are his favorite studies"; of Abraham Baldwin, "Having laid the foundations of a complete classical education at Harvard College, he pursues every other study with ease"; and of James Wilson, "Government seems to have been his peculiar study, all the political institutions of the world he knows in detail, and can trace the causes and effects of every revolution from the earliest stages of the Grecian commonwealth down to the present time." "We had before us," said Pierce Butler, "all the ancient and modern Constitutions on record"; and Gouverneur Morris testified, "The framers of this Constitution had seen much, read much, and deeply reflected."

2. *Why the Prestige of the Classical?* Over the past lay a reflected glory. But there was more. The literature of Greece and Rome abounded in narrative interest before the rise of the novel. Remote from contemporary passions, complete in its rounded story, it lay bathed in a kind of marmoreal calm, such as encouraged reflection. Politically, it presented the perennial problems in a manageable size. And finally, the story was that of mankind, inclusive, set in the clear light of the Greek passion for the natural, the avoidance of excess, the light of reason. But deeper still, the questions raised were Greek questions: What is the nature of nature, and of man in nature? The eighteenth century, says Ernst Casirrer (*Philosophy of the Enlightenment*), returned to the persistent problems of philosophy, and established a direct contact with ancient thought, the opposition of Thrasy-

APPENDIX C

machus and Socrates. And W. G. DeBurgh (*The Legacy of the Ancient World*, Pelican Books, p. 163) finds a striking parallel between the arguments of the ancients and those of the enlightenment. The student may well, then trace the emergence of the ancient themes in the modern world.

So Aristotle sees the state as of natural origin, based on man, the community, humanly developed to satisfy natural wants and embody justice, most rational in a mixed form and on a middle ground; and sees law as "reason without desire," something more than personal whim, yet emergent from custom, tradition, precedent, to the abstract ideal correcting momentary passion, embodied in institutions which are themselves founded on nature's immutable design. The door is opened for rational discussion of the state as a human institution.

3. *The Influence of Lucretius.* A subject but partially explored is the persistent, if often underground, influence of Lucretius, and the Epicurean and the Stoic philosophies, especially in the 17th and 18th centuries. A. N. Whitehead, for example, in *Adventures of Ideas* (Macmillan, 1933, p. 125) finds Newton's system the most "simple-minded version" of the Lucretian doctrine of the void, the material atoms, and immutable law as imposed by nature. And indeed, Newton's *Opticks*, Book III, will yield a clear summary of Lucretius' "Matter in solid, massy, hard, impenetrable, moveable Particles," indivisible, "not as occult Qualities ... but as general Laws of Nature, by which the things themselves are form'd."

Thus, too, Hobbes' and Locke's sensory psychology is clearly derived in large measure from the ancient atomism; and leads in turn to the new empiricism, applied in turn to man and society, and to the new corollaries of tolerance, freedom for investigation, education, the search for reasonable explanation, and the rest. See Lucretius, Book IV, for example, that "Not Sense, but Judgment 'tis mistakes"; and "From Sense all Truth and Certainty infer," for "If Sense be false, then Reason too is so." (Translation of Creech.) Thus Hobbes argues (Book I, I) that "the original of them all [i.e., Thoughts] is that which we call Sense (for there is no conception in a man's mind which hath not at first, totally, or by parts, been begotten upon the organ of Sense)." Imagination, he says, "is nothing but *decaying sense.*" The link with Locke's sensory psychology is clear enough.

The full story would have to take into account Pierre Gassendi's *Life ... of Epicurus* (1647), and Gassendi's personal correspondence with Boyle, founder of the table of chemical elements, with Galileo, Kepler, and Hobbes; and John Locke's friendship with Gassendi's pupil and publisher of Gassendi's *Works*, François Bernier. "Nothing in the mind which has not first appeared in the senses," was Gassendi's favorite maxim. His ideas reappear in La Mettrie's *Man a Machine* (1748), and Holbach's *System of Nature* (1770), the latter publicly burned on the charge of "having revived and extended the materialistic system of Epicurus and Lucretius." Diderot, indeed, acknowledged that French liberalism had its roots in Locke, Shaftesbury and Lucretius. Jefferson was a friend of Holbach's, and on at least one occasion opined that Gassendi's work should be translated into English (*Diary* of John Quincy Adams, Nov. 3, 1807). Twentieth century philosophers have found Lucretius the most modern of ancient cosmogonies; for ours is truly an atomic age.

INDEX

Absolute monarch, *see* King, Monarchy, Tyrant

Acts of Parliament, *see* Parliament

Adams, John: his studies, 2, 4, 91, 238, 275, 276, 280; *Dissertation on Canon and Feudal Law*, 2, 117, 244-246; congressional debates, 10, 259-260; library, 12-13, 276; rationalism, 13-14, 148, 190; *Defense of the Constitutions of the Government of the United States of America*, 13, 29, 261, 276; classical reading, 16, 20, 23, 29, 35, 51, 91, 246, 276, 277; and British seventeenth century, 117, 120, 245; and French, 168, 189, 190, 203, 281; and British eighteenth century, 223, 224; and American opinion, 231, 238, 240; and Puritan spirit, 244; selections from Adams, 244-246; and *Declaration of Rights*, 259, 268, 269; *History of Dispute with America*, 260; Works, 274

Adams, John Quincy, 71, 274, 287

Adams, Samuel, 239, 240, 267, 274: library, 12; *Doctrine of the Lawfulness of Resistance*, 239

Addison, Joseph, 9, 12, 215: *Cato*, 9, 80; selections, 219-222

Africa, 60, 166

Age of Reason, *see* Enlightenment, Reason

Agents, *see* Magistrates

Agrarian, 135

Agreement of the People, 98, 113: selection, 115-117

Albany, N. Y., 196, 242

Alexander the Great, 32, 41, 242

Alfred the Great, 138, 253

Allan, Ethan, 217

America, *passim*, especially Part IV, Appendix A: migration to, 9, 108, 161; European view of, 102, 133, 155, 203, 246, 247-251, 254, 255-256. *See also* topics touching American interests, such as Colonies, Religion, Revolution

American colonies, *see* Colonies

American heritage, i, 5, 9, 22, 71, 101, Appendix B, and *passim*

Amercan Magazine, 8

American political ideas: sources of, ix, 3-4, 5-7, 9-10, 11-14, 17-18, 35, 41, 99, 100-102, 115, 143, 148, 179, 189, 196, 214, 245, 276-280; American contribution to, ix, 3, 4, 6, 9, 11, 13-14, 15, 101, 162, 169, 212, 259-263, 281

American reading, vii, viii, 2, 7-10, 12-13, 15, 17, 21, 47, 80, 117-120, 148, 167, 168, 203, 205, 277 and *passim*

American Revolution, *see* Revolution, American

Ames, Russell, 279

Amyot, Jacques, 80

Anabaptists, 101

Analogy, 259, 280

Anarchy, 49, 98, 251. *See also* Tyranny

Ancient world, 5, and Part I, *passim*. *See also* Classical heritage

Andros, Governor Edmund, 8, 227

Anglican Church, 5, 11, 100, 109, 120, 162; in colonies, 10, 11, 249, 279

Anglo-Saxon Chronicle, 12

Anglo-Saxon heritage, 71, 76, 96, 97, 138

Anne, Queen, 219

INDEX

Antipater, 84

Antonius, 59

Antony, Marcus, 72, 74, 89

apathia, 59

Aquinas, St. Thomas, 5, 7, 16, 36, 41, 101, 120; political theory, 279

Arbitrary power, *see* Monarchy, Tyranny

Arbitration, 113, 262

Aristocracy, 14, 44, 47, 49, 134, 169, 181-182, 261, 262

Aristotle, 2, 4, 7, 12, 16, 35, 36, 47, 59, 80, 97, 100, 120, 227, 260, 277, 280, 281, 286: *Politics*, 41-47, 131, 134, 279; selections, 41-47; *Ethics*, 41, 47, 120; quoted, 131, 133, 134, 139, 198

Arms, right to bear, 234, 270, 272

Army, standing, 4, 115, 163, 269, 270: people's, 175

Arnold, E. V., 278

Asia, 60, 166: Asia Minor, 32, 51

Assemblies: American, 114, 248, 250; popular, 133

Assyrian, 137

ataraxia, 59

Atheism, 203, 217-219

Athens, 8, 20, 24, 36, 51, 135, 138: of Pericles, 25-29; of Demosthenes, 32-35

Atoms (Lucretian), 59, 65, 66, 280, 286

Augustine, St., 5, 35, 58, 120: *City of God*, selection, 89-90

Augustus, 71, 72, 73, 74

Aurelius, Marcus, 60, 69

Authority: in people, 3, 13, 17, 130-131, 199, 205, 250-251, 255, 283; in crown, 120, 143, 162-164, 175, 232, 259

Authoritarianism, 5, 95, 96, 98, 108, 120, 143, 279

Averrois, 41

Bacon, Sir Francis, 2, 7, 9, 203, 285

Bacon's rebellion, 6

Bailey, Cyril, 278

Baldwin, Alice, 276

Baptist, 11, 101

Barbeyrac, Jean, 171, 175, 238, 281

Barham, Francis, 52, 58

Barker, Ernest, 282

Barlow, Joel, 9, 205

Barr, Mary M., 169, 280

Bayle, Pierre, 169

Beccaria, Cesar de, 169, 244, 280: *On Crimes and Punishments*, 169, 279

Becker, Carl, 14, 275, 276: *Heavenly City of the Eighteenth Century Philosophers*, 14, 276

Behaviorism, 143

Belgium, 203

Bentham, Jeremy, 235, 276

Bernier, François, 287

Bestor, Arthur, 274

Beverly, Robert, 7

Bible, *See* Scriptures

Bill of Rights: American, x, 261, 272-273; British, 16, 94, 99, 101, 113, 145, 149, 239, 241, 259; history of, 161-163; selection, 163-164, *See also* Constitution

Biographie Universelle, 204

Blackstone, Sir William, 99, 189, 215: in America, 12, 179, 249, 260, 282, 284; *Commentaries on the Laws of England*, selections, 234-238

Block, Herman, 278

"Bloodless" Revolution, *see* Revolution of *1688*

Bodin, Jean, 12, 167

Bolingbroke, Henry St. John, Lord, 12, 215, 282, 285; *On the Study and Use of History*, 224, 225-226; *Idea of a Patriot King*, 224, 224-225

Books, importation of, 6, 7, 9, 285. *See also* Censorship, Libraries

Boorstin, Daniel, 276

Boston, 8, 106, 219, 232, 238, 285

Boston Courant, 222

Boston Gazette, 244

Boston massacre, 244

Boston Port Bill, 70

Boucher, Jonathan, 11, 100, 276

Bowen, Catherine, 278

Boyd, Julien, 274

Boyle, Robert, 9, 66, 285, 287

Bracton, Henry de, 96, 108

Bradford, Andrew, 8, 282

Brewster, William, 7

Britain: eighteenth century in, 4, 6, 21, 23, 41, 47, 60, 167, 169, 280, and Part IV *passim;* seventeenth century in, 17, 244, and Part II, *passim,* especially 94-102; ancient, 71, 76-78, 187, 236: in Tacitus, 76-78, 178

British colonies, *see* Colonies

British Constitution, *see* Constitution, Bill of Rights

British Journal, 222

British Law, 10. *See also* Blackstone, Constitution, Rights

British liberties, *see* Liberty, Rights

British Revolution, *see* Revolution of *1688*

British rights, *see* Rights

INDEX

253, 255, 261, 283. *See also* Liberty, Rights

Civil Rights, 173, 271. *See also* Rights

Civil state, society, 43, 229-231, 254. *See also* Man, in society

Clarke, John, 189

Classical heritage, 4-9, 12, 15, 18, 21-23, 101, 245: the classics, 7, 9, 12, 133, 277-278, 286, and Part I, *passim*

Claudius, 72, 216

Clergy, 169, 181, 207, 224, 254: in colonies, 10-11, 226-227, 245, 246, 276. *See also* Church

Climate, 180

Clough, Arthur H., 80

Cockman, Thomas, 52

Coke, Edward, 10, 12, 94, 95-97, 99, 108, 118, 120, 147, 227, 234, 260, 275, 276, 278, 281, 284: *Commentaries*, 12, 96; *Institutes*, 94

Colleges, American, 10, 245. *See also* Harvard, Yale, Princeton

Colonial Congress, *see* Congress

Colonial federation, 9, 214

Colonial libraries, *see* Libraries

Colonies, American: history of, ix, 6, 95, 113, 213-215; reading in, 7-10, 12-13, 15, 17, 21, 47, 62, 80, 117-120, 133, 136, 148, 167, 168, 203, 234, 249, 253, 285-286, and *passim;* character of, 162, 167, 168, 204-205, 227, 233, 238, 242, 244; opinion in, 213-214; rights of, 239, 241-242, 255-256, 267-268

Colonies, British, 6, 95, 97, 147, 161-162, 204-205, 238, 247, 280. *See also* Colonies, American

Colonies, Grecian, 24, 243

Colonies, Roman, 243-244

Columbia, college, 9

Commager, H. S., 275, 280

Common interest, 59, 261

Common law, 94-99, 101, 106, 107, 108, 118, 234, 238, 267, 268, 279: *in* Aristotle, 45; origin, 97; judges, 108

Common man, 17, 148. *See also* Man

Common pleas, 107

Common right, 65, 101, 108, 264, 281. *See also* Rights

Common sense, appeal to, *see* Empiricism

Commons, House of, *see* Parliament

Commonwealth: ancient, 42, 50, 52, 72; British, 100, 122, 123, 125, 130-132, 133, 134, 160, 161, 225, 230, 234, 248; in *Utopia*, 104; in Connecticut,

114-115. *See also* Civil State, Democracy, Republic

Compact theory, 3, 4, 82, 91, 97, 113, 118, 148, 162, 171, 173, 176, 189, 193, 195, 204, 235-236, 280-282: in Rousseau, 195, 196, 200-201; in America, 212, 228, 231, 240, 243, 246, 261, 267, 269

Condillac, Etienne de, 12, 167, 203

Condorcet, Antoine Nicolas de, 166-167, 168, 169, 203

Confederation of colonies, 9, 214: Connecticut, 114

Congregationalism, 11, 100, 227. *See also* Church

Congress, colonial, 240, 242, 247, 259, 268: delegated, 131, 255

Congressonal debates, 10, 242, 259-260, 276

Connecticut, *Fundamental Orders*, 6, 113-115

Conscience, liberty of, 7, 116, 118, 120, 129, 133, 175, 195, 231-233, 246, 270: in Cicero, 54, 59. *See also* Freedom, Religious liberty

Consent of government, 3, 14, 35, 57, 91, 99, 100, 101, 122-123, 135, 148, 156-157, 159, 162, 231, 243, 253, 254, 259, 263, 268, 272

Continental Congress, *see* Congress

Continental stream, 4, 17, 279, and Part III, *passim*

Constitution, 96, 133, 190: Athenian, 32; Roman, 51; British, 2, 94, 224, 243, 245, 254, 259, 268; American, 113, 190, 261, 272-273; American state constitutions, 169, 203, 258, 261, 273, 276

Constitutional Convention, 275

Contract theory, *see* Compact theory

Cooper, Anthony Ashley, *see* Shaftesbury

Counter-Reformation, 22

Counter-Renaissance, 278

Corcyra, 28, 29

Cordas, Crementius, 74

Corruption of war, *see* War

Corwin, Edwin, 275

Coupland, Reginald, 280

Court, general, of Connecticut, 114-115

Courtiers, nature of, 183

Courts, church, *see* Ecclesiastical courts

Courts, judicial, *see* Jury system

Courts, royal, 14, 97, 183

Covenants, 100, see Compact theory

289

INTELLECTUAL ORIGINS

Crassus, 72

Crawley, R., 25fn, 31fn, 277

Creech, Thomas, 12, 66-69, 176, 278: translated Lucretius, 66-69

Crevecoeur, St. Jean de, 203

Crime, 54, 263, 280

Cromwell, Oliver, 100, 115, 116, 118, 119, 125, 133, 136, 182, 227, 262

Crown colonies, see Colonies, British

Curti, Merle, 275, 280

Cyclic theory of government, 47, 49

Cyprian, 227

Davidson, Philip, 275

Davies, John L., 37, 277

Davis, Elmer, 277

Dawson, J. G., 277

De Burgh, W. G., 286

Declaration of Independence, x, 2, 10, 16, 64, 189, 203, 242, 254, 259, 260, 269, 272, 278: selection, 272

Declaration of Rights (1688), 16, 94, 99, 101, 113, 145, 149, 239, 241, 260: history of, 161-163; selection, 163-164

Declaration of Rights, American (1774), 16, 260, 268, 269: selection, 268-269

Declaration of Rights, Virginia (1776), x: selection, 269-270

Declaration of the Rights and Grievances of the Colonists in America (1765), 239

Declaration of the Rights of Man, 169, 210, 212, 256

Declaration of the Rights of the Colonists (1772), x, 259: selection, 267-268

Deism: in colonies, 8, 9, 10, 17, 101, 120, 162, 261: link with Stoic, 60; Volney, 206; Shaftesbury on, 217-219, 282. *See also* Empiricism, Latitudinarian, Liberalism, Religion

Demagogues, 29, 45. *See also* Tyranny

Democracy, 42, 47, 49, 100, 134: distrust of, 17, 41, 44; Athenian, 24, 27, 36; defined, 27, 44-45, 47, 134, 182, 185, 261; Aristotle on, 44-45; American, 94, 95, 113, 133, 261

Democritus, 59

Demosthenes, 2, 12, 21, 234; *Philippics*, selections, 32-35

Descartes, 7, 170, 203

Despotism, 29-31, 141, 182, 183. *See also* Tyranny

De Tocqueville, Alexis, 263

De Tracy, Destutt, 167, 262

De Witt, Norman, 278

Dickinson, John, 10, 12, 21, 23, 274, 281

Dictators, 72, 73. *See also* Despotism Tyranny

Diderot, Denis, 12, 287

Digby, John, 65

Disobedience, a duty, 11, 232-233

Dissenters, 10-11, 101, 113, 162, 246, 249. *See also* Protestant, Religion

Distribution of electorate, 116

Divine law, 21, 41, 99

Divine mind, 55

Divine rights of Kings, *see* King, Monarchy

Domitian, 71, 76

Dryden, John, 80, 215

Duane, William J., 259

Dulaney, Daniel, 239: *Considerations on ... Imposing Taxes ...* 239

Dunker, Dunkard, 11

Dutch, in New York, 11, 162, 168

Dwight, Timothy, 9, 169

Ecclesiastical courts, 96, 97, 98, 108, 163: origin, 98

Ecclesiastical powers, 13, 14, 101, 118, 144, 164, 181, 188, 206-207, 245, 253-254, 262, 271

Eclecticism, 6, 22

Economic issues, 5, 9, 96, 100, 133

Edinburgh University, 10

Education, colonial, 9-10, 17, 21, 62, 133, 203, 249-250, 253, 285. *See also* Colonies, reading in

Edward I, 95, 97, 98, 110, 204: Confirmation of, 99, 106-108

Edward III, 110, 111

Edward IV, 278

Egypt, 80

Eighteenth century, 4, 6, 21, 23, 41, 47, 60, 167, 169, 280: in America, 4, 5, 6, 7-8, 9, 13-14, 15, 16, 17, and Part IV, *passim. See also* Empiricism

Election of officials: in America, 4, 114, 248, 269-270; German, 79; in *Utopia*, 102; British, 116, 132, 163

Election sermon, *see* Sermons

Elizabeth, Queen, 113

Ellis, James, 12

Ellis, William, 41, 42, 277

Emerson, Ralph W., 262, 278

Emperor, the good, 90

Empiricism, 2, 4, 6, 13-14, 35, 36, 65, 95, 100, 101, 133, 139, 143, 147-148,

INTELLECTUAL ORIGINS

French Revolution, *see* Revolution, French

Freneau, Philip, 162, 206

Friends, Epicurean, 53-54

Frontier, American, 3, 4, 6, 13, 17, 36, 95

Fuller, Nicholas, 97

Fundamental Orders of Connecticut, 6, 113-115

Galileo, 128, 287

Galloway, Joseph, 260, 280

Garden, the Epicurean, 59

Gassendi, Pierre, 66, 285, 287

Gaul, 76

General Court of Connecticut, 114, 115

General Laws of Massachusetts Colony, 6

General Magazine, 8

General will, of Rousseau, 195-196, 201-202, 206, 235

Geometry, 99, 143

George I, 213

George III, 238

German, Germany: ancient, 71, 76, 78-80, 97, 187: princes, 162, 175; printing, 203; states, 261

German Lutheran, 11

Gettysburg speech, 24

Gibbon, Edward, 12

Gillies, J., 41, 42

Glanville, Ranulph de, 96

Glauco, 36-41

God, law of, 5, 11, 21, 89, 98, 101, 138, 173, 259: Nature's God, 3, 16, 101, 173, 272, 281; ancient, 52, 59, 60. *See also* Natural Law

Gods, pagan, 60, 65

Golden mean, defined, 45

Goldsmith, Oliver, 17, 215

Good life, Aristotle, 46-47

Gordon, Thomas, 2, 12, 71, 222: *Tacitus*, 71

Goths, 89

Government: as trustee or agent, 3, 13, 55-56, 96, 100, 148-149, 231, 245, 254-255, 260, 269; of laws not men, 3, 44, 51, 133, 134, 138, 148, 206; aim of, 4, 55, 231, 233, 253; based on reason, 13, 14, 212, 262; for public good, 36, 60, 90, 193; natural in origin, 42, 47, 48, 101, 156-158, 189, 197-198, 205, 282; forms of, 42-45, 47, 133; as cyclic, 47, 49; mixed government, 47, 134, 141, 144, 227, 231, 277, 286; in colonies, 114, 115, 250-251; popular govern-

ment, 135-136. *See also* Magistrates, Parliament, Tyranny

Gracchus, Tiberius, 21, 28, 87-89, 260, 277

Gray, Thomas, 215

Great Awakening, 9

Great Charter, *see* Magna Carta

Great Protestation, 108-109, 118

Greece: civilization, 5, 22, 24-27, 51; literature, 17, 20, 21, 80; study of language, 22, 60; wars of, 24-35, 217; thought, 59, 144; pagan rites, 65; as model, 74, 245, 246, 247, 260, 279, 286

Greek city state, *see* City state

Greek colonies, *see* Colonies, Grecian

Greenwood, Isaac, 285

Grimeston, Edward, 47

Grimm, Baron, 203

Grotius, Hugo, 2, 7, 9, 10, 12, 17, 100, 148, 167, 170-175, 197, 234, 238, 241, 244, 260, 280, 281, 285: *De Jure Belli et Pacis* (On the Rights of War and Peace), selections, 170-175

Gummere, R. M., 278

Gustavus Adolphus, 172

Guthrie, William, 12

Gwinnett, Button, 10

Habeas corpus, 111

Hacker, Louis, 275

Hadrian, 90

Hadzit, George, 278

Hall, John, 133

Hamilton, Alexander, 2, 143, 168, 179, 235, 261, 274, 283

Hamilton, Andrew, 8

Hampden, John, 117, 118, 239

Hampton, Mr., 47

Hancock, John, 61

Happiness, of governed: pursuit of, v, ix, 64, 269, 272, 281; aim of government, 47, 55, 82, 167, 189, 225, 231, 253

Harazsti, Zoltan, 274, 276

Harrington, James, 4, 5, 8, 11, 12, 35, 96, 99, 100, 113, 117, 119, 133-136, 148, 170, 188, 231, 260, 276, 279, 282: *Oceana*, selections, 133-136

Harris, George, 91

Hartford, Conn., 113

Harvard, college, 7, 10, 12, 22, 171, 189, 227, 239: library, x, 61, 285

Harvey, Ray F., 189, 280

Hawles, Sir John, 94, 119-120, 145

INDEX

Haydn, Hiram, 279

Healey, John, 90

Hebrew, study of, 22

Hedone, 35

Heidelberg, 171, 175

Helvetius, Claude, 167, 203

Henry, Patrick, 23, 32, 148, 238

Henry I, 96

Henry II, 97-98, 106, 118

Henry III, 97

Henry VI, 108, 278

Heraclitus, 59

Hereditary offices, 259, 269

Herodotus, 24

Higher law, *see* God, law of

History: uses of, 13, 15, 20, 144, 203, 214, 224, 225-226; aim of, 24, 25, 73-75; *Use of History*, 225-226. *See also* Bolingbroke

Hoadley, Benjamin, 2, 117, 120, 234

Hobbes, Thomas, 7, 12, 20, 24, 96, 99, 100, 134, 143-144, 147, 170, 171, 176, 189, 194, 195, 198, 235, 276, 278, 283, 286-287: *Leviathan*, selections, 143-144

Holbach, 287

Holland, 120, 170, 203, 261

Hollis, Thomas, 285

Homer, 7, 12, 43

Hooker, Richard, 5, 7, 36, 41, 97, 99, 100, 101, 120-123, 148, 149, 151, 171, 227, 260, 279: *Laws of Ecclesiastical Polity*, selections, 120-123

Hooker, Thomas, 227: *Fundamental Orders of Connecticut*, selections, 113-115

Hopkins, Stephen, 10, 16, 239, 242-244: *The Rights of the Colonies Examined*, selection, 242-244

Horace, 12, 281

House of Commons, *see* Parliament

House of Lords, *see* Parliament

Hudson valley, 168

Huguenots, 11, 168

Humanism, 5, 18, 22

Humanitarian, 9

Humanity, service to, 168, 170. *See also* Deism, Religion

Hume, David, 12, 214, 275

Hutchinson, Thomas, 11

Iberian, 76

Ideologists, French, 167-169, 202-209, 280

Immigration, to America, 9, 108, 161

Immunities, 6, 228

Impressment, 117

Inalienable rights, 11, 146, 148, 195-196, 238, 245, 269, 272. *See also* Rights

Independents, 6, 100, 115

Indians, 8

Individualism, 17, 261; religious, 97

Industry, 149

Injury, to others, 57-58

Injustice, *see* Justice

Inns of Courts, 10, 95

Inquisition, 128

International law, 167, 170-175. *See also* Grotius

Iphigenia, 67

Irony, 216

Israel, 123-124, 234

Italy, 23, 97, 128

James I, 95, 98, 108-109. *See also* Great Protestation

James II, 119, 120, 145, 148, 241: abdication, 162-163. *See also* Declaration of Rights

Jay, John, 258, 261

Jefferson, Thomas, v, 13, 14, 239, 244, 251, 259, 264, 270, 274, 276, 279: library, 12; classics, 20, 22, 71, 276; Plato, 35, 36; Epicureanism, 59, 64, 66; "happiness," 59, 64, 89, 189, 281; Coke, 94, 95; American ideas, 136, 261; Deism, 162, 206, 217; French *philosophes*, 167, 169, 170, 203, 205, 282; Montesquieu, 179, 184; Burlamaqui, 189; history, 224; Blackstone, 235; *Summary View*, 260; American contribution, 262

Jesuit, 180, 204

Jewish, 11

John, King, 245

Jones, Howard Mumford, 168, 280

Jowett, Benjamin, 36, 37fn, 39fn, 42, 43fn, 277

Juba, 219-222. *See also* Addison's Cato

Judges: King's, 97; of Henry II, 97; and common law, 108; functions, 145-147, 159, 187

Judicial review, 96, 235

Jurisprudence, 52

Jury system, jurors, 97, 99, 107, 115, 119, 164, 233, 268, 269, 270, 272, 279: origin of duties, 97, 145-147; freedom of, 146-147

Jus gentium, see Law of Nations

Justice, 59, 144, 258, 264, 270, 272: origin, 36, 39, 49, 52, 130, 194, 200,

293

INDEX

Literacy in colonies, *see* Education

Littleton, Thomas: Coke's *Commentaries* on, 12, 94, 96; *Tenures*, 96. *See also* Coke

Livy, Titus, 4, 12, 20, 21, 23, 74, 80, 133

Locke, John: in America, 2, 4, 7, 8, 9, 10, 11, 12, 15, 101, 113, 117, 118, 136, 214, 227, 231, 234, 260, 262, 279; in England, 5, 14, 41, 42, 60, 64, 66, 95, 96, 99, 100, 120, 143, 147-161, 170, 215, 224, 253, 276, 278, 279, 280, 281, 282, 283, 286-287; *Essay on Human Understanding*, 147; *Essay on Toleration*, 261, 283-284; *Two Treatises on Civil Government*, selections, 147-161; on the Continent, 168, 189, 195, 287; psychology, 143, 280, 286-287

Logan, James, 8

Logic, 5, 63. *See also* Reason

Logos, 60

London Chronicle, 239

London Journal, 222

Louis XVI, 161, 162

Lucretius, Titus, 12, 65, 66-69, 176, 218, 260, 278, 286-287; *De Rerum Natura* (On the Nature of Things), selections, 66-69

Luther, Martin, 188

Lutheran, German, 11

Lyceum, 59

Lycurgus, 50, 80-83

Lyon, Hastings, 278

Mably, l'Abbé Gabriel, 12, 167, 203

Machiavelli, Nicolas, 7, 12, 118, 119, 133, 134, 136, 167, 285

Madison, James, 4, 14, 23, 162, 169, 170, 179, 260, 261, 274, 275, 279, 283

Magazines, colonial, 8, 9, 214

Magistrates: as agents or trustees of the people, 2, 4, 13, 100, 116, 130-131, 137, 142, 148-149, 212, 231, 245, 253, 254-255, 261, 269; how chosen, 49, 80, 114; as tyrants, 57. *See also* Tyranny

Magna Carta, 94, 95-96, 97, 106, 107-108, 110, 111, 119, 138, 141, 233, 239, 245, 260, 278, 283: selection, 106

Majority will, *see* General will

Man: as political animal, 43; origin, 48, 68-69, 70, 195; in natural state, 48, 68-69, 70, 143-144, 148, 149-153, 176, 195, 200-201, 227-229, 267; nature of, 52, 176; as citizen of world, 59, 63; in society, 65, 171, 177-178, 191-192,

229, 235, 252. *See also* Equality, Freedom, Liberty, Rights, Society

Martial law, 111, 112

Mary, daughter of James II, 162, 164

Maryland, 8

Maryland Gazette, 8, 215

Massachusetts, 6, 11, 12, 118, 203, 212, 239, 251, 260, 275: state constitution, 212, 261; assembly, 239; general laws, 276

Materialism, 66

Mathematics, 5, 101, 143, 169, 281, 282

Mather, Cotton, 7, 227

Matthiessen, F. O., 277

May, J. L., 279

Mayer, J. P., 276

Mayflower Compact, 113

Mayhew, Jonathan, 2, 11, 100, 125, 231-234, 279, 282: sermons, 231-233; "The Snare Broken," 233-234, 282

Medical men in colonies, 10

Metaphysical heritage, 3, 5, 6, 10, 14, 63, 89, 101

Mercantile policy, 10, 162

Merchants, 32, 96, 147

Methodist, 11

Middle class, 45, 96, 101

Mill, John Stuart, 263

Miller, John C., 274, 275

Miller, Perry, 15

Milton, John, 2, 5, 7, 9, 11, 12, 17, 22, 96, 99, 100, 113, 117, 123, 125-132, 170, 234, 260, 261, 278, 283, 285: *Ready and Easy Way to Establish a Free Commonwealth*, 123, 131-132; *Aeropagitica*, 125-129; *Eikonoklastes*, 125; *Tenure of Kings and Magistrates*, 125, 129-131

Mirour of Justice, 96

Mixed government, *see* Government

Molière, 168

Monaghan, Frank, 276, 278

Monarchy: under law, 3, 44, 51, 131, 134, 137-138; divine rights of, 5, 35, 96, 120, 133, 149, 162, 224-225, 232; absolute, 5, 56-57, 62-63, 72, 81, 95, 123-124, 129, 131-133, 137-138, 139, 140, 143, 144, 169, 179, 195, 204, 224, 225, 234, 279; overthrow of, 46, 69, 194; defined, 47, 48, 49, 101, 181-183; duties of, 107, 118, 147; limitations on, 147, 148, 169, 174, 181-183, 224, 225, 231, 240, 248. *See also* King, Tyranny

Monroe, James, 23

INDEX

Pamphlets, 9, 118, 120
Pandect, 9, See also Justinian
Pantheism, 60
Paris, 120
Parks, William, 215
Parliament, Part II, passim: history of, 9, 10, 96, 99, 108-113, 115-117, 118-119, 123, 128, 142, 143, 145, 161-163, 181, 213, 233, 242, 245, 255, 256, 260, 268; acts of, 9, 120, 125; freedom of, 99, 109, 110, 117, 132, 162-163, 181; King under, 108, 119, 131, 136, 137, 141, 142, 147, 161, 181, 235; House of Commons, 108, 109, 118, 142, 163, 212, 213, 239, 248, 268; House of Lords, 163, 246; as affecting American colonies, 231, 238, 244, 248, 256, 260, 267, 268
Parrington, Vernon, 275
Passive obedience, 162, 223, 242
Patterson, F. A., 278
Paul, St., 129, 244
Peloponnesian, 24. See also Thucydides
Pennsylvania, 6, 9, 162, 203, 239: assembly, 10; convention, 212
Pennsylvania Journal, 8
People: power in, 45, 47, 100, 206-208, 212, 230, 240-241, 250, 254-255, 261; under tyrants, 49, 50, 57; laws for, 55; safety of, 193. See also Agreements of the People, Democracy, Magistrates
Perfectibility, 203
Pericles, 23, 24: funeral oration, 25-30
Peripatetic, 59, 86
Persians, 32, 46
Petition, right of, see Right of petition
Petition of Right, 1628, 98, 109-113, 118, 162: selection, 109-113
Petition of 1301, 99
Peyre, Henri, 166
Philadelphia, 8, 20, 24, 71, 102, 234, 242, 247, 268, 281, 285: French ideologists in, 168, 203, 204, 205
Philadelphia, College of, 9, 10, 284
Philip of Macedon, 32-35. See also Demosthenes
Philippics, 31-35. See also Demosthenes
Philosopher King, 41
Philosophes, the, 17, 167-169, 204, 282
Philosophical Dictionary: Bayle, 169; Voltaire, 169
Philosophy: ancient, 5, 59, 80, 245; scholastic, 14, 16, 35, 96, 99, 143, 279, 286. See also Deism, Empiricism, Enlightenment, Epicurean, Stoic

Physical sciences, 101
Physiocracy, 133, 203
Pierce, William, 285
Pietist, 100
Pilgrims, 11, 108
Pitt, Sir William, 246, 247, 282
Plain Dealer, 215. See also Parks
Plantation Agreement, Providence, R. I., 6, 7
Plato, 2, 4, 7, 12, 35-41, 41, 51, 59, 80, 89, 277: The Republic, 35-41, 102, 278; quoted, 55, 70, 82, 86, 139, 219, 222, 227, 234
Plutarch, 7, 12, 21, 23, 80-89, 219, 227, 229, 260, 279, 283: Lives, selections, 80-89
Plymouth, 3, 7
Political history, western Europe, 276
Political institutions, ancient Germany, 78-80
Political liberty, 252-253. See also Liberty
Political society, beginning, 42, 68-69, 121, 156-158, 197-198, 205, 252, 269. See also Society
Political thought: American, ix, 9, 35, 41, 212, 214, 246, 262, 277, 284, and passim; Roman, 47, 57, 59, 187; French, 166, 167-170, 196
Politics, 12, 41: selections, 42-47. See also Aristotle
Polybius, 47, 260, 277: General History, selections, 47-51, 277
Pompey, Gnaeus, 72-74, 85-86
Poor: in Italy, 87-88; in More's Utopia, 104-105
Pope, Alexander, 7, 9, 12, 17, 164, 215, 219, 244: Essay on Man, 215
Popular government, see Government
Porch, Stoic, 59
Power, corruption of, 29-31, 36, 143, 198-200. See also Tyranny
Praemunire, 97
Prerogative, royal, see King
Presbyterian, 11, 101, 115, 120, 232
Press, freedom of, see Freedom of press, Printing
Presses, colonial, 4, 8, 9, 23. See also Printing
Price, Richard, 12, 215, 283, 284: Observations on the Nature of Civil Liberty, 254-256
Priests, 207, 224. See also Church, Clergy, Religion
Priestley, Joseph, 12, 20, 215, 251-254, 262, 284: Essay on the First Principles

INDEX

Resistance, right of, 3, 11, 12, 100, 174-175, 197, 280: religious, 231, 233, 249

Restoration, 65, 99, 118, 131, 136, 161

Revelation, no political, 4, 13, 23, 148, 190, 281

Revolution, American, 6, 11, 21, 95, 118, 202, 203, 204, 213, 214, 246, 254, 256, 259, 282, 283

Revolution, French, 42, 71, 167-170, 180, 202, 251

Revolution of 1688, 5, 8, 17, 120, 148, 161-164, 168, 204. See also Declaration of Rights, James II

Rhode Island, 118, 242

Rhode Island College, 9

Rich, the: in Italy, 87-88; in More's Utopia, 105-106

Richelieu, Cardinal, 171

Right (justice): classical, 14-15, 52, 65; British, 94, 119; continental, 172, 173, 190, 281; American, 229, 232, See also Right reason, Rights

Right, common, see Common right

Right, force as, 198-200, 217-219

Right of petition, 163, 233, 234, 269

Right reason: classical, 52, 54, 58-59; seventeenth and eighteenth centuries, 103, 135, 136, 173, 176-177, 204; American, 227-229, 280. See also Reason

Rights: American, ix, 2, 3, 8, 10, 13, 16, 214, 233, 234, 238-239, 240, 241, 242, 243, 246, 260, 269, 272; British, 6, 7, 8, 10, 14-15, 17, 94, 99, 109, 112, 117, 118, 119, 163-164, 214, 233, 234, 236-238, 238-239, 240-242, 243, 246, 247, 276, 278, 283; inalienable, inherent, 11, 146, 148, 195-196, 238, 245, 259, 260, 269, 272; native, 99, 117; civil, 173, 209, 271, 284. See also Freedom, Liberty, Natural liberty

Rights, natural: in America, 1, 2, 3, 4, 8, 14, 15, 16, 148, 209-210, 214, 233-234, 240, 241, 246, 264, 267, 268, 271; British, 148, 237, 240, 241, 246; continental, 190, 197-201

Rights of Colonists, 16, 260, 267-268, 278: selection, 267-268

Rights of man, 3, 6, 10, 13, 14-15, 16, 41, 148, 169, 212, 214, 236-238, 246, 267, 269, 272, 281

Robynson, Ralph, 102

Roman Catholic, see Catholic

Roman courts, see Ecclesiastical courts

Romans, 75, 76-77, 216, 236

Romans, xiii, 1, 100

Romanticism, 17, 195

Rome, 2, 20, 22, 59, 61, 73, 75, 85, 89-90, 98, 135, 144, 187, 219-222, 244, 246, 247, 260, 277, 286: republic, 5, 10, 15, 47-51, 55, 56, 60, 71, 72-73, 80; empire, 5, 14, 21, 60, 89, 135, 216; political institutions, 47-51; government, 47-51, 72, 83, 220; constitution, 51; world, 59; senate, 59, 71-72, 74, 75, 85-86, 135, 219, 221, 222; virtues, 83, 85, 88, 220-222; laws, 90, 98, 278; colonies, 243-244

Rossiter, Clinton, x, 259, 275, 276, 280, 282

Rousseau, Jean Jacques, 12, 166, 167, 176, 197-202, 203, 235, 260, 261, 278, 283: Discourse on the Origin and Foundations of Inequality Among Men, 196; Social Contract, selections, 196-202

Royal power, royalty, 5, 47, 163, 168. See also King, Monarchy

Rulers, as agents, see Magistrates

Rush, Benjamin, 59

Russia, 162, 185

Rye House plot, 137

Sabine, George, 171, 276, 277, 280

Saint-Just, Louis Antoine, 168

Sallust, 12

Samuel (Biblical), 123-124

Sanctions, 100, 101, 260, 280, 281

Santayana, George, 94, 101

Santillana, Giorgio, 278

Satire, 215

Savelle, Max, 276

Saxons, 236

Scholastic philosophy, see Philosophy

Science: eighteenth century, ix, 5, 9, 13, 96, 251, 254; seventeenth century, 100

Science of government, see Political thought

Scipio, 74, 89

Scotch-Irish, 11

Scriptures, 15, 23, 100, 120, 123-124, 143, 199, 227, 234, 281: selection, 123-124

Seabury, Samuel, 2, 11, 143

Secularization of politics, see Separation of

Selden, Sir John, 99, 108, 117, 118, 176, 236, 278

Self-preservation, 130, 143, 159, 171, 197, 200, 227, 228, 267, 281

INTELLECTUAL ORIGINS

Whitehead, A. N., 262, 284, 286
Whitman, Walt, 265
Will, general, 3, 206, 230: in Rousseau, 195-202, 235
Will, Stoic, 61-63
William and Mary, College of, 10, 189
William of Orange, 120, 162-164, 242
William the Conqueror, 96
Williams, Basil, 280
Williams, Roger, 100, 113, 118
Williamson, Thomas, 102
Wilson, James, 112, 189, 212, 234, 262, 275, 281, 284, 286: "Speech at Convention of Pennsylvania," 161
Windsor, Conn., 113
Winthrop, John, 276
Wise, John, 11, 16, 176, 226-231, 282: *Vindication of the Government of the New England Churches*, 11, 16, 176; selections, 226-231

Witenagemot, 96
Witherspoon, John, 189
Worcester, Mass., 180
Wordsworth, William, 195, 262
Wright, Benjamin F., 275
Wright, Ernst, 280
Wright, L. B., 277, 285
Wright, T. G., 7, 285
Writs of Assistance, 239
Wythe, George, 278

Xenophon, 7, 24

Yale, college, 9, 10, 285
Yonge, C. D., 52

Zeller, E., 59, 278
Zenger, Peter, 8
Zeno, 59, 82

THE AMERICAN EXPERIENCE SERIES